To

Kate Adams

Thank you for all you
do for NationsBank —

Hugh McColl

The Story of **NationsBank**

The Story of

The University of North Carolina Press Chapel Hill & London

NationsBank

Changing the Face of American Banking

Howard E. Covington, Jr. & Marion A. Ellis

Foreword by L. William Seidman

© 1993 The University of North
Carolina Press
Manufactured in the United States
of America

The paper in this book meets the
guidelines for permanence and
durability of the Committee on
Production Guidelines for Book
Longevity of the Council on
Library Resources.

Library of Congress
Cataloging-in-Publication Data
Covington, Howard E.
    The story of NationsBank : changing
the face of American banking / by
Howard E. Covington, Jr. and Marion A.
Ellis ; foreword by L. William Seidman.
    p.   cm.
    Includes index.
    ISBN 0-8078-2093-8 (cloth : alk.
paper)
    1. NationsBank—History.   2. Banks
and banking—United States—History.
I. Ellis, Marion A.   II. Title.
HG2613.C354N383   1993
332.1′0975—dc20   92-50814
                              CIP

97 96 95 94 93 5 4 3 2 1

Contents

Illustrations

Foreword

In my six years as chairman of the Federal Deposit Insurance Corp., the nation's safety net for banking since 1933, I watched the industry change dramatically.

New competition, deregulation, new technology, and geographic expansion combined to make banking a decidedly different business than it was when I arrived in Washington in 1985. The Federal Reserve System, traditionally considered the lender of last resort for banks, became the next-to-last-resort lender. The deposit insurance system became the last resort for protecting depositors of failing banks and, thus, the stability of the system, which was shaken by the disappearance of more than one thousand banks because of outright failure or through mergers and acquisitions.

Much of the leadership in American banking, traditionally provided by money-center banks, came from a few select, aggressive, and innovative regional banks. NationsBank emerged as one of the most successful of this category.

When it became obvious in early 1988 that First RepublicBank of Texas, the largest bank outside of New York, Chicago, and California, with $32.5 billion in assets, was doomed, only a handful of healthy institutions could be considered eligible to help the FDIC handle this giant. Most expert observers did not count NationsBank, then NCNB of Charlotte, North Carolina, as part of that select group.

Because of the danger of real disruption in the financial system, we at the FDIC were very interested in finding qualified bidders for First Republic. We were elated that NCNB came up with an innovative and cost-effective plan to take over First Republic. There had never been a transaction like it. It was a creative approach that changed the way the FDIC dealt with similar transactions in the future.

I had never laid eyes on Hugh McColl before the spring of 1988 when he entered my office at the FDIC and said his bank wanted to bid on First Republic. Subsequent meetings and telephone conversations during that four-month bidding period often ended with McColl railing against the regulatory environment that prohibited the FDIC from moving as fast as he wanted. On occasion, he stormed out of my office and declared that he would withdraw NCNB's bid. His performance was pure, first-rate theater. We knew he wanted the deal and believed he would be back. He was eager, his people were ready. You have to give McColl credit. He stuck with it, and the result was a brilliant deal for his bank and a most helpful solution for the FDIC.

A reader of the history of McColl's bank will see that he was only following in the footsteps of his predecessors—most notably former NCNB chairmen Addison Reese and Tom Storrs—who had taken a much more aggressive position toward the business, first in North Carolina, where state laws permitted statewide banking, and then within the region, as NCNB broke through interstate barriers.

McColl represents a new breed of bankers, real competitors who will eventually help modernize our banking system to provide a broad range of services in a nationwide branching system.

Some argue that NationsBank has been lucky in its success. That is true if luck is defined as Governor George Romney of Michigan defined it for me years ago. He said, "Luck is where preparation meets opportunity." NationsBank has been prepared for its opportunities from the beginning.

L. William Seidman

Preface

Thirty years is a relatively short time in the life of most financial institutions of the size and range of NationsBank. Chief executives of banks in America's traditional financial centers can trace their lineage directly to predecessors who managed through the panics of the late nineteenth century, the creation of the Federal Reserve System, or the despair of the Great Depression. Such accounts have been recorded in other books.

When Addison Reese began putting together NCNB (North Carolina National Bank) in 1960, he recognized the contributions of the antecedent institutions whose founders organized their banks in the nineteenth century. But Reese's vision was firmly focused on the future and a new kind of bank that would challenge the status quo in North Carolina. He was more intent on building a new culture than on nurturing those that he inherited.

Reese's basic vision has remained steady for more than thirty years. Only the scope of his goal has changed. His successors, Thomas Storrs and Hugh McColl, have taken NationsBank far beyond the borders of a single Southern state, positioning it to be among the first to offer customers a nationwide bank. Through these three chief executives, the NationsBank corporate culture and heritage were formed. This is the story of that vision and the people who continue to extend its reach.

Most institutions that grow and expand as rapidly as NationsBank find little time to spend on filling their archives with the detail necessary to tell the complete story. Only writers lament such a loss. Executives are more intent on the opportunities of tomorrow than reflections on the past. Their quest hurries an organization forward, but at the expense of preserving the trail that led to the present day.

Fortunately for us as writers, many of those who experienced the development of NCNB and the creation of NationsBank are still available to relate their part of the story. Moreover, they were encouraged to do so for this book by Hugh McColl, whose service with NationsBank predated NCNB and whose rapid rise through the ranks permitted personal experience in nearly all of the bank's major successes and shortcomings. He was not reluctant in his recollection of either, and his acceptance of this project facilitated the full participation of others.

In addition, the culture of NationsBank has been one that promoted internal and external communication, much of which helped to tell the story of the early years. We drew upon editions of early corporate newsletters and magazines to trace developments from the beginning.

Of particular assistance in defining the development of the first half of the life of NCNB was a series of interviews conducted by John Jamison, a former newspaperman and NCNB corporate communications officer. Jamison was commissioned by Thomas Storrs in 1982, following the bank's entry into interstate banking, to interview many of those who had been present at the merger of the Greensboro and Charlotte banks to form NCNB, as well as others whose careers preceded the formation of NCNB. Jamison reached nearly all of the principals, and he captured material that otherwise would have been lost to us nearly a decade later.

Jamison's complete and unedited interviews were part of the NCNB archives when McColl revived interest in a book on NCNB after the bank's inventive and surprising victory in outbidding major competitors to acquire First RepublicBank of Texas. Initially McColl had in mind a comprehensive account of the Texas coup. As part of that, members of the NCNB Texas team were encouraged to write their own recollections of the experience. In discussion with the authors, however, the project was expanded to include the development of the company to that point and, with the further C&S/Sovran merger, the subsequent reshaping of the nation's banking industry.

As the writers commissioned by NationsBank for this task, we were familiar with the growth and development of NCNB. We had both worked as reporters at the *Charlotte Observer* during the three decades of NCNB's existence, often reporting as a team on major projects, including the paper's Pulitzer prize–winning series on occupational health in the textile industry published in 1980. More recently, we have worked together on freelance writing projects. We are also each involved with a periodical publication—Ellis with a monthly business publication in Charlotte, and Covington with a regional gardening magazine in Greensboro. Ellis is the author of a history of Myers Park Baptist Church in Charlotte. Covington is the author of a history of Belk Stores, published by the University of North Carolina Press in 1988, and a history of Linville, a mountain resort in North Carolina, written for the occasion of its 1992 centennial.

We were offered complete and unrestricted access to the people and the archives of NCNB for this project, which was supervised by Executive Vice President Joe Martin, a scholar and a participant in the bank's major expansion efforts of the last decade. Martin's appreciation for the bank's culture and experience was demonstrated in his own detailed recollections, which he reinforced with his notes and memoranda produced during or immediately following crucial events in Florida and Texas. As a published author, Martin was sensitive to the importance of detail, as well as to the need for accuracy and editorial freedom in order to produce a manuscript that would be both meaningful and interesting.

We also wish to thank the members of Martin's corporate communications staff, headed by a former *Charlotte Observer* colleague, Richard Stilley, who facilitated the location of photographs, speeches, and other items requested during the research for the manuscript.

We also appreciate the interest of Pat Hinson, Hugh McColl's chief assistant, who always could find time in her boss's busy schedule for interviews as needed during our two years of research. She also was able to provide a unique perspective on the growth of NCNB and Nations-Bank: her own career at the bank began in the late 1950s when she took a job as a typist for American Trust Co.

Finally, we thank our spouses, Gloria Covington and Diannah Ellis, who overlooked the stacks of material that overflowed our work area, accommodated schedules that interrupted family affairs, and provided counsel following extended writing sessions that often left us all drained.

The Story of **NationsBank**

Chapter 1 **Who Are Those Guys?**

Thrusting into the Carolina sky above what a generation ago was merely another ambitious Southern city, a sixty-story office tower designed by Cesar Pelli stands at the center of Charlotte, North Carolina. The spires atop the building, which reach high enough to redirect the landing patterns of airliners, are a symbol for NationsBank, the newest major contender among the nation's financial heavyweights.

With more domestic deposits than New York's Citibank, market capitalization to rival J. P. Morgan & Co., more branch offices than almost any competitor, and assets of nearly $120 billion, NationsBank is a curious phenomenon. Its leader is CEO Hugh McColl, an ex-Marine who favors military metaphors. He's the one who inspired the tongue-in-cheek name "the Taj McColl" for the company's new office tower.

McColl leans back in a chair in the small conference room beside his modest-sized office. With his feet propped on a round table topped with Formica, he answers questions with the smile of a winner or, as he puts it, of someone who enjoys the absence of losing. He is fifty-seven years old, intense, with deep-set, heavy-lidded, penetrating eyes. He's a Southerner who respects his South Carolina heritage and loves duck hunting, but he's equally comfortable in his black BMW and Brooks Brothers shirts. He is a competitor savoring victory and pausing before the next challenge.

"For the first time we are bigger than we think we are," McColl says, in a staccato voice. He never rambles, getting to the point quickly. He is smiling but serious. "We are more important than we think we are, which is rare for us. Now we have to prove we can run what we have and we can run it better than anybody else."

His task is to manage the hottest banking franchise in the nation. NationsBank was born January 1, 1992, in a merger between NCNB of Charlotte and C&S/Sovran of Atlanta and Norfolk. At the time of the union, NCNB was the tenth-largest bank in the country and C&S/ Sovran was twelfth.

Together they became a super regional, the leading bank in a market that reaches south from Maryland and the District of Columbia to Key West, Florida, and west to the edge of Texas at El Paso. "We've got a huge task," McColl says. "No one has tried to merge a multistate, multibank holding company with another multistate, multibank holding company. There is no model."

More remarkable is that just twenty years ago, NCNB ranked only number two in North Carolina, trailing its nemesis, Wachovia Bank & Trust Co., which had been the commanding leader in North Carolina banking since the days of the Depression. And neither bank had more than $3 billion in assets.

In 1982, NCNB successfully led banking across state lines and established a foothold in deposit-rich Florida, fully two years ahead of any interstate competitor. And six years later the company doubled its size, to $65 billion, with the acquisition of First RepublicBank in Texas through a unique and controversial partnership with the Federal Deposit Insurance Corporation.

McColl is heir to a corporate culture that has put NationsBank on track to become a truly nationwide bank, a concept totally foreign to those who created NCNB in 1960. He believes that it will be Nations-

Bank and a handful of others from outside New York City that will command the banking industry in years to come. They will establish markets from coast to coast, while once-powerful New York banks recover from bad real estate loans, their reputations riddled by unpaid debts from less-developed countries.

McColl can trace this growth directly to NCNB's first CEO, Addison Reese, and his successor, Tom Storrs, who instilled an aggressive, competitive spirit in the young talent that joined their new bank, challenging their employees to do battle with "the Wachovia," based ninety miles north of Charlotte in Winston-Salem. Reese and Storrs shaped NCNB into a company that strived to be different from its competitors. The result was an organization that frequently broke from the ranks of banking tradition. McColl may have led the troops to Texas, but it was the spirit of Reese and Storrs that inspired NCNB to outwit Citicorp and Wells Fargo to claim the rich prize in Dallas.

A record of the company's remarkable growth hangs in McColl's private, windowless conference room on the twenty-third floor of the old forty-story tower on the southeast corner of Trade and Tryon streets. Covering two walls, mounted like hunting trophies, are thirty-five stock certificates representing the sixty-plus banks acquired during NCNB's rise to prominence since 1960. Accenting the green-and-white documents are political cartoons lampooning McColl and NCNB and an eye-catching photograph of a lighting bolt striking the company's round office tower on the Tampa, Florida, waterfront. "BLITZKREIG," screams the type just below it.

Next to the light switch is an outline drawing of the states of Florida and Texas with the keys to hotel rooms that served as McColl's headquarters during NCNB invasions of those two states. A foot-long bronze lion reclining on a piece of marble is in the center of the conference table. Near the door an old cavalry sabre lies atop a credenza. Next to the sabre is a broken cornerstone with the name "Republic Bank" chiseled in it. Of these mementos of conquest, perhaps this is the most significant.

The Texas coup, which catapulted NCNB well past its regional rivals—including First Union, Wachovia, and Barnett in Florida—into the ranks of the largest of America's banks, was a watershed in American banking, wrote banking analyst Carter Golembe in 1988. "Ten or twenty years from now," Golembe said, "and perhaps even earlier, those of us who are still around to comment on financial trends are likely to cite this move by NCNB as one of the most important signs that a fundamental change was taking place during the 1980s in the U.S. banking scene."

Golembe observed that his list of the nation's twenty largest banks, when ranked by market capital, included only four based in New York. Philadelphia and Chicago banks no longer ranked in the top twenty. Six of the top twenty were from the southern states of Florida, Georgia, North Carolina, and Virginia. Indeed, Golembe's prediction of change came true sooner than he or anyone else had anticipated. By the end of 1991, the nation's financial institutions had experienced the most shocking disruptions since the bank failures of the Depression. During the four years ending with 1991, more than 750 banks failed, including a record 206 in 1988. The failures began in the farm states of the Midwest, then spread to the Southwest, and finally moved into New England.

The losers were gobbled up by a handful of institutions that quickly became regional powers, forming the nucleus of a group seemingly destined to become America's first nationwide banks. The leaders in the banking industry were no longer concentrated in New York. Instead, the focus shifted to cities like Charlotte, headquarters to both NationsBank and First Union Corp. (which is approaching $65 billion in assets and a ranking in the nation's top ten banks); Columbus, Ohio, home to Banc One (which has quadrupled its size to rival that of First Union); or west to San Francisco, home of Bank of America.

The success of these banks was possible, in part, because America had too many banks—12,000 institutions coast to coast. Banks weakened by competition from nonbank companies such as communications powers that issued credit cards, auto manufacturers that made car loans, and brokerage houses that offered interest-bearing checking accounts found themselves vulnerable to the strong banks. The consulting firm of McKinsey & Company predicted in 1991 that consolidation would continue among the nation's 125 largest bank holding companies. In that scenario only 5 to 15 institutions would remain by the end of the decade, but the resulting mergers would save the industry $10 billion in annual operating expense.

The new breed of banks would be characterized by clearly defined cultures and innovative and aggressive corporate personalities, rather than the storied banking traditions in which one's family name, social address, and schooling were of primary importance. The new leaders would be less concerned about convention and more concerned about competition.

Banc One, for example, led by John McCoy Jr., established "boutique branches," located in shopping centers and featuring neon lights and partitioned service areas. Customers can arrange vacation travel, negotiate a home loan, open a checking account, or take advantage of a relocation service all in the same office. Branch executives hold "sidewalk sales" offering a quarter point off loans, while customers eat free hot dogs and hamburgers cooked on an outdoor grill by bank employees. And Banc One offices remain open on Saturday and Sunday afternoons.

Banc One focuses on individual consumers and small- and medium-sized businesses; 80 percent of its commercial loans go to companies with sales of $50 million or less. Since 1984, the bank has quadrupled in size, partly because of its entry into the Texas market, where it purchased MCorp with an FDIC-assisted plan pioneered by NCNB.

BankAmerica, meanwhile, pared down its global ambitions and is following a similar strategy. The San Francisco–based bank cut its foreign operations almost in half and decided that, rather than compete with money-center banks as it had for eight decades, it would concentrate on becoming the premier consumer bank in the western United States. Founded in 1904, BankAmerica barely survived disastrous losses on loans to Brazil and other less-developed countries, watching its stock fall from $32 a share in 1980 to $7.625 on October 21, 1987, ending that year with losses of $955 million.

The bank fended off a takeover in 1986 from First Interstate Corp. of Los Angeles, then effected a $4 billion merger with Security Pacific Corp. in August 1991, shortly after NCNB and C&S/Sovran announced their merger. The resulting merger pushed assets to $190 billion and extended business to 2,400 branches in ten states, ranging from California to Colorado.

BankAmerica is building a franchise in the West equal to the one under the NationsBank logo in the East. The two big banks together cover the Sunbelt states, with BankAmerica coming from the west through the south and NCNB expanding from the east. A merger of the two into one nationwide franchise at some point in the future is not outside the realm of possibility in many analyses.

"If you believe that history is prologue, then you know that we are going to buy a company of $100 billion soon," McColl says. "Not tomorrow, not next week, not necessarily next year. But if you take a company that has multiplied by more than ten times in a period of eight years it is conceivable to think we will double the company inside of five. It is inconceivable to think we wouldn't."

McColl is not shy about challenging the traditional power blocs to ensure the expansion of the NationsBank franchise. "Our pattern puts us more and more at odds with most banks. It's not clear that we won't break away from the American Bankers Association," he says, smarting from the ABA's opposition in 1991 to congressional reforms allowing nationwide banking. "I'm not sure it is worth our money to fund organizations that fight us. Like Citibank, we are out in a different ball game."

In the late 1970s, NCNB was not seen as the most likely contender to reshape the nation's banking industry. Most analysts failed to mention NCNB as a prime candidate for leaping over state lines, and one touted Wachovia as the most likely expansion-minded bank in the South. Like many regional banks that had captured the attention of Wall Street with their dynamic growth in earnings before the recession of 1974–75, NCNB was still picking up the pieces from its bout with the battered economy. But NCNB's CEO, Tom Storrs, McColl's predecessor, was looking for ways for the bank to survive and compete.

If Storrs had followed the conventional line of thinking about banking, NCNB's future would have been limited by the finite number of markets and the modest growth of consumer deposits within North Carolina's borders. But Storrs was a man who had pushed for expansion into international finance in the early 1970s, before most regional banks saw the opportunities abroad. His vision was anything but conventional. In 1980, he organized a task force to find ways for NCNB to expand its business across state lines.

Storrs didn't know when he created his task force that one of the bank's attorneys, Paul Polking, would find a gap in the Florida legislation prohibiting out-of-state ownership of banks that provided an opportunity just right for NCNB and no one else. In June 1981—literally overnight—bank officials hung the NCNB sign on a small, country bank in Lake City that they bought before they ever set foot in the small town in north Florida.

The move stunned and then angered Florida bankers. Within six months, however, NCNB's beachhead was secured when the purchase was approved by the Federal Reserve Board. The board agreed that a 1972 Florida law left NCNB the right to expand into other kinds of banking because it already owned a nondeposit trust company in Florida.

Between mid-1982 and the end of 1988, NCNB's Florida banking assets increased from $21 million to more than $7.4 billion as the bank acquired one bank after another. While bankers in Florida and the remainder of the Southeast may not have liked NCNB's incursion, the bold move across state lines represented an inescapable confirmation of Storrs's prediction. State barriers to out-of-state ownership of banks disappeared in June 1985, when the United States Supreme Court ruled that states could make interstate bank compacts.

McColl, Storrs's chief of staff in the Florida expansion, became his successor in 1983 and guided the bank to the next plateau. His style contrasts sharply with that of most members of the banking fraternity, and some observers and competitors have misinterpreted McColl's penchant for talking business in military terms as a rattling of sabers or macho blustering. It is more fundamental than that. He calls the Marine Corps his graduate school of business.

"I believe we will accomplish more if people feel pride in themselves and the institution, and I learned that in the Marine Corps," McColl says. "You can take the ninety-seven-pound weakling and you put him in that green uniform and pretty soon he thinks he can kick in doors by himself, but the team will see that he doesn't get killed. That really is part of my philosophy of management: Give your troops victory. Troops love victory. Pay them well. Give them the room to run. Be tough about standards, and be tough about what you expect."

Rugged and fit at just under five feet seven inches tall, McColl is the ultimate competitor—at banking, sailing, or tennis. He even competes against himself, working large, monochromatic jigsaw puzzles by the hour, a bottle of beer in his hand, concentration evident in his face. He has been told all his life not to settle for second best; he has been expected to be the winner, the leader. A significant childhood memory is the story "The Little Engine That Could," which his mother read to him. The slogan stitched on a sofa pillow in his office warns, "The trouble with being a good sport is you have to lose to prove it."

The vitality of the place keeps McColl's top executives sharp and interested, leaving them little time to wander off to the competition. His nervy manner alerts his competitors that he means business, that they will have to work hard to defeat him and his company.

McColl is highly charged; he usually requires five or fewer hours of sleep a night. He devours information, believing that a chief executive must always be collecting data. "The most dangerous thing about this job is that you are never told the truth," he said once after he became CEO. "The truth never makes it to the top. It gets filtered. The way to avoid letting the truth get filtered is to go down in the ranks and have the reputation that you are down there checking on things and that you may know more about their area of responsibility than they do."

McColl isn't a sedentary boss. He roams the territory, often in his shirtsleeves. Executives are not surprised when he pops into a conference room just to see what's going on. Once, when he found a door locked, he hunted down a key and let himself in while a meeting was under way.

He asks questions of employees at all levels, something he calls "eclectic interference," even when he knows the answers. When he doesn't know, he will check later to verify that what he was told was correct. He expects nothing less of those who work for him. Shortly after NCNB purchased a bank in Florida, McColl and other NCNB executives were reviewing the real estate involved in the sale with the officers of the acquired bank. McColl asked the comptroller how many square feet were in the bank's downtown office building. The man didn't know, which McColl found curious since the comptroller was responsible for negotiating leases. The next day, he asked the same man the same question. Again, he was told, "I don't know." Before long, the comptroller left the company. "He wasn't smart enough to work for us," McColl said later.

Such incidents spawned complaints in Florida that NCNB was ruthless, uncaring, and coldly methodical in its dismissals of dozens of executives and others in banks that it acquired. One former top executive there summarized NCNB's corporate culture, often personified by McColl, as that of "a snotty-nosed kid aching for a fight." McColl was profiled by *Fortune* magazine in 1989 as one of America's seven toughest bosses. According to associates and friends, the honor was unwarranted. The article triggered a flood of more than four hundred Valentines from NCNB employees shortly after it appeared in February.

McColl may seem to some to be a stormy Marine, but he is intensely loyal to his friends and uncommonly supportive of "members of his team." He mixes with subordinates whenever possible. He joins bull sessions of new recruits and looks for other opportunities to get to know the people who work for him. For example, the bank's fleet of planes is open to any employee who can justify the use. As a result, junior officers may find themselves seated next to the CEO, who is as likely to strike up a conversation about a bank project as he is to ask about their family or a weekend golf game. This familiarity, and McColl's ability to recall such encounters, breeds loyalty that any CEO would envy.

Executives and department heads who have failed to share McColl's respect for individuals and who have trifled with subordinates have felt his wrath. Once, on a visit to the bank's bond trading department, McColl asked why an employee was sitting on a bench instead of in her own chair. The chair was on order, the woman's supervisor said. How long had it been on order? McColl asked. Two or three months, he was told. McColl reached for a nearby phone and called the department head responsible for office furnishings. He listened patiently to an explanation and then replied, "Yes, yes, I understand. But I'll tell you what—if you can't get her a chair, if we don't have one available within the next twenty to twenty-five minutes, then you can bring her your chair."

Under McColl's leadership, NCNB established flexible hours for working parents and a pre-tax child-care-expense reimbursement fund. Maternity leave was extended from four to six months, and the concept was expanded to include time off for fathers as well. These policies attracted the attention of the *Wall Street Journal*, which in its centennial edition in 1989 selected NCNB as one of twelve companies in the world to watch in the future. *Fortune* also chose McColl as one of the year's twenty-five most fascinating business people—the only one in banking—in its January 1989 issue.

A fifth-generation banker, McColl is nevertheless a maverick in an industry dominated by clubbishness. By his own admission, he is not likely to be nominated as president of the prestigious Association of Reserve City Bankers, an honor won by both his predecessors.

Hugh McColl was raised in a family of bankers and merchants in Bennettsville, South Carolina, a town of 10,000 about ninety miles southeast of Charlotte. The county seat of Marlboro County, Bennettsville is surrounded by the remains of Old South plantations and still depends heavily on the area's agrarian economy. It is Scotch Presbyterian country, where tradition and family mean everything. McColl is proud of his heritage, even though an Edinburgh limousine driver once told him that in Scotland the McColls were "a damned bunch of sheep thieves."

McColl's father, "Big Hugh," ran the Bank of Marlboro and kept it open through the Depression. When the family finally sold it, he turned to other McColl enterprises. "I encouraged all my boys to go into banking," the elder McColl said. "I was a banker. My father was a banker, and my grandfather was a banker." His two other sons also went into banking, Kenneth with South Carolina National Bank in Greenville, South Carolina, and James with Citizens & Southern National Bank in Columbia, South Carolina. His only daughter, Frances, died in 1990.

McColl credits his mother for his competitive nature. She was an artist who studied in New York City before returning to Bennettsville, where she kept a studio behind the McColl home near the center of town. She also was a musician and a daredevil who once dove off a trestle bridge into a river and flaunted the rules against outrageous behavior at Winthrop College by taking an airplane ride while she was a senior. The stunt cost her a place in line with the graduating seniors.

She didn't allow a television set in the McColl home, instead encouraging her children to read. Completion of *Beau Geste*, a romantic book about brotherly love, was a rite of passage for the three McColl boys. "I was raised on sayings like 'Come home with your shield, or on it.' That was Mother. She raised us on Siegfried, Beowulf, and heroic figures."

During high school, where he lettered in four sports and was class president, McColl kept the books for the family business, a cotton-ginning operation. The elder McColl demanded accuracy, once causing young Hugh to miss a weekend at the beach with his friends while he stayed home to find a penny lost in the balance sheet. He had the books balanced by Sunday night.

At the University of North Carolina at Chapel Hill, his father's alma mater, McColl was a mediocre student in the business school. "You could put all I learned about banking and finance in an ashtray," McColl recalled. He spent a lot of time partying and served as president of his fraternity, Beta Theta Pi, where he earned the nickname of "Motormouth McColl." He lettered in lacrosse and once bit through his tongue after a particularly vicious hit.

McColl entered the Marine Corps after graduating in 1957. He joked that he was on the rebound from a love affair and joining the Marines was the closest he could come to joining the French Foreign Legion, which he had read about in *Beau Geste*. On more careful reflection, he said he was impressed with the coach of the lacrosse team at Chapel Hill, a Marine captain in the Naval Reserve Officers' Training Corps.

McColl got his commission, and his unit shipped out for Lebanon in 1958. His exposure to one of the world's hot zones was uneventful. Throughout his tour in Lebanon, he remained on a troop ship and played no-limit poker games, winning the equivalent of three years' pay. Once, however, during a training exercise after the Lebanon crisis, he jumped from a helicopter into the sea, and the scuba air tank strapped to his back struck the back of his head, cutting a large gash and knocking him unconscious. A sergeant saw a trail of McColl's blood in the water and followed it down to pull his unconscious platoon leader to the surface, saving his life.

"I grew up some in the Marines," McColl said. "We had to get up early. We had to work for people we didn't particularly like. We had to be there on time. You know, it is a terrific school of management. I remember walking down the road, in the rain and mud. It was miserable. Then, sort of like a light went on. They've got me, I thought. I actually think I'm supposed to be here. I saw nothing wrong with walking down this road, carrying a weapon, freezing to death. They had won. They were good at it."

He might have stayed in the Marines, McColl says, but he didn't like having to serve time in grade before he could be promoted. McColl still turns to the lessons from his old officer's manual. "You learn a lot about letting the troops eat first, about not asking someone to do something you wouldn't do. The standard has to be set by the officers. Those are good rules in a company. You've got to look after your troops. They'll look after you."

In 1988, less than five years after McColl assumed the NCNB chairmanship, he felt his troops getting restless. They had been through some tough battles in Florida, had pushed interstate banking onto the industry's agenda nationally, and then had taken advantage of the merger opportunities that followed, buying Bankers Trust of South Carolina and picking up smaller operations in Maryland and Georgia. Big changes were afoot as regional competitors like First Union and Wachovia in North Carolina, Citizens & Southern in Atlanta, Sovran in Virginia, and Barnett and Southeast in Florida continued to grow in importance and size, feeding on the prosperity of the Sunbelt economy.

Change was also taking place in Washington, where a former businessman and business school dean, L. William Seidman, took over the chairmanship of the Federal Deposit Insurance Corporation. Just three years into the job, Seidman was faced with the possibility of the agency's first operating loss in fifty years. Two of the biggest banks in Texas—the $12 billion First City Bancorp of Houston and the $32.5 billion First RepublicBank of Dallas—were on the FDIC's critical list. While McColl and his peers in the Southeast were flush from expansion, major cracks were appearing in other parts of the nation's banking system.

Still recovering from the FDIC takeover of Continental Illinois Bank in Chicago, the biggest bailout of American business ever, Seidman faced a year that would record more bank failures than any in history. In early April 1988, he agreed to a conference with Hugh McColl, whom he had never met. Together they would change the direction of banking in the United States.

Chapter 2 **An Unlikely Candidate**

When L. William Seidman assumed the chairman-
ship of the Federal Deposit Insurance Corporation in 1985, he wasn't
aware of the challenges that lay ahead. In fact, he wasn't sure where in
Washington the agency's offices were located. Upon his arrival on the
scene, he found the agency with its smallest staff of field bank examiners
ever, at a time when banks teetered on the brink of the greatest period
of calamitous change since the 1930s.

Organized in 1933 to insure the money of individual depositors, the
FDIC was an independent government corporation, created by Congress
to reassure bank customers that their money was safe. At the time, the
nation was in the grip of the Depression; thousands of banks had not
reopened after President Franklin Roosevelt's Bank Holiday in 1933.
The FDIC's stamp of approval on a bank meant that customers' deposits

were guaranteed, at that time up to $2,500. To pay its own expenses and to establish the insurance fund, the FDIC assessed member banks a modest fee.

Over the years since then banks had failed from time to time, but the resources of the FDIC were always more than sufficient to cover depositors' claims. In time, the agency had even reduced the amount that banks paid in insurance premiums. The operation became relatively routine. When a bank was in trouble, the agency had two basic choices: Close it and pay off depositors from the insurance fund, or take it over and sell the assets to some healthier institution. For the most part, the agency's work was little noticed outside the banking community.

By the time Seidman was installed as chairman, however, the FDIC had stepped beyond its passive role of simply insuring deposits. And the risks were greater. Now the agency insured deposits up to $100,000, and during the 1970s it had begun extending loans to troubled banks and using other extraordinary devices to keep banks from failing.

Business, politics, and banking, either individually or collectively, had been part of Seidman's professional life for years. A Republican from Michigan and an accountant whose family firm was one of the largest in the nation, Seidman had his first look at the inside of government in 1974 when newly appointed vice president Gerald Ford, another son of Grand Rapids, asked him to help organize his administrative staff. Seidman had been called to Washington for a minor appointment in the Department of Housing and Urban Development, but the events leading to the resignation of Richard Nixon and Ford's elevation to the presidency soon put him in the White House as one of seven assistants with direct access to the Oval Office.

It was a heady time, and Seidman enjoyed the work and the perquisites of the job as domestic economic adviser to the president. He and his wife, Sally, reluctantly left Washington when Jimmy Carter's Democrats gained control in two years. Nine years later, in 1985, he got a call from an old Washington chum who asked how he would feel about becoming chairman of the FDIC. By then, Seidman had served a stint as vice chairman of Phelps Dodge Corp., a multinational copper mining and manufacturing concern, and three years as dean of the Arizona State University Business School in Tempe.

Seidman, then sixty-five, was pleased to be back in Washington, but he brought part of the Southwest with him. His office at the FDIC became a showcase for his collection of Hopi kachina dolls, Navajo rugs, and other artifacts and examples of Native American art. He wore a silver-and-turquoise ring and watchband. A 12,000-acre ranch in New Mexico, where he raised Corriente cattle, remained a favorite retreat. The new chairman also brought recent experience as the chairman of an Arizona state commission that had studied opening the state to interstate banking and recent membership on the board of an Arizona bank holding company.

Seidman infused the stuffy bureaucracy of the regulatory environment with freshness. A short, stocky man, bald except for a border of fuzz above his ears, he was plainspoken and quotable, and he had uncommon press savvy. When other bureaucrats ducked for cover at the first sign of bad news, he grabbed the microphone. Seidman was about to move the nondescript FDIC into the front lines of banking regulation.

One of only a few businessmen ever to be appointed chairman of the FDIC, Seidman assumed responsibility at a time when the agency's fundamental premise was being challenged by revolutionary changes in banking. The transition had begun quietly in Boston in 1971 when the FDIC helped prop up a struggling, black-owned bank in a black neighborhood because, the FDIC directors argued, it was "essential" to the community it served. The bailout, the first in the FDIC's history, involved advancing $1.5 million in loans as part of a $2 million package to revive the bank. Also in 1971, the FDIC was faced with the collapse of Detroit's Bank of the Commonwealth, the first billion-dollar institution to fail.

Then, in 1974, Long Island's $3.7 billion Franklin National Bank failed, shocking the banking industry, which had never encountered a bank failure of that magnitude. By the end of the decade, that large sum had been surpassed by First Pennsylvania Bank in Philadelphia, with more than $9 billion in assets. The FDIC bailed it out also, arguing, as it had in the Boston case, that the continued operation of the bank was necessary to the community. This time the bank's "community" was defined as the state of Pennsylvania.

The FDIC's role was changing because the banking industry was changing. A bank was no longer one company doing business from one location on Main Street in the bank president's home city, although that was the romantic notion one could divine from the way banking legislation was written. Chastened by the collapse of banking in the 1930s, state and federal laws had placed banks under strict controls, limiting the kinds of businesses they could conduct with the restrictions of the Depression-era Glass-Stegall legislation.

Largely because of these controls, the familiar structure of American banking remained in place, with the major New York City banks, rich with enormous deposits and billions in corporate and international business, at the top of the heap. These money-center banks were considered to be the epitome of banking. They bespoke stability and refuge for investors in hard times, often extending credit to smaller banks in the provinces to keep them afloat.

The next tier of banks included those that dominated a particular state. These state leaders collected the local equivalent of blue-chip customers and carefully managed their resources. Many represented generations of business leadership drawn from a special fraternity. In the South, where the growing Sunbelt was boosting bank stocks, Citizens & Southern in Georgia had a hundred-year reputation. Wachovia in North Carolina was the essence of stability. Each was a leader within its borders. On the bottom tier of the banking hierarchy stood the community banks, which seldom ventured beyond their home base for business.

This system was earmarked for oblivion in 1981 when NCNB found that loophole in Florida law and entered the lucrative, deposit-rich Florida market. By 1985 Southern states had joined together in an agreement to allow banks within the region to cross state lines. The compact kept New York banks at bay but allowed NCNB and others to become regional powers. Similar legislation to permit interstate banking, such as that proposed by Seidman's study commission in Arizona, won approval in other parts of the country.

By the late 1980s, NCNB was ranked among the top banks in Florida, South Carolina, and North Carolina and had operations in three other Southern states. First Union Corp., another North Carolina bank, was also in Florida and Georgia. Citizens & Southern, from Georgia, had established itself in the Florida market, as well as in South Carolina. NCNB's leaders, and others, now believed it was their fate either to expand or to be absorbed by some larger buyer.

Perhaps more troubling to banks were the changes taking place in the marketplace. Banks no longer were the sole source of money for individual corporate customers. In the 1980s, a savings and loan charter permitted even more flexibility than a bank in serving some customers.

Wall Street began to bypass traditional banking sources in huge corporate buyout deals. Consumers could find traditional banking services available at Merrill Lynch. The increasing size of leveraged buyouts, with multimillion-dollar fees that traditional bankers had never thought possible, created a frenzy during the early part of that decade. Banks that had been the models of conservatism found themselves scrambling for a piece of this business. In their zeal, some banks loaded their investment and loan portfolios with risky corporate credits.

American bankers enviously eyed their foreign competitors, who could underwrite securities deals and perform many other functions that were prohibited in the United States by Glass-Stegall. In addition, they liked the looks of the foreign banking structure: there were large banks and not so many of them. In the United States, for example, 14,000 banks competed for business at all levels, while in Japan, Germany, France, and England combined there were only 1,500.

Risk increased with size, and so did the workload of the FDIC. From 1980 to 1985, the number of bank failures accelerated. By the end of 1985, the FDIC's list of problem banks included more than 1,000 institutions, five times more than five years earlier. In 1984 and 1985, there were more than 200 bank failures, a number greater than the FDIC had faced since before World War II.

One of the first major shocks to the system came in 1984 with trouble at Continental Illinois, a $41 billion Chicago financial institution with a $34 billion loan portfolio filled with loans in default from the decline of the Texas and Oklahoma oil economies. Here, for the first time, was a bank whose failure had national and international implications.

At first, regulators and Continental's management believed the bank might survive. In May 1984, however, Continental's management was publicly fighting rumors that the bank was considering bankruptcy. These denials only fed talk of the bank's problems. Concerned international investors with large amounts on deposit in the bank began making withdrawals, creating an electronic "run" that drained billions of dollars with the click of a computer key. Deposit transfer orders from around the world flashed into the bank, sometimes removing millions in seconds.

The Continental case presented the FDIC with a problem of a new magnitude—the bank was too big to close. Regulators believed that a straight payoff of depositors, at first estimated to cost more than

$3 billion, might lead to a national banking panic. Regulators also feared that a wave of problems would wash over smaller banks that had their money deposited at Continental. (More than 175 banks had at least half of their capital in Continental; 66 did all of their correspondent banking there.) With no buyer stepping forward to take over, the FDIC's only option was to guarantee the continued operation of Continental and assume control. The agency guaranteed not only the deposits but the investments of bondholders in the bank holding company because there was no way to separate the two.

The agency was roundly criticized for its bailout of Continental Illinois, which required an infusion of cash and credit far larger than anything Congress had ever considered for Lockheed, Chrysler Corp., or New York City. Immediately, smaller bankers complained that they were not given the same quality of protection as large banks because they weren't "too big to fail." After the FDIC arranged for Continental to continue in business, and even to buy other banks, it faced loud criticism that it was creating a "nationalized" bank.

The Continental failure was just the first tolling of the bell. Next to waver were Texas banks that had survived their initial problems with energy loans by making deals on escalating real estate prices. At the time real estate appeared to provide a big enough cushion for the future.

The first to join the real estate chase were Texas savings and loan institutions. Traditionally, Texas thrifts were the hometown banks for most consumers; the big banks weren't interested in individual checking accounts but fought instead for $10 million and $100 million business deals. Changes in laws regulating thrifts in 1981, however, had freed these institutions, with millions in customers' cash, to invest in speculative real estate deals and join the pursuit of junk bonds sold to finance corporate buyouts. Texas thrifts began lending money for all manner of grand schemes and packing their investment portfolios with risky paper in a very volatile market.

The banks soon followed. Total real estate loans at the big banks in the state's four largest metropolitan areas—Dallas–Fort Worth, Houston, San Antonio, and Austin—reached a peak of $32.8 billion in 1986, a 50 percent increase in just three years.

The fever was not limited to Texas. The rest of the Southwest was a hot spot, as was New England, where a series of mergers had doubled the size of the $20 billion Bank of New England almost overnight. The bank was riding the economic boom called the Massachusetts Miracle. It was a financial bonanza built on lavish investment—in office parks, shopping malls, and other ventures—with little or no controls.

In Texas, banking itself became a hot commodity. More than 140 new banks were opened in 1981 and 1982. In 1984, 137 opened, and an even 100 were chartered in 1985. Insiders referred to the Office of the Comptroller of the Currency, which issues national bank charters, as Conover's Candy Store, after Comptroller C. Todd Conover.

With years of 10 percent annual economic growth to bolster their confidence, Texas bankers thought the good times would never end. The state seemed virtually immune to economic disasters of the manufacturing centers of the Midwest and the Northeast. In 1981, Texas Commerce Bancshares chairman Ben Love had predicted that his bank would grow in size from twenty-second in the nation to among the top fifteen.

Texas bankers had survived the recession of the 1970s, which had brought banks from all across the land to their doorsteps seeking lines of credit. They saw no reason to change now. In the November 28, 1984, issue of *Inside Texas*, a Dallas business newsletter, Texas economists predicted growth for the state's economy in 1985. RepublicBank's Ed McClelland said that the number of nonagricultural jobs in the state had increased some overall, a sign that growth might be on its way. McClelland's optimism wasn't founded on hard numbers. His bank's profits had taken a 10 percent tumble the year before.

In the December 1984 issue of the same newsletter, Bill Gruben at the Dallas Federal Reserve cautioned: "If there is an improvement next year, I certainly think it's going to be very mild. The downside risk has increased." RepublicBank's Joe Fortson said, "The overall level of real estate activity is abating in response to supply on hand." But he apparently couldn't resist predicting the beginning of a weak turnaround, adding, "But I don't expect state [housing] starts or [building] permits to plummet drastically during 1985."

The optimistic predictions were totally discounted when oil prices plunged from $28 a barrel to $10 a barrel in January and February of 1986. Millions of dollars of loans to oil drillers and others connected with the energy business went into delinquency. Unpaid real estate loans grew to 14.63 percent of all loans in 1987 in Texas, the highest of any region in the nation. The fate of many Texas institutions became certain.

As Republic, the staid leader of Texas banking, and all other Texas banks continued to struggle with the state's troubled economy, changes in the state's banking laws that had been adopted elsewhere were finally being considered. The call for new laws to allow branch banking became louder. Some analysts would later say that Texas's restrictive branching laws meant the state's banks, which could not open offices outside their hometown, were forced virtually to stand alone against an onslaught of problems without income from more profitable operations in another city.

In 1987, leaders of the two largest bank holding companies in Texas, InterFirst Corp. and the venerable RepublicBank Corp., agreed to merge in a frantic effort to save enough through consolidation to avert disaster. There was some hope that by combining departments and eliminating three thousand jobs, the two would be able to garner enough resources to gain stability. But the savings weren't sufficient. The 1987 losses totaled $657 million.

Although Texas led the list, it wasn't the only state with problems. In 1987, the FDIC supervised fifty bank failures there, about one-fourth of all failures across the nation, and the numbers were growing. In addition to the failures, a dozen Texas banks (out of nineteen nationally) had received financial assistance from the FDIC.

The newly merged First Republic began 1988 with a whopping 27.2 percent of its real estate portfolio in some stage of default. Real estate and foreign loans made up most of the $4 billion in nonperforming loans. The situation worsened in the first quarter of 1988, with $1.5 billion in losses, and $700 million in the second. By the middle of 1988, First Republic's net assets had dropped from a pre-merger combined level of $41.1 billion—$22.6 billion for Republic and $18.5 billion for InterFirst—to $26.8 billion. The largest bank in the state of Texas was sliding into default.

Even a $1 billion loan in March from the FDIC did little to help. As a guarantee for the loan, all forty-one of the bank's operating units (forty banks in Texas and the credit card bank in Delaware) were pledged as collateral. The note was due in September.

Seidman and other FDIC officials were deeply troubled by First Republic's deteriorating situation. They knew that resolving the bank's problems would severely test resources and stretch the legal obligations of the FDIC. The agency had more than $18.3 billion in its insurance fund, but a failure at First Republic would drain it by billions. That bank alone would apparently require as much as $10 billion, perhaps $14 billion, and it was only one of more than 13,000 banks whose customers had come to rely on the FDIC to protect deposits of up to $100,000.

As First Republic edged closer and closer to the brink, Seidman also was presiding over the bailout of First City, a Houston bank holding company that owned sixty-one banks throughout Texas. Some of them were solvent, but others were not. The holding company, meanwhile, owed more than $225.8 million in the form of notes and bonds to private investors. If all the banks were closed and the holding company failed, the shareholders, bondholders, and other creditors would receive next to nothing.

The recapitalization of First City was consummated in mid-April 1988. It involved $970 million in FDIC assistance, accompanied by $500 million in new equity capital from private investors headed by A. Robert Abboud, former chairman of the First National Bank of Chicago. The FDIC chose a so-called open bank transaction, effecting recovery without closing the bank entirely, but at the last minute the success of the deal was thrown into doubt when New York speculators took advantage of the rules that applied to open bank transactions.

The FDIC couldn't close the deal until the holders of 90 percent of the holding company's bonds agreed to sell them at either forty-five cents or thirty-five cents on the dollar, depending upon the type of security. Speculating investment brokers, who make profits by buying up blocks of stock or bonds and reselling them later, had purchased an estimated $55 million of First City debt at a discounted price and were holding out for full payment (i.e., 100 cents on the dollar) before they would agree to the FDIC's proposal rehabilitation plan. These bondholders were gambling that the FDIC wouldn't allow the First City holding company to fail; if it did fail, the FDIC would face the expensive payoff of depositors. The bondholders were also counting on the FDIC to save the bank to prevent a crisis of confidence in Texas banking.

"In effect," the FDIC's chief negotiator, John Stone, recalled later, "the arbitrageurs said, 'We'll hold the gun to the public's head. We'll put you in a position, FDIC, where we are going to profit out of this misery because we don't think you'll close this down.'"

The FDIC caved in, allowing those who held about a third of the bond debt to get full payment, while others were left with less, as little as thirty-five cents on the dollar, depending on the type of bonds. "If we had let First City crater, it could have had negative public impact," Stone said later.

The First City deal was still high priority at the FDIC on April 5, a Wednesday, when Seidman met with Hugh McColl, the CEO of NCNB, which, he was told, was interested in bidding on First Republic.

McColl's request for a meeting seemed curious. With about $28 billion in assets, NCNB was not the obvious choice to bail out First Republic, which was about the same size. Regulators were looking to financial powers like the $205 billion Citicorp and the $45 billion Wells Fargo as the most likely candidates to take over. In fact, Seidman's predecessor at the FDIC, William Isaac, told the *New York Times* that only Citicorp, Wells Fargo, the $99 billion Chase Manhattan of New York, or the $73 billion Security Pacific of Los Angeles, plus a few Japanese banks, would be big enough to handle the collapse of Texas's largest bank. Some analysts even said the FDIC would find no serious bidders and would probably have to take over the bank and operate it itself, as it had done in the case of Continental Illinois.

That was traditional thinking. For McColl, Texas seemed just the next logical step for a bank like NCNB—motivated by a growth culture that demanded expansion.

Chapter 3 **Watching Wachovia**

In the mid-1950s, when New York bankers talked about North Carolina, they usually were talking about Wachovia Bank & Trust Co. With offices from the mountains to the coast, The Wachovia, as it was called, had the backing of the monied interests of Winston-Salem, was run by the astute Robert Hanes, and held 20 percent of all bank deposits in North Carolina.

In addition to its considerable financial clout, Wachovia exercised its accumulated political influence in Raleigh. State government was one of its leading depositors, and Wachovia's political connections guaranteed the bank ready access to the governor, attention from the legislature, and a seat on the state banking commission, which approved new branch locations, issued charters for state banks, and regulated the banks under its jurisdiction. The bank also had been one of the prime movers behind the North Carolina Citizens Association, which was formed to see that the voice of business was clearly heard in Raleigh.

In the business community, a Wachovia loan was a treasured commodity. Businessmen who could secure Wachovia underwriting for their plans had an extra edge when they approached potential investors. If Wachovia was interested, the business community believed, then the deal had been reviewed by the best. With that solid reputation behind them, Wachovia's vice presidents on the loan platform and its officers soliciting corporate accounts had their pick of business customers in North Carolina.

The bank also was well known outside the state. Hanes had been president of the American Bankers Association and enjoyed a national reputation as the chief executive of a well-run and profitable bank. He was known as an intense competitor among top officers at other banks who made the rounds of the national corporations in New York or Chicago in search of corporate banking business.

Bankers at other institutions with visions of growth were not embarrassed by their envy of Wachovia's position. Some, like Addison Reese at American Commercial Bank in Charlotte, considered competition with Wachovia one of the reasons for going to work each day. Reese's competitive spirit was fierce when it came to Wachovia. He would tell his young loan officers that getting one dollar's worth of business away from Wachovia was worth two dollars to American Commercial. It was not by accident that American Commercial's new building, then under construction, would top out higher than Wachovia's on the Charlotte skyline. Reese was making a statement.

His building might be taller, but Reese didn't fool himself by that symbolic gesture. Wachovia was a formidable opponent. In a day when banks were measured by the money they had on deposit, Wachovia had twice as much cash in its vaults as American Commercial.

Reese did believe that North Carolina banking was poised for change and that there was nothing to prevent him and his bank from meeting Wachovia's challenge. The state's liberal branch banking laws had been on the books since the early part of the nineteenth century, when a Wilmington bank appealed to the state legislature to open an office about ninety miles away, in Fayetteville. The legislature had complied and in the intervening 150 years had seen no reason to restrict branch banking as most states had done.

The potential was perhaps more apparent to Reese because he had not been reared in the North Carolina banking community and to some extent had entered the business reluctantly. He once said he believed there were two things he would never do: follow his family in the theater business or become a banker. He considered bankers to be stuffy people whose dull, uneventful lives were spent hunched over desks and wearing green eyeshades.

Reese's great-grandfather had owned and managed Ford's Theater in Washington, where President Abraham Lincoln was assassinated in 1865. Young Addison grew up in Baltimore, in the home of his maternal grandparents; his parents had divorced when he was three. Reese's grandfather, Charles E. Ford, ran Ford's Theater in Baltimore and frequently invited performers and traveling troupes into his home. Dorothy and Lillian Gish, the most beautiful women Reese had ever seen, sat around the Ford dining table on one occasion.

When seventeen-year-old Addison entered Johns Hopkins University, he went in search of a career. After his third year, as the Depression bore down harder and harder on his family, he quit school, still uncertain about his future. Times were tough, but with the help of his father he found a job as a laborer at a paper mill in Ypsilanti, Michigan. In a few months, the Depression canceled that job, and he returned to Baltimore in his Model A Ford, taking the only job he could find, in the private banking house of Franck-Rosenberg. Within a few months that firm went into liquidation.

Through the intercession of a family friend, young Addison secured an appointment as an assistant national bank examiner and finally found financial security on the government payroll. Reese still didn't consider banking to be his life's work, but the experience was an eye-opener nevertheless. On loan to the Reconstruction Finance Corporation, which was extending credit to problem banks and rehabilitating shaky ones, Reese saw the mistakes that had led to the financial downfall of many community institutions.

"Seeing all those banks that had failed," Reese once recalled, "never having been sure just what I could do before, I said to myself and to any others who would listen, 'One thing I *know*—I can run a bank better than any of these people in these busted banks. I know I can.'" By 1936 he had qualified for a senior examiner's position and, at twenty-nine, was the youngest person appointed to that job in the nation's banking system.

Reese got his chance to manage a bank when the Nicodemus National Bank in Hagerstown, Maryland, offered him a position in 1941. With the help of a family friend, a retired industrialist who had taken Reese and his brother under his wing, he borrowed the $1,700 needed to buy the stock for a seat on the board and began his career. He returned to the bank after service in the Army Air Corps in World War II, during which he earned the rank of major, and was named president and chairman of the board in 1947. This was where Torrence Hemby of Charlotte found him in 1951 when Hemby went searching for a possible successor to lead his American Trust Co.

Hemby, president of American Trust since 1943, had been on hand for forty-five of the bank's fifty years and had seen deposits grow to nearly $141 million. He fit the traditional image of the banker of the day, taking a conservative attitude toward his duties, conditioned by a vivid recollection of the Depression. Hemby was a balding man with a firm countenance and steel-rimmed glasses. A neatly folded white handkerchief placed carefully in the breast pocket of his suit coat was his nod to fashion.

While there was no question that Hemby was in charge, he did still work under the watchful eye of Word H. Wood, who along with George H. Stephens had first opened the doors of American Trust Co. under the name of Southern States Trust Co. on July 15, 1901. At the close of business that hot summer Monday, their new company had accepted $1,739.77 in deposits. The bank was little more than a storefront operation, its fifteen-by-sixty-foot space at 216 South Tryon Street. The bank didn't even have a vault. The initial capital of slightly more than $31,400 included $768.62 for furniture and fixtures. Until the fledgling institution secured more capital and found better facilities, Ernest Davis, the teller, bookkeeper, and general clerk, took the day's accumulation of valuables to another bank for safekeeping overnight.

The business grew. At the end of the first eighteen months, the directors paid a dividend of 6 percent of earnings and authorized the opening of a branch office in Davidson, a country village and college town about twenty miles north of Charlotte. Five years later, in January 1907, the directors asked the state legislature, which chartered financial institutions, to change the name to American Trust Co.

It was the custom of the day for bankers to sit behind their desks and wait for business to walk in the door. Deposits weren't actively solicited from prospective customers; the business of banking was a low-key, private matter that shunned publicity and promotion. Wood began to change that.

In 1906, Wood hired young Torrence Hemby and sent him right back out the front door. Wood told the young man to scout the Carolinas for new business from local, hometown banks that needed a source of funds and banking services of their own. To Hemby's surprise, he was quite successful. In farming communities and mill towns, Hemby found new correspondent banking business for American Trust. His first client was in Rock Hill, South Carolina, a textile town just across the state line from Charlotte.

The bank became a booster for the region's economy, particularly the textile industry that was relocating from New England to the South and would generate most of the dollars that found their way through American's books. In recognition of its close ties to the region and its new industry, the bank adopted as its logo an illustration of a woman drawing yarn at a simple pioneer spinning wheel. It promoted its position, soliciting business with newspaper advertising long before others did.

In the summer of 1951 Hemby and Wood savored fifty years of business written against a backdrop of periods of remarkable economic growth, punctuated by a deep economic depression and two world wars. The Depression had closed 215 banks across North Carolina, hitting small and large communities alike. Not a single bank in Greensboro, the second-largest city in the state, had reopened after Roosevelt's Bank Holiday. American Trust not only survived, it helped others survive, extending credit to its correspondent banks so they could remain in business, and it continued to pay dividends through lean years.

As he looked ahead to the next period of growth, Hemby had surveyed the bank officers who had returned to their jobs following the war. Three senior banking officers with desks outside his glass-enclosed office near a corner of the main floor appeared to be in line to succeed him, but he decided he would go outside the bank to find the man he wanted. It wasn't his first venture beyond the existing staff. Hemby had recently hired James B. Bostick away from a New York bank to become understudy to B. W. Barnard, who would soon be retiring as head of the bank's trust department.

Through friends at Central Hanover Bank in New York, Hemby heard about a forty-two-year-old banker from Baltimore named Addison Hard-

Downtown office of the conservatively managed American Trust Co., the bank that brought future NCNB chief executive Addison Reese to Charlotte in 1951.

castle Reese. Reese was president and chairman of the board of the County Trust Company of Maryland, a bank about one-third the size of American Trust, which operated branch offices throughout southeastern Maryland. Hemby made further inquiries and finally invited Reese to Charlotte for meetings with a committee of his directors. They liked what they saw.

Reese and his wife, Gertrude, settled into one of Charlotte's finest neighborhoods, Myers Park, where they bought a home on Sherwood Avenue, a winding, tree-lined street. The shady quiet of Sherwood Avenue and the greens of the Charlotte Country Club golf course were retreats from the challenges of the bank, where Reese found he had to prove himself to a board that was not immediately comfortable with his ideas for growth and expansion outside of Charlotte.

The American Trust board was an impressive group that included such leading Charlotte businessmen as James G. Cannon of Southeastern Factors Corp.; Frank Dowd of Charlotte Pipe and Foundry Co.; W. H. Belk, Jr., one of the region's leading retailers and heir apparent to the Belk family of department stores; Frank Sherrill, president of the S&W cafeteria chain; Philip Van Every, president of Lance, Inc.; and George C. Snyder, president of the Charlotte Coca-Cola Bottling Co. From outside the city, Hemby and Wood had recruited Harold Lineberger, a textile manufacturer from Gastonia; Donald Russell, president of the University of South Carolina; and James L. Coker, president of Sonoco Products Co. in Hartsville, South Carolina.

Four out of every ten dollars of the American Trust Co.'s deposits came from its correspondent banks in communities throughout the Carolinas. American Trust board members valued those relationships and didn't want expanded branching operations to disturb the status quo. "Naturally," Reese once recalled, "they felt branching out might lose them much correspondent and collateral business as well as a number of depositors."

If the board's nervousness bothered Reese, he didn't show it. Bostick, the other newcomer at the bank, recalled, "Ad came in with a great enthusiasm for making [the bank] grow and for creating a different kind of bank. He had to be careful in the early stages, because obviously Torrence Hemby was of the old school. He didn't want to move too fast, and Ad was a diplomat enough to realize that and not push hard in the early stages. He got himself immersed in community affairs before he really went gung ho in terms of expanding."

While Reese was totally committed to his new bank home, there was a part of him that stood outside the old-boy network that characterized Southern business and institutions. He made his appearances at official functions but was often the first to leave, preferring to spend the evenings at home with his wife. Reese drew some criticism from his colleagues in the bank about the distance they believed he put between himself and others. Some took him to task because he would occasionally lapse into referring to Baltimore as home. He would never lose his attachment for the place, nor his love of Nantucket, where he vacationed each summer.

When Reese joined American Trust, all concerned understood that he was Hemby's choice to succeed him. Certainly that was Reese's understanding. Hemby had told him if he could "cut it," then he would be president within a year. After two years, however, he was still executive vice president, and one former associate recalled that Reese "got a little fidgety in there." Reese and Hemby worked well together, but Hemby was reluctant to relinquish control. "Torrence hated to give it up," director Harold Lineberger later recalled.

Julian Robertson, a Salisbury textile executive, joined the American Trust board in 1953. Robertson, Frank Dowd, and Hemby were "weekend neighbors" at Myrtle Beach, where they each had a beach house. The men frequently discussed business, and Robertson recalled that Hemby often talked about Reese. Though Reese was Hemby's clear choice, Hemby privately remained ill at ease about his handsome and distinguished protégé. But he never displayed a hint of doubt in Charlotte, and in 1954 the board finally named Reese president of the bank. Hemby became board chairman.

Difficulty in transferring leadership was a common malady among banks in the mid-1950s. More often than not, the presidents and board chairmen were the first generation of managers. Like Hemby, they had built their banks from small operations to major financial interests. They held power closely, and only in their later years did they give any thought to succession. Promotions came slowly, if at all, and bank employees clung more to the security of their positions than to the promise of something better. At American Trust, for example, 34 of the 309 employees in 1953 had been with the bank more than twenty-five years. Few, if any, of the men who were running banks had college degrees, and they felt little compunction to recruit new employees who did. Now that this generation of founders was aging out, bank directors were concerned about the future.

This management crisis set in motion changes that would shape the development of banks over the next twenty years. These changes, primarily in the form of acquisition of small institutions by medium-sized banks, were already under way in Charlotte as Reese moved into the second half of the 1950s.

Next door to American Trust, on the southwest corner of South Tryon

Street, just one block off the square at Fourth Street, stood the twelve-story Commercial National Bank building. It was a historic location. A brass plaque on the spot reported that Jefferson Davis, president of the Confederacy, had been standing there in 1865 when he learned of President Lincoln's death. The Commercial National building, opened in 1913, was as narrow—just forty feet across at street level—and tall as the American Trust building was broad and short. In fact, from a distance the American Trust facilities appeared to form something of a three-story skirt at the foot of Commercial National.

Ivey Stewart, a banker of about the same age and disposition as Hemby, was the president at Commercial, which, while not the largest, was one of North Carolina's oldest banks, founded in February 1874. Though its total deposits were only about a third of American's, Commercial had a strong retail base with a demonstrated competitive edge among the growing suburban population of Charlotte. In 1948 it was the first bank in the state to open a drive-in branch, which it put in a Charlotte suburb. As Charlotte's population grew, so did the bank's number of depositors. More than half the bank's $70 million in deposits came from demand deposits of individual customers.

Like Hemby, Stewart was a conservative banker of the old school. He remembered the bitter years of the 1930s and was determined not to see his bank fall into the same condition again. There were no frills, except for the employee cafeteria on the basement level, where a lunch of an entrée and two vegetables sold for thirty cents. Dessert was fifteen cents. Employees were expected to work hard for their pay. Pat Hinson started work in 1956 as a secretary in the credit department, taking the place of another woman who had quit under the pressure of the job. At the end of her first day, Hinson left in tears. A credit officer had given her forty pages of dictation that she was expected to produce quickly, without any erasures, on a manual typewriter. When she later asked for an electric typewriter, her request was refused.

Even in the face of some rising demand for consumer loans and new types of personal accounts, Stewart remained resolutely in tight control of conservative lending policies. It was said that in the mid-1950s when a young loan officer proposed the notion of loaning money so a customer could buy an automobile, Stewart approved the idea on the condition that the buyer park the car behind the bank and leave it there until the loan was repaid. Then the owner could have the keys.

Stewart, Hemby, and Reese, along with other bankers in the growing population centers of North Carolina, were marching toward the same inevitable conclusions that major changes were ahead and fresh new leaders would be needed. In addition to the management problems facing a number of small banks, bankers were watching their markets change. Easy, inexpensive transportation, expanding retail markets, and communication—television had come to the Carolinas—were removing the relative isolation of small-town businesses that had characterized the Carolina economy during the first half of the century. American Trust advertised "air mail field pick up" as part of its night transit service to correspondent banks. Bankers looking to the future recognized the potential advantages of statewide branching as the early stages of automation began to help bankers cope with a growing volume of paper and number of transactions. Competitors who had worried about growth in a single city now began thinking beyond their traditional local boundaries. But expansion required resources, and that meant merger.

Board members from American Trust and Commercial National had talked about merger for some time. The subject first came up shortly after Reese came aboard. The idea made sense financially, and there were no questions about the basic soundness of the two institutions. But directors could not agree on who would be the new bank's president and who would sit on the new board of directors. "It was all people problems," William H. Barnhardt of Charlotte, a Commercial National director, recalled years later.

The Commercial board also had entertained a merger proposal from Carl McCraw, who was president of the Union National Bank, located just across the street. Commercial and Union National were competing for the same growing consumer market, and McCraw was eager to expand. But American Trust and Commercial National seemed to be the more natural partners, and the Commercial board rejected McCraw's overtures.

While their board members engaged in talk of merger at monthly meetings, on the golf course, or at social functions, Stewart and Hemby stayed out of the fray and had little more to say to one another than what was dictated by banking industry politics and civil Southern society. They were competitors, and the proximity intensified the relationship. About this time, however, they each had a visit from John "Jack"

Van Lindley, Jr., of Greensboro, the textile manufacturing center about a hundred miles north of Charlotte.

Lindley was a member of the executive committee of Jefferson Standard Life Insurance Co., a regional insurance company with headquarters in Greensboro. Jefferson Standard also owned a controlling interest in the Security National Bank of Greensboro, where Lindley held a seat on the board and a considerable block of stock. Lindley's proposition to both men was simple and straightforward: Jefferson Standard wanted out of the banking business and was looking for a merger partner that would leave it a comfortable percentage of ownership but relieve it of day-to-day operations.

Well connected in Guilford County and beyond, Lindley was a good choice for the role of matchmaker. His grandfather, a Quaker with large landholdings around Greensboro, had been something of an entrepreneur, building a fortune from his farming and an insurance company that he merged with Jefferson near the turn of the century. Lindley inherited the family business just in time to see it all plunged into jeopardy during the Depression. He had learned what he knew about banking from the far side of the desk, negotiating loans to keep his nursery operation in business. "I didn't know anything about banking except you wrote checks and got money out of it," he once said.

Lindley also kept his hand in politics. He had been a member of the Greensboro city council, and when North Carolina voters elected William B. Umstead governor in 1952, Umstead rewarded Lindley for his support with a seat on the state road commission. After Umstead's death in 1954, his successor, Luther Hodges, who moved up from lieutenant governor, named Lindley to the state banking commission. It was the perfect perch from which to learn who was who in the banking business, as well as who might be looking for a possible merger with Security National, which already had offices in more than a dozen cities.

Lindley, a quiet-spoken man with a broad smile, was a wily negotiator who claimed he was just a simple farmer. He became Jefferson's ambassador-at-large and was constantly on the move, often making calls from public phones along the highway to set up important meetings. His friends included congressmen, federal banking officials, state politicians and officeholders, and businessmen in some of the more important boardrooms around the state.

When Lindley began talking with Charlotte bankers, he had already visited with Branch Banking & Trust Co. and First Citizens Bank & Trust Co., two banks with headquarters in eastern North Carolina. Those negotiations had gotten rather far along before they broke down on the fine points of the transactions. Finally, Lindley found his way to Tryon Street, where he made as many as two and three visits a day. He talked to McCraw at Union National Bank, but not enthusiastically. The bank was not at the top of the list, because of its relative size in Charlotte. He talked with City National, paid a call on Stewart at Commercial National Bank, and, one morning, showed up at Addison Reese's office at American Trust.

"I don't know which one I stirred up first," Lindley recalled years later, "but I got along very well with Mr. (Ivey) Stewart at Commercial when I talked to him. And he was interested in thinking about it, as I remember.

"I walked into Addison's office one afternoon over across the way and told Addison that I'd come down from Greensboro and that there was some interest on the part of Security in talking to the American Trust about the possibility of a merger. Well, I think Addison turned a little bit white, and he looked through the glass door and saw Torrence sitting there, and he knew real well that if he didn't go immediately and tell Mr. Hemby that he was talking merger, Mr. Hemby would not like it."

Reese quickly excused himself and returned a few moments later with Hemby at his side.

"Jack," Reese said, "this is Mr. Hemby. If you'll tell him what you just said to me, why, we'll see whether he's got any interest."

Lindley repeated his suggestion, and the three talked further and then agreed to get together again in a few days.

Before Lindley could get back to Reese and Hemby, some of the directors of Commercial National and American Trust met—Lindley recalls it as an accidental gathering at a cocktail party—and renewed their discussions about merger, this time with a bit more urgency. Neither bank wanted to be left behind if Security pressed its bid. In addition, Commercial National's Stewart now was talking about retirement. He had asked William Barnhardt, one of his directors, about assuming the chairmanship. Barnhardt's refusal further set the stage for merger. As word reached Lindley about these new talks, he backed off. "There was nothing further for me to do except hold up," he recalled, "and they went on together and formed the American Commercial."

The merger of Commercial National and American Trust combined the retail business of one and the correspondent banking business of the other. American was the larger of the two, with more than $184 million in resources. On November 29, 1957, American Commercial Bank, with combined resources of $234 million, opened for business. Combining the offices was easy enough. Construction workers simply knocked a hole through the walls and connected the main floors of the two banks. Reese was named chief executive when both Stewart and Hemby finally moved into retirement.

It wasn't quite as simple as that. Hemby and Stewart had run their own banks for too long just to walk out and leave. For some time, the operation ran like two banks, Reese later recalled. "To get those two fellows together so as not to injure their personal pride," he said, "was probably one of the most difficult tasks I ever had. They were both great bankers, but they also had been competitors for years."

The merger stunned McCraw and Union National. Suddenly, they were competing not against Commercial National, which was roughly their size, but against what appeared to be a giant of a bank, $200 million strong in assets, which was more than twice as large. He called an immediate council of his top executives, including two men he yanked back from Atlantic City just as they arrived there to attend an American Bankers Association meeting. Executives got on the telephone and touched base with major accounts, and McCraw began looking for another merger partner. He dispatched a young executive, C. C. Hope, to New York to meet with an experienced bank stockbroker to learn all he could about arranging mergers.

McCraw targeted First National Bank of Asheville as a likely partner. First National had about $45 million in assets with branches in surrounding mountain communities. With Hope driving the car and Mc-Craw working out the analysis during the 120-mile trip over mountain roads, the deal was finally arranged. In 1958, First Union National Bank was created, and McCraw's appetite for expansion was temporarily sated.

The American Commercial merger was just the first step for Reese. Six months later, in May, he announced plans for a $3 million building

Addison Reese (center) balanced the interests of Torrence Hemby, president of American Trust Co. (left), and Ivey Stewart, president of Commercial National Bank (right), after the two banks merged to form American Commercial National Bank in 1957.

Eighteen-story Charlotte office building begun for American Commercial National Bank but finished as the new home of North Carolina National Bank following the 1960 merger creating NCNB.

to replace the two aging structures that had been home to the banks. In his statement, Reese predicted that in the next twenty years Charlotte's population would increase to 500,000 and employment in the area would double. A year after the merger, the cost of the building had increased to $4.5 million.

The structure, to be the tallest welded-steel-frame building in the Southeast, would be 259 feet tall, with eighteen stories, including a penthouse and a floor for mechanical facilities—three stories more than the new building planned for West Trade Street by Wachovia Bank & Trust Co. On April 27, 1959, at a ceremony to mark the beginning of construction, Reese picked up a brick that had been part of the old building and hurled it through one of the tall, imposing front windows of American Trust Co.

That fall Reese completed an agreement with First National Bank of Raleigh, which merged with the new American Commercial Bank of Charlotte on November 30. Finally Reese had broken free of the bounds of Mecklenburg County and stepped across the state into the capital city. He had long believed that no bank could claim authority within state banking circles unless it was represented in the state capital. But the statewide bank he envisioned remained outside his grasp.

Chapter 4 **The "New" NCNB**

The men who ran Security National Bank in Greensboro harbored the same notion as Addison Reese in Charlotte did: Wachovia needed a statewide competitor. That is why the one bank that Jack Lindley did not approach as he rode the circuit looking for a merger partner was Wachovia, even though the bank had its headquarters just twenty-five miles west, in Winston-Salem. While the Jefferson Standard Life Insurance Co. interests that controlled Security National Bank did want a smaller share in a larger bank, they were not interested in being swallowed up by Wachovia, no matter its reputation. A merger with Wachovia, they thought, would guarantee that the Greensboro interests would have little say in the future of the new bank.

Security National was a proud institution that had risen from the ashes of the Depression. On the national Bank Holiday, March 6, 1933, every bank in Greensboro closed its doors and never opened them again. Greensboro, a major textile manufacturing center and home of the Jefferson Standard and Pilot Life insurance companies, found itself without a bank. For textile executives or mill workers, the closest bank was fifteen miles away in High Point. One, two, three, finally four and five months passed without any banking activity at all in Greensboro. Lowell Thomas reported the city's plight in a national broadcast six months after the Bank Holiday, noting that Greensboro was the largest city in America without an operating bank. Jefferson Standard and other large employers were forced to go to other cities, principally New York, to find the cash they needed to make payrolls and keep their businesses running.

With the backing of Jefferson Standard and $300,000 from the Reconstruction Finance Corporation, Security National organized to do business on August 7, 1933, and planned to open its doors on Friday, August 25. Much to the chagrin of the organizers, the telegram from bank regulators in Washington authorizing the new bank didn't arrive until the following day, a Saturday. In order to comply with requirements that the bank start business on the day authorization was received, bank president N. S. Calhoun made a nominal deposit to have the required transaction on the books.

"Nobody knew where he got the cash," Cornelius M. "Neil" Vanstory, Jr., who later became Security president, recalled years later. "All of us were broke."

On the following Monday, the thirty-two officers and employees— from bank president to janitor—gathered in the bank lobby for a group photograph. They all looked properly serious, with not the least suggestion of the relief they felt for Security and the financially beleaguered city. In early 1934, the city gained another financial institution when Guilford National Bank opened with the support of Pilot Life Insurance Co. and the RFC.

By the early 1950s, Security had achieved a commanding position in the Greensboro banking market and advertised resources of $70 million. Its main offices were on the ground floor of the city's largest building, the seventeen-story Jefferson Standard headquarters at the main downtown intersection of Market and Elm streets. In addition, the bank had offices in Burlington, High Point, Raleigh, Wilmington, and the small eastern North Carolina tobacco town of Tarboro, the hometown of a major Jefferson stockholder.

Security was making money, but it was not an aggressive player in the financial markets, largely because of its relatively modest size and the still-vivid example of 1933. President Calhoun instilled a conservative spirit at the bank and required tight controls on credit. For example, the bank's High Point office was not permitted to make a loan of more than $1,000. These policies continued even beyond Calhoun's retirement in 1950. Recalled Lindley, "He was a conserver, not a growth banker."

A change in the bank's status was inevitable. First, the wave of bank mergers was bound to upset the comfortable balance of bank power in Greensboro. More important, Howard Holderness, who had succeeded Julian Price as chief executive at Jefferson Standard, was worried about the impact of ill feeling among Jefferson Standard customers, some of whom still recalled the wave of foreclosures by bankers during the Depression. It had not been that long since Depression-era bankers, cast as responsible for the nation's problems, were called "banksters." Now, as a result of Jefferson Standard's 1945 merger with Pilot, the Jefferson board was responsible for banking business at Security as well as at Guilford National Bank, effectively controlling the banking industry in Greensboro. "They didn't mind making the profit," recalled Lindley, "but they didn't want to get the blame for having all that control."

Lindley had been scouring the Carolina countryside looking for a suitable mate for Security. He had been close to the altar a few times when, in October 1958, Huger S. King of Greensboro, who had been elected president of the Richardson Corp. five months earlier, approached Holderness and asked if the insurance company would be interested in selling a portion of its stock in Security National.

The Richardson fortune was founded on the Richardson-Merrill Corp., which produced Vicks VapoRub, among other popular consumer products. Lunsford Richardson was a pharmacist in Greensboro when he concocted the first batch of his famous liniment, and his family had long been prominent in the city's affairs. King's entry helped relieve part of Holderness's concern and with the endorsement of Vanstory, then chief executive of Security, the Richardson Corp. became a stockholder in the bank. Before the deal was closed, Vanstory asked King if he was interested in pursuing mergers for the bank. "Why, that's the only reason I would buy it," King responded. The bank not only sold a block of stock to Richardson but took King onto its board and executive committee.

King was a prominent citizen of Greensboro. A senior partner in the law firm of King, Adams, Kleemeir & Hagan, he counted among his clients the Richardson family and had served two terms as mayor. Richardson Corp. owned a majority interest in a life insurance company and a reinsurance company, and King had combined the interests into a holding company, Piedmont Management Cos., Inc.

In less than a year, King had scouted a possible acquisition for Security while trying to buy the B-C Remedy Co. King learned that Depositors National Bank in Durham, whose trust department managed a block of stock in the company that made B-C headache powder, was available. It wasn't a large bank, but it was, as King called it, "a deep freeze." The bank had lots of money in the vault and few obligations. It catered mainly to commercial accounts and a small group of wealthy customers, and it had not ventured far from that kind of safe business. Bank board chairman and principal stockholder C. T. Council boasted of Depositors' no-loss record in consumer loans. During the previous decade, however, his bank had loaned a modest $30,000 to people financing cars, buying appliances, or making home improvements.

Council's conservative view of banking was shared by Scovill Wannamaker, whom Council had hired from the RFC in the 1930s to manage his bank. Council agreed to sell to Security in September 1959 after negotiating a good price for his bank and a permanent position with Security for Wannamaker. It was a good deal for Security, which added $14 million to its base and secured a foothold in another major North Carolina city. And it saved Depositors from a real management crisis, for within a year of the merger, Council was dead and Wannamaker was seriously ill.

The bank merger circuit was getting busy as North Carolina prepared for a new decade. Bankers were coming to realize there were only two kinds of banks in the state, the acquirers and the acquired.

Like Reese, Carl McCraw at First Union was trying to build a statewide bank from his base in Charlotte. "You saw him everywhere," King recalled. McCraw had made a run at Depositors, King said, and tried to scuttle the Security merger by offering Wannamaker a Cadillac limousine for as long as he was with the bank if he would help swing the sale to First Union.

Security's board members knew that sooner or later their bank would need an address in Charlotte, which was the location of the Federal Reserve branch. They considered two routes to that goal: opening a new branch office and building the business from scratch or merging with an existing bank.

McCraw was eager to oblige with a merger. One meeting was held at Lindley's home in Greensboro, with Vanstory and Lindley representing Security and McCraw and his assistant, C. C. Hope, there on behalf of First Union. McCraw even pursued King to New York City and the Richardson-Merrill offices in midtown Manhattan for a two-day bargaining marathon at the Commodore Hotel on Forty-second Street. McCraw produced a written proposal, but King privately preferred a merger with American Commercial as a way to get a Charlotte connection. Neil Vanstory, who was now president of Security, also was cool on First Union; McCraw's aggressive style was unsettling to him. King, however, was more receptive. "It was a quality bank and stood well in the community, and in the state, and I rather thought we had the same type of institution," he said later. But negotiations stalled.

The Charlotte connection was particularly nettlesome to Vanstory. A proud and imposing leader, Vanstory was a forceful spokesman for the Greensboro banking interests. A tall man with broad shoulders and a square jaw, Vanstory was known to be outspoken, even embarrassingly blunt. He ran a bank where his chief loan officer, Hugh P. Beal, would telephone young loan officers at their desks as they talked to a loan applicant and bark, "What the hell does he want?" The junior officer would stutter an answer as best he could without revealing the question or the source of his discomfort to his customer. At the same time, Vanstory encouraged promising young bank officers to call him by his first name and often asked them to accompany him on business trips to New York, where he called on national accounts with the smooth efficiency of an accomplished salesman.

He had been a vigorous and active mayor of Greensboro and had close ties with two powerful interests in the city, the Richardsons and the Cones, whose textile company was the city's largest employer. The story is told that during his one term as Greensboro's mayor, from 1945 to 1947, he received a telephone call at 3:30 A.M. from a woman complaining about a broken streetlight. The next day he took care of getting the light repaired and waited until 3:30 A.M. to call the woman back to tell her the light was in working order.

Vanstory once told a Greensboro newspaper reporter: "I found you couldn't please everybody and get anything done. If you kept putting off something because it was controversial, you ended up making everybody mad. But, if you went ahead and did it, you made only half of the people mad. I didn't run away from criticism."

While Vanstory had been on board at Security National on opening day, he had left a few years later to go to New York and work for Chemical Bank. He returned to Greensboro to become treasurer of Spencer Love's Burlington Industries, another large textile concern. In 1950 he was the administrator of Moses H. Cone Memorial Hospital when the Security board asked him to become chairman and chief executive officer of the bank. In ten years he had more than doubled the resources of the bank and, like Reese, had visions of a bank that would challenge Wachovia for statewide dominance.

At the beginning of 1960, Vanstory was making plans for a name change at Security, but it didn't involve another bank. He recommended to his board that the bank change its name to Security First National Bank & Trust Co. He liked the ring of the word "First," and he believed that emphasizing the trust functions of the bank would be good for business. The board unanimously approved. Before Vanstory could get new stationery printed, however, events began to unfold that would change not only Security's name but its future as well.

Vanstory reported to the board on February 16 that he had reopened merger talks with Guilford National Bank. With $41 million in resources from Guilford to add to Security's bottom line, the Security board approved a share-for-share exchange. Missing from the minutes of the February 16 meeting was any mention that Addison Reese had also begun merger talks with Guilford National Bank. One week later, on February 23, Vanstory reported that news to his board. American Commercial's bid was rebuffed, and a merger of Security and Guilford was scheduled for stockholder approval on March 31. The new bank, hailed by Greensboro's leaders as a boost for the city's position, was due to begin business April 10.

Vanstory appeared to have scored a coup. He placed a high value on the merger because it moved Security into closer parity with American Commercial, its nearest rival. The deal also thwarted Reese's efforts to gain an advantage in Greensboro, which would have been another major addition to his expansion.

In making his move on Guilford, Reese had gained the support of Guilford's president, Patrick N. Calhoun, but he couldn't overcome the influence of the insurance interests on the board, which voted in favor of Security. With the Guilford merger, Security would hold about $210 million in assets and progress a notch as a major player in North Carolina banking circles. In addition, the resulting board included some of the biggest names in Greensboro business. Calhoun, president of Guilford, was offered the presidency under Vanstory's chairmanship, but he left Greensboro for a job with American Commercial. Some Greensboro business interests now believed their city would be home to one of the state's largest banks, an ambition for more than a generation.

On April 8, at the board meeting to appoint officers for the combined Security-Guilford operation, Vanstory made an announcement that would reverberate in Greensboro for years to come: American Commercial and Security had reached tentative agreement on "consolidation"— the word "merger" was avoided—and these arrangements already had the approval of the Comptroller of the Currency. The news stunned some of the board members seated around the table. As they read the terms of the deal, the assembled new board realized that half of them would not have a bank board seat within ninety days, when the merger was complete.

Bank officers in Charlotte and Greensboro announced the plan in the local newspapers. The early reports of the pending merger of the Greensboro and Charlotte banks were incomplete, but this much was known: The bidding for Guilford had finally brought American Commercial and Security to the bargaining table. If there was to be a statewide competitor to Wachovia, the combined resources of these two banks presented the best opportunity. The agreement crafted by Jack Lindley, representing Greensboro interests, and Harold Lineberger, representing Charlotte interests, included five major points for merger that had the endorsement of investment bankers in New York as well as the Comptroller of the Currency.

The deal required compromise on both sides, but it was an attractive arrangement. The new bank would use Security's charter and become a national bank. Since national banks were not permitted to operate an insurance company, American would have to divest itself of a lucrative part of its business. The new bank would have dual headquarters and operate under a new name. A final point would cause Greensboro interests to balk: the comptroller's office required one address for official business, and that would be in Charlotte, the Federal Reserve city. The rest of the agreement spoke to board membership, meetings, and appointment of officers. All understood that Vanstory would be chairman and Reese president.

For Lindley and King from Greensboro, Lineberger and a few others from Charlotte, the agreement was the result of months of work. But board members fresh to the inner sanctum at Security needed background on events leading to the announcement. Lindley obliged with the details.

The latest round of negotiations had begun late in 1959, while Lindley and Vanstory were out of the country on a trade trip to Europe with North Carolina governor Luther Hodges. King had arranged a meeting with Reese and Lineberger at the Holiday Inn in Salisbury, midway between Greensboro and Charlotte. "We had a long talk," said King. "I had tried to break the cigarette habit, took up cigars and Harold smoked cigars. We got poor Addison in there and stayed all morning. You couldn't see across the room when we got through."

King brought along Security's controller, who had prepared charts showing the growth of deposits at Security and at American Commercial. The Charlotte base was much larger than Greensboro's and American Commercial's total deposits were greater than Security's, but King had his chart maker show total percentage of market. The charts portrayed American Commercial less favorably than Security. Throughout the discussion, King recalled, Reese would turn the charts back toward the wall and then, a few minutes later, King would turn them back around again.

Further meetings were held. On his return, Lindley took the point position as negotiator for Security National, and he was well armed. While Reese would have to pull a number of his directors together to represent a majority stock interest, Lindley, representing Jefferson Standard, could make proposals on the spot, knowing he had enough votes in Greensboro to back them up. "If I had had to come back and get a decision every time, we never would have gotten it," Lindley said later.

Bank directors gathered for lunch in Charlotte hotel rooms, at sessions with investment bankers in New York and in Greensboro. The Charlotte interests were concerned about what Jefferson would do with its large block of stock. There were equity issues to overcome and personality clashes that blocked the way. Lindley maneuvered around these obstacles and depended on Lineberger to smooth over objections to Reese, whose patrician appearance and cool personality did not sit well with some. Lineberger, an American Trust director since 1946, had attended prep school with Vanstory and had grown up in an environment similar to those across the negotiating table. He was able to relate more effectively and keep Vanstory from bolting.

Whatever issues divided the two camps, they shared one common goal: both sides wanted to challenge Wachovia. That interest was also shared by the Comptroller of the Currency, who wanted to see a strong national bank—Wachovia operated under a state charter—emerge in North Carolina. In fact, the new bank would become the largest national bank in the Southeast. With a national charter, the new bank also would be free from the supervision of the North Carolina Banking Commission, whose members included officers from competing banks, including Wachovia.

The early public announcements were sketchy because not all the details had been worked out when the news broke in April 1960. At concurrent board meetings on April 8, Security and American Commercial representatives explained that American Commercial shareholders would own 56.5 percent of the stock in the new bank and Security would hold the remaining 43.5 percent. American Commercial would select thirteen of the board members and Security twelve. The new bank would have total resources of about $500 million, making it a sizable financial institution with nearly a thousand employees working in forty offices in twenty cities. The new bank would be the second largest in the state, behind Wachovia with its $658 million in resources.

A sensitive issue had been management. During negotiations with Security, Lineberger had insisted that the chief executive would be Reese. King and Lindley had no problems with Reese and were impressed with his vision and energy. This plan didn't sit well with Vanstory and others in Greensboro, however. Reese's election would tilt the direction of the bank toward Charlotte and leave the Security managers appearing to have sold out their city's largest bank to Charlotte. To appease them,

Lineberger agreed that Vanstory would be chairman of the board and the bank would operate with dual headquarters, one in Charlotte and one in Greensboro. The negotiators also agreed that directors would alternate meetings between the two cities. The division of labor and power relieved the anxieties, at least temporarily. Lindley and King acknowledged years later, however, that they knew Greensboro's position would slowly erode until all power of the bank eventually settled in Charlotte.

The consolidation was a Pyrrhic victory for Vanstory. He would emerge as chairman of one of the state's largest banks just slightly more than a decade after taking over the conservative, staid Security National, and he had gained a foothold in Charlotte for Greensboro banks. At the same time, the bank that he had built to a position of strength had virtually been sold out from under him.

Missing from the initial releases was any reference to the new bank's name because that was one thing that had not been agreed to. Business writer Rolfe Neill of the *Charlotte Observer* speculated that the new name would be American National Bank of North Carolina. At subsequent meetings in Charlotte on April 11 and back in Greensboro on April 13, a select committee of board members from the two banks worked out the final details. C. T. Council complained that early news reports made it sound like the new bank would be headquartered in Charlotte, and he didn't like that. He also objected to a long, awkward name such as American Security Commercial National Bank. Others agreed the name should be simple, but the first offering that reached consensus was American Security National Bank.

The group endorsed the Vanstory-Reese axis at the top and recommended three executive vice presidents. One was Patrick N. Calhoun, the former president of Guilford National, and the other two were Julian J. Clark and Herbert M. Wayne of Charlotte, who came from American Commercial. The committee also affirmed the dual headquarters and decided that, according to a report appended to the corporate minutes, "due to the many years of experience in handling out-of-town branches it was logical that this operation would remain in Greensboro." The correspondent banking business, corporate banking, and other business would be the responsibility of the Charlotte office.

Greensboro bankers also were concerned about Reese's new building, which was not yet finished. Before the deal was closed, he filed a detailed report showing that the Charlotte headquarters would cost just under $8.4 million—almost double the first estimate—and include another $1 million worth of improvements and furnishings. Accompanying this report were his estimates that the Charlotte business would grow from just over 62,000 accounts to nearly 86,000 accounts by 1964. Installment loans, the new consumer business, had almost doubled in the previous year, he reported.

At another meeting on April 21, as board members were about to finish their agenda, a committee that had been studying the proposed new name, American Security National Bank, reported problems. The name was unwieldy and looked to the past rather than the future. Lindley put forward the name National Bank of North Carolina. It included the word "national," as required by regulations, and it projected a statewide image. But older members of the group cautioned against its use. Thirty years earlier one of the more stunning bank failures had been the collapse of the North Carolina Bank & Trust Co. Security National, which had taken over some of that bank's offices, had suffered from that hangover even with a new name. Despite the warnings, the board adopted the name National Bank of North Carolina unanimously.

Within a week, however, the name was back on the agenda. The comptroller's office had disallowed the suggestion. Joseph M. Bryan, board chairman of Pilot Life, then suggested that the committee turn the words around and call the new bank North Carolina National Bank. That name stuck.

Negotiations to resolve the name had been tricky, but a more unpleasant chore awaited leaders of the two banks—deciding which half of each bank's board of directors would be asked to step aside. The new bank could have no more than twenty-five directors, and each bank already had that many on its own board. "That didn't win any popularity contests," King recalled some years later. For example, the treasurer of Cone Mills Corp. was named to the new board of the Guilford-Security merged bank, attended one meeting, and then was left without a seat.

The new board was an impressive lineup of North Carolina businessmen. The Greensboro interests were represented by Vanstory; King; Lindley; Council; Bryan; W. C. Boren III, president of Pomona Terra Cotta; Wilbur L. Carter, Jr., executive vice president of Southern Life Insurance Co.; businessman Fielding Fry; John B. Hatfield, general manager of the Sears Roebuck & Co. distribution center; W. G. Clark, Jr., of Tarboro; James M. Peden of Raleigh, president of Peden Steel Co.; and Orton A. Boren of Greensboro, president of Boren Clay Products, Inc.

Directors coming from the former American Commercial board were Lineberger; Reese; James L. Coker, president of Sonoco Products Co. in Hartsville, South Carolina; Frank Dowd of Charlotte Pipe and Foundry; T. A. Upchurch of Durham (a former member of the Raleigh bank board); James J. Harris, a leading Charlotte insurance broker; Julian Robertson of Salisbury, a textile executive; Thomas M. Belk of Belk Stores Services, Inc.; John C. Erwin, president of Allison-Erwin, a distributing company; William H. Barnhardt, president of Southern Webbing Mills in Greensboro; H. F. Kincey of Charlotte, president of N.C. Theatres, Inc.; James G. Cannon of Charlotte, of American Credit Corp.; and David R. Johnston, president of Johnston Mills Co. in Charlotte.

North Carolina National Bank began operation on July 1, 1960, a Friday. Most customers probably noticed little difference from the previous business day. In Greensboro, for example, the Security and the Guilford offices were not consolidated, and employees settled in at their desks and teller cages the same as they always had at bank offices located two blocks away.

At topping-out ceremonies for the new Charlotte building that November, Reese noted that fifty years earlier ground had been broken for the Commercial National Building. He pointedly corrected a Charlotte reporter's reference to the "new" North Carolina National Bank, saying, "We are not new. We're the oldest bank here." He did have to reach back to the 1874 date on Commercial National's charter for that, however.

The first stage of NCNB's headquarters building captured the attention of Charlotte. It was to be the tallest building in the state and the first Charlotte office tower since 1925 tall enough to require an aircraft beacon on top. The broad lobby, which opened to a mezzanine-level balcony, was strikingly different from the traditional cloistered appearance of the main floor of older bank buildings. The wall immediately behind the tellers would feature sculptures from eight to twelve feet tall and weighing as much as six hundred pounds. Designed by Charlotte sculptor Louis J. Martin, these twenty-five-by-one-hundred-foot figures represented industry, transportation, agriculture, medicine, education, and science.

Reese wasn't finished expanding, however. Before the end of 1961, he added two more banks to the fold. One was in Statesville, the county seat of Iredell County, located just north of Charlotte. The other was the First National Bank in Winston-Salem.

At the close of the year, eight and a half years after arriving in Charlotte, Addison Reese had the beginning of the statewide bank. North Carolina National Bank had forty offices between Charlotte and Wilmington. Granted, some of the cities where the bank was conducting business were small, but the bank also was represented in every major population center except Asheville in the mountains and Fayetteville in the east. Reese had not caught Wachovia, but he was particularly pleased to have an NCNB office in the heart of Wachovia's hometown of Winston-Salem, where he was in a much better position to keep watch on his adversary.

Chapter 5 **Armed Peace**

The challenge facing Addison Reese in early 1961, as he looked ahead to his first full year as president of North Carolina National Bank, was both exciting and daunting. His vision of a new state-wide bank capable of challenging the prevailing leader was now more clearly in focus than ever before. Virtually overnight Reese had succeeded to management of the second largest bank in the state, with offices from the mountain foothills to the coast.

But Reese knew as keenly as anyone that his "bank" was not so much one institution as it was a confederation of separate institutions, each with its own management, its own traditions, its own style, and its own policies about everything from loans to vacation pay for employees. A common name appeared on the front doors of the bank offices, but inside, employees with long and deep loyalties to old institutions were not united.

At best, the merger of the Security National and the American Commercial banks was a delicately balanced compromise. It was a cooperative venture that matched powerful interests in Charlotte and Greensboro who shared both a common goal of building a major statewide institution and anxiety about how such an institution should operate.

The merger committees had made the management challenge all the more difficult by agreeing to operate this new bank from two headquarters. To further complicate matters, Reese found himself with a board of directors jealous of its power, composed of members who wanted to be intimately involved in the details of the bank's management.

In short, NCNB had no policies, no guidelines, no corporate culture to establish how decisions should be made and few managers with any experience in large organizations. Every issue that arose required an answer on the spot, and many of these issues got put on the board's agenda by members who often were looking out for "their" officers or interests associated with the predecessor banks.

At the same time, Reese had a unique opportunity to forsake the disadvantages of traditional banking and create a new bank as it should be, from lending policies to filing cabinets. The opportunity was fleeting and it was rare. Few bank mergers would create a new organization as large as NCNB at the outset.

As if the long-range challenges weren't enough, Reese had major questions to answer immediately. At the top of the list was who would manage the day-to-day operations of the Greensboro headquarters. Hugh P. Beal, the most senior officer under Vanstory, was nearing retirement and was not encouraged to stay longer than necessary. Some of the harshest criticism to the merger proposal had come from Beal, a conservative banker of the old school who was uneasy with the balance of power. At one Security National board meeting before the final merger vote, he suggested that the deal was a sellout of the Greensboro stockholders. Reese needed a new, fresh manager, someone without the political baggage of either city but who could command the respect of Vanstory and the former Security National bankers.

Reese and Vanstory found the man they wanted in Thomas Irwin Storrs, the bright, tough-minded manager of Federal Reserve operations in Charlotte who had only recently moved there from the Richmond district office. Trained as an economist, with a doctorate in economics from Harvard University, but with no practical banking experience on his résumé, Storrs had nonetheless impressed Carolina bankers immediately upon his arrival. Vanstory had asked him to come to work at Security during their first meeting a month after Storrs arrived in Charlotte in 1959. A short time later, Reese had sent word that if Storrs was interested in joining American Commercial, there was a job waiting for him.

Storrs deflected both offers. He didn't believe it proper to move to Charlotte to take one job and then immediately leave for another. In the spring of 1960, however, while considering an offer to leave North Carolina to become president of a small insurance company, he called on Reese and Vanstory to see if their earlier interest was still alive. Both assured him that he had a job at their new bank. When they expressed interest in having him aboard, Storrs traveled to Greensboro for a meeting with Jack Lindley.

"I asked him several questions," Storrs recalled years later. "The one that sticks in my mind particularly is what his ambition for the company was. He said that all he wanted was the best bank in North Carolina, and he thought that things like size and such would take care of themselves.

"And then he went on to say that Wachovia, by its overwhelming dominance in the state not only in banking but in politics and business in general and the civic and social life of the state, had been so great that it was becoming a little bit fat and that the situation cried out for a competitor who could meet it and deal effectively as a competitor."

That was enough for Storrs. He attended the September board meeting, was elected to office, and on October 1, 1960, reported for duty as head of the Greensboro operations. Reese had his man in Greensboro.

Reese and Vanstory had been forced to go outside the bank to fill the important job in Greensboro for more than political reasons. Neither American Commercial nor Security had a reservoir of talent. Most of the experienced officers in the two banks were either close to retirement or conditioned by the Depression to conservative banking, an attitude that didn't complement Reese's vision.

In addition, there was a wide age gap between senior officers and promising newcomers in the lower ranks. Banking had not been attracting the best and brightest minds from the college campuses in the late

Thomas I. Storrs, NCNB executive vice president (left), and C. M. Vanstory, Jr., NCNB's chairman, made their headquarters in Greensboro, where Vanstory's Security National Bank was located.

1950s, and bank owners had not prepared second- and third-level managers for the top jobs. New bank presidents survived into the job more often than they learned and earned their way to the top. One Charlotte bank got a new president in the 1950s who was sixty-five years old. On college campuses, the banking industry's reputation for stuffy people and low pay had stifled interest among graduates in making a career in banking. Bank managers compensated for the low salaries with titles and job security, but most eager college graduates still steered clear of a career that led to a long, narrow corporate ladder.

Despite the enthusiasm from Reese and Vanstory to introduce new blood to the business, some top officers still harbored a paternalistic approach to employees, who were treated more like a big family than a professional organization. Herbert Wayne, the executive vice president in charge of Charlotte operations, made the rounds on Monday mornings to ask employees if they had attended Sunday school and church. His Monday inquisitions earned him the name "the Bishop." Wayne's questions about church attendance were not idle chatter; the right answer was important to one's future. Once, after an employee told him that a person's religious preference was a private matter, Wayne reported the incident to Robert L. Kirby, the American Commercial personnel manager, and complained that the man had a bad attitude.

Kirby had joined American Commercial in 1957, leaving a job in the personnel department of Burlington Industries in Greensboro. Even before the merger with Security, Reese told Kirby that he wanted to hire a new kind of banker. Kirby said Reese explained his vision of building a bank that could compete with Wachovia, saying, "If we're going to give the state a choice, let's really be different. Let's don't look like them, act like them, let's don't have a cookie cutter here, let's don't have a company mold."

"I was told, 'You go for all the different backgrounds you can find,' " Kirby recalled. "Don't get all Southerners, don't get all Baptists, don't get all University of North Carolina graduates." Then Reese told him that someday they would be recruiting women and blacks. Reese's words shocked Kirby. Women only recently had taken positions in the teller cages, and blacks still were relegated to custodial jobs.

While Kirby's marching orders were bold, his resources were thin. The early classes were limited to five trainees a year. He wasn't permitted to hire more, no matter what. He broke the rule in late summer of 1959, however, when a young applicant named Hugh McColl reported for work even though Kirby had told him there were no vacancies in the trainee class. Kirby admitted McColl when he learned that one of the bank's senior vice presidents had gotten a call from McColl's father, one of the bank's good customers, who asked, "What's this about you don't want my boy Hugh up there?"

McColl had applied at American Commercial because of his family's ties to the bank, and because Charlotte was close enough for him to continue his courtship of Jane Spratt, the daughter of a prominent lawyer and bank president in nearby York, South Carolina. He had met her

J. Van Lindley (left) of Greensboro and J. H. Lineberger of Belmont, North Carolina, who played key roles in merging the Charlotte and Greensboro banks, were members of the first board of directors of NCNB.

at the Southern Railway Depot in Charlotte just as the two were leaving for Europe in separate groups, and he had courted her all across the Continent, once buying forty dozen roses from a flower cart in Belgium and sending them to her room. They married the month after he started work.

The American Commercial training program was a frustrating exercise for young men like McColl, who were eager to get ahead. Kirby usually assigned the class of five (now six) to a rotation of service in the various bank departments. Each man spent a certain amount of time at each stop on the tour, watching but not working. When each left for his next stop on this modified open house, he prepared a paper on what he had learned.

The department managers disliked the system, and some of them gave the trainees a cold welcome. When McColl hit the transit department, the critical point in banking where what goes out is reconciled with what comes in, he ran square up against Benny Shaw. "I want to make one thing clear while you are here," Shaw told McColl. "I didn't ask for you, I don't want you, and I don't like college guys. And I don't like you."

McColl tried to win Shaw over and finally succeeded by working well beyond regular closing time to help clerks balance the books. The search for the missing penny at his father's business was not wasted.

Once trainees got beyond the old war-horses of the bank, they sensed that indeed they were part of something different, something exciting, though not quite defined. The spirit began to build after the creation of NCNB. Kirby used this growing sense of excitement about North Carolina's newest bank in his recruiting. "Here's your chance to kind of become a pioneer," Kirby told candidates for bank jobs. "Here's a chance to catch this train that is pulling out. Don't miss the ride."

Reese knew he needed to reach these young trainees early and encourage them to help pull his train. By 1962, the New York management consulting firm of Cresap, McCormick, and Padgett had started to work on an organizational plan that would tie all the disparate interests together and build a bank for the future.

CMP's first task was to inventory the company and determine exactly what people were doing, how skilled they were at their jobs, and how deep the management talent was within NCNB. Under CMP direction, some of the brightest of the young recruits were assigned to help carry out a management audit that covered every office in every city. Carrying notepads and checklists, young men who had just completed the training program were asking top-level officers to explain their duties and responsibilities in detail. They were not always met with smiles. The survey included such questions as how much time senior officers spent in managing their people, how much in generating new business, how much on civic affairs or at the country club. The assignment accomplished two things: CMP got the data and the young people got a look at the entire banking operation.

"People were very sensitive about these reports," recalled Sam Sloan, who served as the liaison between the bank and CMP. Sloan was typical of the new kind of employee signing on at NCNB. He had a degree in economics from Davidson College and a grandfather who ran a savings and loan in Gastonia, but he had not planned a career in banking. Just before he was due for release from a two-and-a-half-year Army stint, a friend told him about a new bank in Charlotte. He applied, was accepted, and was serving his time in the training program—which included leading tours to the top of the new building—when he was assigned to management services.

"People were sensitive because they knew that the report went to the chairman, the president of the bank, all of the executive vice presidents, and so on," said Sloan. "You had to watch out that somebody would try to give you an impression just to tell you what you wanted to hear. You had to be diplomatic about asking questions because some people felt threatened by it."

CMP took the material collected in the survey, talked with Reese, Storrs, and other senior officers, and created an organization for a bank. The plan included the first job descriptions ever written for some bank officers and defined duties and responsibilities more clearly than ever before. It placed a premium on management of people.

The resulting reorganization sent shock waves through some NCNB departments. Senior officers who had handled the larger accounts that added prestige and status to their jobs became managers of people instead of managers of money. Certain bank functions were consolidated at regional operations centers in Greensboro and Charlotte, which further chipped away at the prerogatives of top officers who previously had operated virtually independent of the Charlotte headquarters. National business was pulled from local branch operations and concentrated under a new national division in Charlotte, now headed by Pat Calhoun, formerly of Guilford National in Greensboro.

At the same time, other changes were taking place. Julian Clark, the bank's chief credit officer, wrote new loan policies for NCNB offices to follow, which created further concern among older bank officers in the branches. These policies were the first formal loan guidelines that some of the officers had ever seen. They were brief by current standards, but they were something new for many of the top employees in the branches, who previously had made decisions on loans to favorite customers with little peer review. Now their loan commitments would be reviewed by a committee and others under Clark's direction rather than approved by only one person.

The changes drew resistance, and Reese developed a straightforward strategy to pressure the local units and keep the business moving forward. To help him implement the changes and build the organization he would need in the future, he hired Dr. James Farr, a New York psychologist, whom CMP had used in other projects.

Farr came highly recommended by CMP. When he arrived in Charlotte, he didn't know he was embarking on an assignment that would engage him as a member of the NCNB organization for seventeen years. Though he had more cosmopolitan clients than a relatively small bank organization in a sleepy Southern city, Farr liked Reese and his ambitions for NCNB from the first. He found Reese to be "very handsome, gentlemanly, very bright, a very attractive person. I found him very smart, very motivated, not driven, but definitely motivated to build a bank. He was very people-oriented and very definite about where he wanted to go, but he had a soft approach."

At their first meeting, Farr said, Reese outlined the assignment, saying, "I have just merged sixteen small units that have spent years as competitors, and I'm trying to merge them into a single unit. How do I exert my leadership in a manner that will get the proper response by all the people I have to treat with kid gloves because they are chairman of the board of their unit?"

Farr was dispatched to the outlying branch offices to work with local bank officers and branch managers. "We didn't want to come in with an axe," he recalled, "but the other side of the problem was that Reese was absolutely committed to having an effective organization. My job was to really make local officers totally aware of how their performance was fitting in and what the new goals and strategies were, and to make them aware of contradictions and conflict.

"There were a lot of them who when they became aware of what was negative and conflicting, gradually adjusted. The others slowly faced up to the fact that they didn't want to adjust and there was no way out and they resigned and quit. Addison let it happen over time, but with a very definite focus that people either measure up to our growing standard or they will not be allowed to slow down the bank, and he did it as lovingly as possible."

After a hiatus of just more than a year and while still building its organization, NCNB entered into another round of negotiations that continued the bank's growth. On March 30, 1962, the Bank of North Wilkesboro joined, extending the bank's reach into the mountain foothills. Three months later, on June 8, the Bank of Wilmington became a part of the growing NCNB.

The Wilmington merger was a defensive move. When the Wilmington bank went on the market, NCNB sought a merger to increase its business in this important coastal city to strengthen its competitive position with Wachovia. The merger also added a touch of history. The bank traced its origins to the Bank of Cape Fear, which opened in 1804 and established the state's first branch office in Fayetteville in 1814 when the North Carolina legislature authorized branching of state banks.

Along with Reese, top officers of the other leading banks were combing the state for acquisitions. Chasing right after NCNB was First Union; Carl McCraw would dispatch his chief assistant, C. C. Hope, to small communities across the state. It was a game of cat and mouse. If Hope saw a banker from NCNB or Wachovia in a small town in the middle of the week and during the heat of the day, he could usually count on the visit being associated with a merger. To avoid detection on his trips, Hope would remove the Charlotte city license plate from the front of his car. The number of independent banks declined steadily as First Union, NCNB, and Wachovia grew.

Recounting NCNB's accomplishments of 1962, Reese could talk about growth of the new national division and the strengthening of the industrial development department, the only one of its kind in a North Carolina bank. Young loan officers scrambled for accounts. Bill Covington, who had forsaken a higher starting salary at First Union to join NCNB, was one of the early members of the national division. He learned that a good place to scout for new business was in NCNB's own transit department, where checks cleared. After regular business hours, he would stop by the department to look over the checks from correspondent banks to learn where potential corporate accounts had their banking business.

The national division was a hot spot. Hugh McColl had moved there after working in the correspondent banking department under L. W. Henderson, whom McColl remembers as "the meanest, toughest guy that ever worked in the company. But he knew a lot, could teach you a lot, and chose to do it by letting you make a lot of errors, then chewing on you like a drill sergeant." During his first five years with the bank, McColl traveled 60,000 miles, driving a Volkswagen because it got good gas mileage and saved him money.

The corps of young bankers also included Luther H. Hodges, Jr., a former classmate of McColl's at the University of North Carolina at Chapel Hill. At six feet two, Hodges even looked the part of the well-groomed banking leader, a perfect Reese protégé. His father had been governor for more than six years, having succeeded Governor William Umstead, who died midway through his term. Because of his father's background in business and as an adviser for the government in postwar Europe, the younger Hodges was a well-traveled young man even before he got to UNC, where he earned a degree in economics and a Phi Beta Kappa key. He took a master's in business administration from Harvard University and was considering a career in banking, but he accepted a teaching job at the business school in Chapel Hill in 1961 to give himself a year to sort things out.

Hodges had been raised in the bosom of the state's political and economic establishment and knew only one bank, Wachovia. His father was close to Robert Hanes, Wachovia's chief executive. But, Hodges recalled years later, he was hearing more and more about NCNB when he returned to Chapel Hill for the faculty position: "Somebody told me that Bob Hanes was the banker of North Carolina of the 1950s and Addison Reese was the banker of North Carolina in the 1960s." Hodges arranged to meet Reese and soon found himself forsaking a possible position with Wachovia and prestigious New York banks for a slot at NCNB.

The entry of Hodges into the ranks of Reese's young managers upped the stakes. McColl was particularly keen on the pecking order and believed that Hodges had an edge because of his political connections. At one point Reese's in-house psychologist, James Farr, took McColl aside and delivered this advice: "McColl, if you will quit worrying about your relative position with other people, they will start worrying about you."

"I took it to heart," McColl said years later. "It became quite prophetic."

In November 1962, Reese invited North Carolina governor Terry Sanford to help dedicate the second phase of the new building at 200 South Tryon Street. Many of the bank's 1,738 employees stood on the mezzanine and around the broad, marbled lobby to watch.

Reese had just more than a decade of North Carolina banking experience behind him as he headed into 1963. During that decade the state had shown strong economic growth. International trade had doubled and retail trade showed a similar increase. Per capita income had risen

50 percent. Ten percent more people lived in North Carolina than when Reese moved to Charlotte. Textiles, tobacco, and furniture remained the leading income producers for the state, but more specialized and more technical businesses were opening. NCNB was now a part of that growth, with more than $300 million in loans outstanding to businesses and individuals in the state.

NCNB was steadily building its reputation as an aggressive bank that would go after business that Wachovia and other banks ignored. In addition, managers of commercial accounts pared their costs and did whatever they could to lure business away from Wachovia and other competitors. The bank sought new ways to attract the middle market and position itself as the bank for the small- to medium-sized businesses that were experiencing rapid growth.

Creative approaches to new business were encouraged and rewarded. In 1963, for example, NCNB got special approval from the Comptroller of the Currency to lend money on lots at Duke Power Company's Lake Norman, the largest man-made lake in the state and an attractive site for second homes along hundreds of miles of waterfront. Other banks wouldn't touch the business, but NCNB gained approval to make the loans without securing deeds of trust.

In September 1963, Reese negotiated a merger with the Bank of Chapel Hill, firmly establishing NCNB in the promising territory known as Research Triangle Park, a concentrated research and light industrial area already being promoted as the industrial development of the future. Ironically, the park was created largely through the leadership of Wachovia's Robert Hanes and his successor, Archie Davis. Former governor Hodges also was an important figure in its development.

At the end of 1963, NCNB's resources were nearly $654 million. In March a $1.5 million computer system had gone on-line. The bank had fifty-eight offices in eleven of the state's most prosperous communities and plans for several new branches in 1964.

Late in 1963 Reese called a special meeting of the bank's top officers, city executives, their chief lieutenants and headquarters officers. The bank was approaching the end of its third year and was building its own record, not one that was a compilation of its predecessors' achievements, Reese said. He cited growth in deposits and specifically praised the work of city executives C. M. "Sodie" Allred of Raleigh, John Knox of Statesville, Elmsley Laney of Wilmington, Gordon Malone of Burlington, and

Allen Preyer of Durham. Their offices had impressive increases in deposits and net operating income, and Reese gave them credit for boosting the overall assets of the bank. But Reese had more than numbers on his mind. The management plans put in motion months earlier were now clear, and Reese was eager to move ahead with a program that would set the tone of management development for years to come.

"I know all of you are pretty well sold on the idea that management development is a good thing," Reese told the city executives and senior bank officers. "You're in favor of it like motherhood, perhaps, but many of us find ourselves so caught up in the daily task of controlling costs and improving earnings that we relegate our responsibility for management development to a position of secondary importance."

Then, with emphasis, he said, "In fact, if this bank is to survive in today's competitive market, you must develop managerial talent."

NCNB's real objective, he said, "is simply this—that for every key position in North Carolina National Bank we want two replacements, one fully qualified to step in tomorrow morning if need be, the other to be ready within two years."

Reese said more was to come. In future months, they should be prepared to move promising managers into new positions, bypassing those who might be senior to them if they didn't show the same potential. "Management, unfortunately, involves demotions as well as promotions," he said. "Managers should be prepared to move people between different banking offices, quashing forever within NCNB deep-rooted traditions to the contrary." He concluded his pronouncements, unsettling to some in the room, with the statement "I believe that I have made it clear that in the future you and your subordinate managers are going to be judged, to some extent at least, by the quantity and quality of the managerial talent you produce."

Reese's remarks left no doubt that his search for bright young talent was no casual affair. He wanted adaptable people who weren't hidebound by traditional banking practices. The bank didn't try to hire away Wachovia's bankers or look for new officers among the crowded junior ranks in New York. Instead, the personnel department was interested in people who could conceptualize, who had good people skills, who had an interest in community relations. "We needed that more than we needed brilliant credit men," said Robert Kirby, who continued his quest for a new style of banker.

Within his top management, Reese had in Julian Clark one of the best credit men in North Carolina banking. Clark had come from the American Trust branch and was well known in banking circles as an experienced manager of lending. A graduate of Davidson College and the son of a banker from Bladen County in eastern North Carolina, he had spent his entire career at American Trust before becoming one of Reese's executive vice presidents. He was a very deliberate man, quiet-spoken and even austere at times, but occasionally he enjoyed a joke with the young lending officers during the morning coffee breaks. Like Reese, he saw his job as getting young bankers off to the right start, from lending policies to the proper attire. When a young newcomer named Joe Claud showed up for his first day wearing a sport coat, Clark complimented his choice but suggested that a suit was more in keeping for a banker, unless he wanted to earn "sport coat" wages. Claud didn't have to be told twice.

Clark also was one of Reese's closest counselors. The two often rode to Greensboro together, arranging their game plan for the monthly board meetings en route. Like other senior officers, Clark handled some of the bank's largest accounts and set the tone for the conservative lending practices.

Also on Reese's team were Executive Vice President Pat Calhoun, who managed the correspondent banking and commercial banking business as well as some operations matters; Storrs, who managed the Greensboro region; and Wayne, who managed the Charlotte region. The dual headquarters envisioned by NCNB's founders remained, at least on paper. The bulk of the retail business—the NCNB branch operation—was based in Greensboro, but even as soon as Storrs was installed, the balance began to shift to Charlotte.

The tip of the scales southward did not sit well with Vanstory and others eager to maintain Greensboro's status as a headquarters office. NCNB's organizers proposed in the initial merger draft that the bank's "big board" would hold only quarterly meetings, but the reality was monthly meetings, with meetings of the executive committee sandwiched in between. The drain on management was steady and unrelenting. Bank officers shuttled back and forth between Charlotte and Greensboro as the board alternated its meeting site. Reese never fully recovered from one session before he was preparing for another.

During these years of growth, the relations between Reese and Vanstory were cordial and cooperative in public, but one person who was close to the board in those days described their relationship as one of "armed peace." The two tolerated one another, and Reese spent many board meetings absorbing complaints and objections from the Greensboro interests. But Reese could count, and he knew where the votes were on the board. He just went quietly about his business, biding his time until Vanstory's scheduled retirement in 1966.

Reese's reputation as a bank builder and the aggressive posture of NCNB in the marketplace were attracting more and more bright young men to the bank. By 1963, some of the small nucleus of college-trained recruits that had joined the bank in the late 1950s had become officers, and the word of their rapid rise through the ranks boosted NCNB's stock on college campuses. In addition, they were loyal to Reese, who gave his young officers more and more authority. Hugh McColl and his peers realized early that "we were going to get ahead if we just went after it because of the basic inertia of the average officer. There were few decisive people and Mr. Reese wanted things to happen. He had a great deal he was going to accomplish and he was using the young people."

Storrs said, "We took people who were freshly out of college or graduate school and pushed them to be executives. Reese had no children, and he looked upon many of these young men really as a lot more than just youngsters in the bank. He was determined that he was going to push their development as hard as he could, not only to fill these gaps that we had but also because he just plain liked them. He gave them authority and responsibility, and it was reflected in the speed of their development and in the expansion of the company."

NCNB's prestige and recruiting potential received a boost in 1964 when Richardson Preyer of Greensboro joined the bank's trust department. Preyer had resigned a federal judgeship to make a run for the Democratic nomination for governor. His unsuccessful campaign had captured the imagination of college students and progressive Democrats, but it had been a bitter and emotional fight against racist politics in North Carolina.

The day after his loss, Preyer received a call from Addison Reese asking him to join NCNB as head of the Greensboro trust operations. "When you are down and out, that is a very heartwarming call," recalled Preyer, who left the bank in 1968 to mount the first of six successful campaigns for the U.S. House of Representatives. "So I went to work with them as head of the trust department and enjoyed that very much."

Preyer's experience in politics and his Richardson family connections gave NCNB an edge in Greensboro. The bank's personnel department also used Preyer to help recruit new people. From time to time, he was asked to call promising applicants and add his personal request that they join him at NCNB.

From his office on the mezzanine level of NCNB's headquarters in Charlotte, Reese was in sight of customers and employees alike. He could step out his door and see the main lobby below. His quarters were small, with only enough room for a desk, a side chair, and a sofa. A few personal pieces of art—landscapes and a sketch of a city square in Baltimore—were on the walls. Ironically, the location placed him in clear view of a large Wachovia sign on a building across the street. The sign advertised Reese's nemesis as "the largest bank between Philadelphia and Dallas." Reese's office was as neat and proper as its occupant; he seldom appeared in the bank without his suit coat, a habit from earlier days when bank officers had their desks in full view and conducted business in the open area of the bank's main floor.

The office was not a forbidding inner sanctum, but it was clear that, except for senior officers, this was a place that one entered when summoned, not when in need of a few minutes of chitchat. Reese respected the chain of command, and he used it. Employees seldom got calls from him, but they would hear from their superiors, who were gathering information for the boss. And if a young officer was called for a meeting, he was expected to be on time and ready to do business.

"I am sure that he was accessible to Julian Clark and Tom Storrs," McColl recalled, "but I was always under the impression that it took a brave man to go see Mr. Reese. There weren't a whole lot of them around. In other words, you got sent for."

The president's style was one of cool efficiency; his schedule one of order and purpose. Reese handled correspondence and memos as soon as they appeared on his desk. When he arrived at about 8:30 A.M., ready for work, he greeted his secretary, Betty Wright (who had been with him since 1954), and moved right to the waiting mail that she would have arranged in order of priority. The most important items were on top, memos and work prepared for distribution to others in the middle, and reading material that he might put in his briefcase for review that evening at home at the bottom. Reese used the telephone to keep in touch with Storrs in Greensboro, who spent a couple of days a week in Charlotte, and to handle outgoing business, but his incoming calls were screened and Betty Wright redirected any that could be handled by a junior officer.

Part of the training rotation for young recruits was a turn as Reese's assistant. The title was more impressive than the work, however. The assistants handled some routine chores, including chauffeuring Reese in his Cadillac across the state to branch operations and meetings. Reese often carried work along with him on these trips and seldom involved his drivers in idle chatter. Assistants also ran errands. One eager young man was impressed the day he was entrusted with the out-of-town delivery of legal papers involving an important bank merger. Throughout the trip, he drove carefully, confident that any accident would surely derail an important deal. To his chagrin, he learned that another set of papers had been sent by air and no one was awaiting his return with eager anticipation. His efforts were just insurance against a plane crash.

Despite Reese's imperious style, a personality often described as aloof, and a manner that kept him a proper distance from employees, he was not only respected but admired by subordinates. His management style and personality often were the subject of coffee-break conversations among the young bankers bucking for promotions and were scrutinized even more closely by a more formal group of junior officers who met regularly with Jim Farr.

Reese, with suggestions from Storrs, Clark, and others, singled out about twenty promising young men who seemed to have the ability to become executive vice president or president and assigned them to study under Farr. The group, with the official title of the Information and Advisory Panel, came to be called the Young Turks. They met a couple of times a month and were given projects that would take them all over the bank. When their work was finished, they would report to the board or the appropriate executive officers.

The strategy was to enable these young people to influence the emerging culture of NCNB without undermining the more conservative philosophies of senior officers. It also gave Reese a direct line to the next generation. Any topic was open for discussion. A young Francis "Buddy" Kemp once suggested boldly to Reese that the leadership of the bank should be entrusted to those with a history with the company rather than bringing in "outsiders." Reese responded coolly that the observation was "interesting" and then reminded Kemp that both he and Tom

Storrs had been "outsiders" at one time. The men often talked about the bank's management, particularly Reese's style and the qualities that set him apart from other corporate leaders.

"We all decided he had it, but we didn't know what it was," said McColl. "It was just power. You knew you were around the chairman. How he walked, how he looked through you. When you were talking to him he looked straight through your eyes and into the back of your head. You knew that whatever you were thinking he knew what it was. In other words, his way of looking at you was so penetrating that he would be reading off the back of your tape. When you were in his air space, you were in *his* air space and he was concentrating on you. Whatever you said was going to be weighed and could be found wanting."

But there was more to Reese's influence than sheer force of personality. For young bankers like McColl and Hodges, Reese was their idea of a banker for the future. He had national connections, having achieved the prestigious post of president of the Association of Reserve City Bankers in April 1965. At home, he was the man who was going to make their lives exciting and offer opportunities that far exceeded what their peers would find in other banks in North Carolina.

The Farr group was an in-house laboratory, a place to test the young men that Reese saw as the managers of the bank in the next generation. It was also a necessity. The paucity of management talent within NCNB presented Reese's new crop of bankers with few role models. Often the recruits—within just a few years—would end up managing men who were their seniors. "Addison really believed in building executives for the future," Farr recalled. "They weren't going to make it if they weren't going to plan now for when they were five times bigger. Part of my assignment was to help develop that future leadership."

Of those within the group of Young Turks, Hodges was considered to have an inside track to the top job someday. He had the right name, he was urbane, handsome, smart. Some said that his good looks and stature made him a natural eventually to follow Reese into the chairman's office. It was only a matter of time, observers said. His position was further enhanced in February 1967, when Reese named him city executive in Chapel Hill.

Another restructuring at the top followed Herbert Wayne's death in January 1965. The following month, the board named Julian Clark executive vice president for finance. Tom Storrs was named executive vice president for administration. Three senior vice presidents—C. M. All-red, J. A. Tate, Jr., and J. H. Witherspoon—were given regional respon-sibilities for management of the branch offices.

Any remaining hope among Greensboro's board members that Reese and the Charlotte interests would not have their way with NCNB evapo-rated in 1966 when Vanstory retired as chairman. Both he and Reese had been given five-and-a-half-year contracts with the bank when it was organized in July 1960. The end of the term coincided with Vanstory's reaching the age of sixty-five.

Vanstory did not leave his post entirely satisfied with what the 1960 merger had wrought. He and some board members from Greensboro, such as Joe Bryan, who represented the Jefferson Standard Life Insurance Co. interests, had resisted the shifting of power to Charlotte. Even though they never did have the votes on the board to stop the steady migration of power south, they had undertaken delaying actions along the way. After his retirement, Vanstory told a biographer, Abe Jones, Jr., of Greensboro, "It would have been a lot easier for me if I'd gone along." But that was not his style, no matter the odds.

When Vanstory retired, he could be proud of the growth and devel-opment that had come from the merger. NCNB had not yet caught up to Wachovia, but it had narrowed the margin considerably. At his re-tirement, NCNB's resources were $949 million and Wachovia's were $1.29 billion. NCNB had seventy-seven offices in fifteen cities and was looking for new sites. NCNB beat Wachovia into the growing Research Triangle Park near Raleigh, but only after fighting off official objections from Wachovia and Central Carolina Bank. Less than a year later, Wa-chovia and First Citizens Bank & Trust Co. filed objections to NCNB's expansion in Raleigh's suburban neighborhoods.

On February 14, 1967, the board of directors elected Reese chairman, elevated Storrs to vice chairman, and named Julian Clark president. The banking operation that Reese now commanded reached from the resort community of Tryon in the state's southwestern mountains to Wilming-ton on the coast. The bank's area of influence roughly followed U.S. 70, one of North Carolina's primary east-west routes. Vanstory had used the highway as his guide to direct expansion of the Security National system, and early in 1967 plans were being made to continue development in this direction with a new branch in Morganton, a busy furniture manu-facturing town about fifty miles east of Asheville.

In 1967, after Vanstory's retirement, the NCNB board elected Addison Reese (right) chairman. Thomas Storrs (center) was named vice chairman, and Julian Clark, the bank's chief credit officer (left), became president.

Before the Morganton branch, all of NCNB's expansion had been through mergers that either strengthened the bank's position in an important market, such as Wilmington, or extended the bank's reach, such as Tryon. The mood within the organization was one of anticipation and eagerness for competitive growth. Reese alluded to this in his opening remarks to the new members of the Morganton board.

"We are the state's largest national bank [Wachovia was a state-chartered bank], the third-largest bank in the Southeast, and the fiftieth in the nation, with assets just under a billion dollars. We think that is a pretty good record for a seven-year-old bank," Reese said. But, he added, "We don't want to be the biggest, just the best. Size will follow naturally."

By the end of the year, with offices being added in Fayetteville through the merger of Commercial and Industrial Bank, the bank's aggressive loan policies had doubled the loan portfolio to more than $580 million in just five years. The nation's economy was heating up under President Lyndon Johnson's domestic spending and a growing investment in a war in Southeast Asia.

"The environment was one of change," remembered McColl. "Mr. Reese was trying to make a statewide company, creating mergers, and he was looking for people who were decisive. Luther and I were both willing to take more risks than anybody in the company. We were very aggressive lenders and did things the bank had never done before.

"We thought we were smart as hell, but it takes getting older and looking back to see what was happening. The country was emerging from nearly twenty years of low inflation rates. Luther and I were aggressively lending money in the face of an ever-rising economic environment. So we couldn't make mistakes. Any errors of judgment we might have made were bailed out, in effect, by the huge overheating of the 'guns-and-butter' Great Society era."

"We were growing fast, and that was the goal to achieve," Richardson Preyer recalled. "I think there was some feeling that Wachovia prided itself on getting the pick of the crop, so to speak—young people coming out of college. NCNB felt that this group was a little elitist and that we at NCNB had a little more common touch. We were going after businesses that weren't R. J. Reynolds, weren't Wachovia-type businesses, but were growing young businesses and we felt that NCNB was on the trail of the fast-growing, newcomer business and younger people in the state. We were not a stuffy bank. We were a more gung ho operation."

The steady and rapid growth of the bank built on itself. The bank that barely six years ago had had no identity and a polyglot heritage colored by competing and often conflicting interests and traditions, was beginning to build a corporate culture. Ironically, that culture was being shaped by Wachovia, the bank that Addison Reese did not want to be. It boiled down to this: NCNB would be whatever Wachovia was not.

"It was a way to unite the troops," recalled Farr, Reese's management consultant. "And it worked for years. Reese intended NCNB to become the biggest bank in the Southeast. The first thing he had to do was beat Wachovia. It wasn't just a model. He was out in fact competing with Wachovia. It was a plan. We were going where we had to go to beat Wachovia. It was something to focus on. It was 'let's win.' And what does win mean? It means getting bigger than Wachovia."

While NCNB had begun to develop a distinct culture within, its image

dominant
new star

in
carolina

The timely emergence of North Carolina National in 1960 was prompted by the demands of a State economy *first in manufacturing* . . . second in total business volume in the entire Southeast. Born of vigor, with antecedents dating back to 1874, the expanded bank's assets exceeded a half billion at the end of its first six months. 51 locations in ten cities cover principal money centers in the State. When your business concerns North Carolina, contact North Carolina National Bank.

Resources $526,696,038   Capital Funds $41,704,336

NORTH CAROLINA NATIONAL BANK

MEMBER FEDERAL RESERVE SYSTEM • FEDERAL DEPOSIT INSURANCE CORPORATION

BURLINGTON • CHARLOTTE • DURHAM • GREENSBORO • HIGH POINT • RALEIGH • STATESVILLE • TARBORO • WILMINGTON • WINSTON-SALEM

The new bank's logo drew upon the public's fascination with the nation's space program. In the early years the bank was called North Carolina National, but bank officers eventually succumbed to the public's name, NCNB.

outside the bank offices was cloudy. Ken Clark, the bank's public relations officer, had joined the company in the summer of 1967. Before he arrived, NCNB's community involvement consisted primarily of participation in United Way campaigns. Successful public relations was measured by column inches of newspaper copy, not by the number of potential customers attracted to this aggressive newcomer. One of Clark's first assignments was to take a look at the bank's public image and, most important, its identifying logo, which appeared in different variations.

At the time of the creation of NCNB, marketing specialists and a special committee assigned to create a new logo for the bank had searched for a new image and symbol for their bank. America was fascinated with space exploration; the Soviet Union's Sputnik was circling the globe. After considering several suggestions, the group had finally settled on a logo that featured an oval with a Polaris starburst in its center. A circle to represent the Carolina moon enclosed one end of the oval. The outline of the circle suggested the orbit.

What had seemed a good idea at the time failed to capture anyone's imagination, although it was committed to bronze and installed in the sidewalk in front of the Tryon Street headquarters. People in the bank couldn't even remember whether this logo would be used with the circle to the side of the oval or turned 90 degrees and placed at the top, where it took on the appearance of a halo. The bank's in-house publication, *The Compass*, used the logo with the outside circle at the top in the halo position. When the new Raleigh building was dedicated in 1966 the logo was hung on the wall with the halo at the three o'clock position.

To confuse matters further, some within NCNB called their company Carolina National, and some printed material of this era set the words "North" and "Bank" in smaller type than others—probably a holdover from the lingering concern of the elders who were still sensitive to the collapse of North Carolina Bank & Trust Co. during the Depression.

Clark hired national pollster Lou Harris to find out what the public thought the name was. What he learned was that people didn't care much for the name Carolina National. North Carolina National Bank was NCNB. "And," Clark recalled, "anytime we suggested something else they threw it right back at us."

NCNB was to be the preferred name, history notwithstanding.

Chapter 6 **What Are We Waiting For?**

During the 1950s, hundreds of banks, including Chase Manhattan in New York, had tried to generate new business with something called credit cards. In 1951, Franklin National Bank in Franklin Square, New York, issued a card to its customers that could be used in the Franklin banking market. As losses mounted on bank cards, however, many imitators were discouraged from entering the new market. For example, Chicago banks, which tried a joint card program in the 1960s, ran into problems early, and during the first six months of 1967, losses amounted to $7.2 million.

North Carolina's First Union National Bank, NCNB's competitive neighbor on Tryon Street in Charlotte, introduced bank cards to North Carolina in 1958. At first, the cards could be used only at assorted retail shops in Charlotte, where the bank had offices. When First Union merged with First National Bank in Asheville and later opened offices in Wilson, North Carolina, in the eastern part of the state, the card business was exported there, but usage was still limited.

One success story was Bank of America, which with its many branches throughout California had succeeded with its card, introduced in 1958. Hundreds of thousands of cards were mailed to Bank of America customers, who used them to buy gasoline, pay for a meal, and purchase high-ticket items such as furniture and appliances.

In 1966, the Bank of America decided to extend its card business across the country. Addison Reese learned of Bank of America's plans in late spring 1966, when he got a call asking if NCNB would be interested in becoming part of a nationwide network of banks that together would offer the distinctive blue, white, and gold Bank of America card.

Reese and Storrs saw the competitive advantages for NCNB if it could get in early and capitalize on the novelty of a card that could be used throughout North Carolina as well as outside the state. If successful, the credit card would give NCNB customers a more efficient way to manage their money, and the bank could earn a fee on a transaction that might otherwise be completed with cash. It also would give the bank a boost in attracting consumer business. Despite NCNB's growth, it still lagged in consumer deposits, a relatively inexpensive source of money for the bank. No matter how much NCNB grew, Wachovia continued to outdistance it in deposits.

Reese and Storrs put NCNB's $25,000 deposit in the mail to the Bank of America without first discussing the new product with their board, some of whom frowned on the plans when they were outlined later. The dissenters said it wasn't appropriate for a commercial bank to be in the credit card business. Had Reese and Storrs waited for board approval, however, NCNB might have lost its claim to the card. About the same time they were filling out the NCNB application, a rival bid was being prepared at Wachovia. It could have been something as benign as the efficiency of the mail service or the NCNB style of fast response, but NCNB's acceptance of the Bank of America offer arrived a day earlier than Wachovia's application, and NCNB secured the unofficial franchise for the state. NCNB joined two banks in the state of Washington, two in Oregon, one in Boston, one in Ohio, one in Philadelphia, and the First National Bank of Memphis as the first to enroll in the new national

BankAmericard system. It was the only statewide bank east of the Mississippi to do so.

The early endorsement of bank cards was just one of several important decisions that during the next six years were timed just right to keep NCNB a step ahead of the competition. Before he retired at the end of 1973, Addison Reese not only would achieve his goal of surpassing Wachovia as North Carolina's largest bank but also would leave behind a long record of success and a competitive culture for the next generation of leaders.

Before the bank credit card was introduced, one survey found that people in the banking industry believed the most exciting thing to happen in banking in postwar America was air conditioning. For generations, the banking business had been as dull as the people who managed it. Customers put money in a bank and wrote checks for periodic withdrawals. For the most part, the people who borrowed money didn't need it. Businessmen and blue-chip clients were simply renting someone else's funds so as not to disturb their own. Credit opportunities for the average worker with a home mortgage and car payments were limited. Innovation in banking meant accepting weekly deposits to the Christmas Club.

Bank cards could change all that—at least they suggested they could. But the new attraction was not without risk. The losses in Chicago, Chase's misfortunes, and the weak response to the First Union effort were not lost on more conservative bankers in the Carolinas. A High Point bank, a correspondent banking customer of NCNB's, had tried a purely local card and soon found itself waist-deep in collection problems. NCNB helped bail out that bank, which was using off-duty policemen to collect delinquent accounts. Indeed, some of the early launches of the Bank of America card posted losses for participating banks because the banks moved too quickly, introducing the card before support systems were in place.

NCNB's marketing director, Robert Provence, knew he had his most challenging assignment when he was handed the bank card promotion. In late 1966, Provence and others from NCNB traveled to San Francisco to meet with other bankers about the launch of the so-called Bank-Americard program. Along with Provence, NCNB sent Connie Owens, who was in charge of consumer credit; Lewis Perry, manager of the credit center; L. W. Henderson, the bank's operations chief, and an account executive from the bank's advertising agency. The group was excited but cautious. Not everyone at the bank had bought into this notion of easy credit for consumers.

Provence didn't question the marketability of the concept, but he did see some problems. For example, he said, the name of the card was awkward. It wasn't really a word, only a collapsed version of "Bank-of-America-card." As a former broadcaster, he could envision announcers stumbling over the card name, and he suggested something with fewer syllables. He also questioned whether a card that had international potential should include "America" in its name. (A decade later, Bank-Americard became VISA.)

The bankers also talked about the importance of making a fast, well-coordinated launch of this new banking product. With the problems that bank cards had experienced, public confidence in the system required a clean start. In addition, all agreed there would be a competitor. In fact, plans for another card already were in the works in a move launched by four California banks that would eventually produce the Mastercharge card, which later became MasterCard.

On their return from California, NCNB's team went to work. First they needed cardholders. City executives submitted names of potential card customers, and each was screened for creditworthiness and repayment experience. Customers qualified if they would otherwise be eligible for a $500 unsecured installment loan. Other bank files were scanned for potential names, producing a combined list of 104,000 names.

Just as important as cardholders was the enrollment of a wide range of merchants with whom customers could use their cards. For a customer to see the value of the card, he or she needed to have places to use it. On the other hand, merchants weren't interested in discounting their prices to the bank for a service that only a few of their customers would use. More cardholders, more merchants. More merchants, more cardholders.

While card customers could be signed up by mail, the merchant end of the loop required more personal involvement. To kick off the merchant recruitment campaign, Provence and others began putting together plans for a meeting the likes of which NCNB had never seen and would never see again. It took place in High Point, a furniture manufacturing center about fifteen miles south of Greensboro. For NCNB, it would be the launch site of one of its most successful and profitable marketing ventures.

On January 28, 1967, a Saturday just a few weeks before the furniture manufacturers rolled out their floor samples for the industry's annual spring show, about five hundred NCNB officers met in one of High Point's furniture exhibition buildings. It was a command appearance. Each had received a personal invitation from Addison Reese to spend Saturday talking business. Throughout the morning, past lunch, and on into the afternoon, Provence and the marketing team explained what the card was, how it worked, and what was needed to make the program a success at NCNB. Not since the bank was organized in the summer of 1960 had all of NCNB's officers been together in the same place at the same time, mobilized to work together on the same project.

"Almost inadvertently," Storrs said years later, "we did something that we should have done five years before, which was to get a great many of the people of the bank together."

Immediately after the High Point meeting, Provence deployed a hand-picked team of 125 of the bank's best young officers, who were pulled off their regular assignments for sixty days and put on the streets to sign up merchants. In addition, every other bank officer was expected to do his best to bring merchants in his market into the program. As soon as a business was recruited, one of thirty attractive young women dressed in blue, white, and gold uniforms visited the owner, delivered point-of-purchase displays, pressed special decals on the doors, and reviewed the operating procedures with the shop owner and the employees.

North Carolina was well suited to a bank card program. The retail business in the state was based in many small- to medium-sized communities where local department stores, restaurants, and shops competed for the customers' dollars. This program was particularly popular in such retail markets because it helped local merchants become more competitive with the larger stores, which had their own credit plans. Large department store chains rejected the bank cards because they competed with the stores' own profitable credit programs.

The merchant campaign was a success. In eight weeks, about 3,500 merchants were signed—twice the goal. By August, NCNB licensed the first of its correspondent banks to issue cards. By the end of the year, fifteen banks in thirty-three communities had added merchants and consumers to the program.

Public reaction was generally positive, but mixed with it was some initial confusion and surprise that a bank would extend $300 worth of credit—the standard limit—without so much as an application or credit check. NCNB even drew criticism from preachers, who complained about the card from the pulpit. Newspaper editorials were not all positive. Critics warned that the cards made it easier for consumers to run up debts they couldn't pay, leaving themselves liable for interest rates that were more than triple those of conventional lending. Customers liked the card. In the first month, the sales and cash advances charged to it topped $1 million.

By all accounts, BankAmericard was NCNB's most successful new product. Initial start-up expenses were heavy—earnings per share were cut by 11 cents to pay for BankAmericard—but by year's end, NCNB customers had used the bank card for more than $10,200,063 in purchases, an amount significantly greater than projected figures. Participating were 4,600 merchants, with a total of 7,400 business locations. More than 185,000 North Carolinians were BankAmericard customers.

The card introduction was well under way when NCNB reached another milestone in its growth. On September 1, the bank reported accumulated resources of more than $1 billion.

In 1967 NCNB appeared to be a business bursting at the seams. It began the year with 1966 earnings up nearly 17 percent from 1965 and pulling out of the tight credit of the previous year. Loan demand was strong; more than half a billion dollars of individual and corporate loans were on the books. The bank had made calls on thirty European banks to explore correspondent relationships. An aggressive management training program was bringing in two dozen recruits a year. The annual report for 1966 also bragged on the bank's conversion from second-generation to third-generation computers. Noted in the report was the announcement that William H. Dougherty, Jr., had joined the corporate staff on January 3, 1967, as management services executive.

Dougherty was thirty-six years old when he packed his belongings into the family car on New Year's Day, forsaking the televised bowl games for the drive from his home outside Pittsburgh to Charlotte. He had just resigned as vice president–finance at the Western Pennsylvania National Bank and Trust Co., where he had gained a reputation as a wizard with the computer management of bank accounting and financial systems. Trained as an accountant, Dougherty had helped negotiate mergers and worked to build Western Pennsylvania into a bank with more than $1 billion in assets. He was made chief financial officer and was in

charge of the treasury departments, legal, and real estate when he resigned and headed south.

Dougherty was a beefy guy with a coal miner's build and a steelworker's heritage. His roots were deep in the blue-collar communities of suburban Pittsburgh, where his father, a machinist, and his father's father
had worked more than a hundred years for the U.S. Steel Corp. In addition to his duties at Western Pennsylvania, Dougherty was mayor of
the suburban community of Liberty Borough, a job his dad had held for
twenty-four years before him. The night the call came from a corporate
headhunter working on NCNB's behalf, he took the message over the
police radio while cruising with one of the town's patrolmen.

The corporate scout told Dougherty he had a job opening at a bank
in the Southeast. Was he interested? Dougherty had never heard of
NCNB, so he assumed the offer was for Citizens & Southern in Atlanta
or Wachovia in North Carolina. Told neither was the client, Dougherty
still agreed to meet. He made arrangements to fly to Charlotte.

Dougherty was sold on the idea of working for a statewide bank, and
he liked what he saw of Julian Clark, Tom Storrs, and Addison Reese.
"I really liked these three men," he recalled later. "You could sort of feel
that something was going to happen at this institution. I was really taken
with Addison Reese and the way he handled me and his warmness, open-
ness, his frankness."

Reese explained that he needed someone to bring the NCNB systems
into line with the growth and development of the bank. The bank had
installed expensive computer systems, but Reese told him they weren't
adequate. He would have complete authority to do what was needed,
Reese said.

What Dougherty found was worse than what Reese had described.
Here was a bank on the verge of recording $1 billion in resources, and
its main banking office in Charlotte hadn't balanced the cash accounts
for more than a year. He found a back room full of checks that had not
cleared. They had been kicked out of the system because of improper
coding or some other error and had never been entered manually. "That
was money," Dougherty said. "That was cash sitting there. They said
there were a lot of problems, but I don't really think that they knew.
Addison Reese was really straightforward in his command, but the problems that I found were overwhelming."

With the help of an assistant, who spent months on the project,

Dougherty finally resolved the imbalance in the teller logs. "It was just indicative of the careless manner that the records were being maintained," he said. "The accounting system would produce at best a balance sheet that may or may not balance. And except for having a consolidated profit and loss statement, we had no idea what the branches were doing, not anything. We were trying to run a bank without any management information. And that's where I started."

Dougherty had been at the bank two weeks and had found himself coming up against one discouraging situation after another. One afternoon, he left his office on the mezzanine level with his shoulders slumped and discouragement written across his face. He saw Reese emerge from his office a few doors away. Reese called Dougherty over, put his arm around his shoulders, and said, "Bill, I know you're the man that can do this job and can take care of it. Don't let it overwhelm you. You can handle it."

The endorsement from Reese was a tonic. "I probably could have taken on the world because he displayed that much confidence in me and from then on we tore it up."

Dougherty laid out a plan to modernize NCNB, starting with a new general accounting system and an entirely new chart of accounts that was flexible enough to accommodate the banking of the future. The system was designed not only to ensure that the books balanced but to provide current financial data so managers could determine whether the bank was making money and where it was being made. For example, the system would allow Reese to figure out if NCNB operations in Raleigh were as profitable as operations in Winston-Salem. This idea was later extended to individual types of business and even to certain large accounts.

Within a year after Dougherty arrived, he had installed another major new management tool. American business had for some time adopted profit planning systems. Banks had ignored the lesson. Now Dougherty was devising a system with which managers could see how well individual locations were performing, thus allowing for better planning and opening new ways to reward employees for performance. With a net return figured for each profit center, NCNB's top executives could measure performance throughout the business. Dougherty didn't know it, but he was establishing more than a system. He was contributing to a corporate culture that years later would be based on accountability at the lowest level possible.

These management data allowed sharper pricing of services and special products, which permitted NCNB to become more competitive. "We could tell how to price consumer services," Dougherty said. "We could always price these services cheaper and develop a large return on assets and return on equity by the customer."

This consolidation of systems resulted in another change also. Under the old system, NCNB looked like a confederation of banks. The new system cut straight through the various defenses that local branch managers had erected to protect their own operations from close scrutiny by Charlotte. The new data gave top management in Charlotte a look inside the daily operations of the city organizations. For the first time, top management knew where the soft spots were in the business. And the depth of the problem could be measured. This new information began to change the way NCNB managed itself as well as its customers' deposits.

"We said that we were going to run this ship lean and mean, and we're going to make it a very accountable place. If you said you were going to do something, then we were going to make sure you did it," Dougherty said. It was a refrain that would set the tone for aggressive expansion into other markets, and it became an anthem in later years.

The system was only as good as the information fed into it. To gather that information required more reporting than most bank employees had seen, particularly fast-moving loan officers who were more interested in getting business on the bank's books than in how it added up when it got there. To produce the management data necessary to plan new products and manage services, someone had to get that information into the system. The reporting began on the front line.

One day Hugh McColl, by now a senior vice president and in command of the national division, stormed into Dougherty's office and complained loudly that his loan officers didn't have time to fill out Dougherty's reports. They would have no time to serve customers, McColl complained, if they were busy with paperwork. Dougherty acknowledged that he had not sold the need for accurate and complete reporting well enough to the people on the line. Once he explained how the data could be used, however, McColl's temper cooled, and he eventually became an advocate for accurate data and the accountability that it provided for management all the way up and down the line.

In August 1968 Reese announced that NCNB's new computer system would be installed in a new $4 million, 123,000-square-foot building that would be erected in downtown Charlotte at the corner of College and Second streets. The announcement came one day after First Union National Bank announced plans for a thirty-two-story office tower to go up just a block away between Tryon and College streets. The announcements by both banks marked the beginning of the transformation of downtown Charlotte from a mercantile center characteristic of the 1940s to a commercial center at home in a forest of towering office buildings. Reese nudged the city to keep pace with its downtown redevelopment plans. "What are we waiting for?" he asked in announcing NCNB's plans.

While Dougherty was trying to bring the bank's back room and accounting systems into the twentieth century, other problems were being attacked in the front office. Dougherty arrived at the same time that NCNB and banks across the land were struggling to find sources of funds to meet the loan demands of their customers.

Banks work on a simple principle: They must take in money to be able to lend money. As the inflationary policies of Washington fueled industrial growth and economic expansion in the South and used up the nation's savings to finance federal deficits, banks found that they were not able to attract enough money through traditional methods, such as savings and demand deposits, to keep up with the loan requests of their customers. Interest rates were climbing, and by 1966 some customers could earn more interest lending money to the United States government by buying U.S. bonds than they could by keeping funds in a savings account at their local bank.

NCNB was no different from any other bank. Demand deposits, such as checking accounts, which had been growing steadily for a decade, now were level. Time and savings deposits had fallen by more than $63 million, from more than $281.5 million to just more than $218 million. NCNB needed cash to be able to remain in the marketplace with loan money available for its customers. In an effort to raise money in March 1966, just before the severe crunch in August, NCNB sold its headquarters building on Charlotte's South Tryon Street in a leaseback arrangement. At the time, the $8.9 million sale was the largest real estate transaction ever recorded in Mecklenburg County.

A similar tight-money situation had spawned a new product in 1961 when Regulation Q limits, which put a cap on the interest rate that banks could offer savers, created another tight-money situation. Then, in an effort to get around the limits, New York's First National City Bank created a market for its certificates of deposit, or "CDs." These negotiable certificates allowed banks to effectively circumvent the low rate ceilings and helped the money-center banks to generate large amounts of cash. The early CDs were sold mainly to corporate customers in denominations of $1 million. In creating a market for their CDs in smaller denominations, First National City Bank could easily generate cash by selling them in bulk when it needed the money, rather than waiting for cash reserves to build up while customers purchased one of the instruments.

By August 1966, CDs accounted for $18 billion of the money-center banks' resources. Walter Wriston, then president and later chairman of Citibank from 1967 to 1984, said in a 1977 interview that CDs "probably changed the world [of banking] as much as anything."

That was fine for the big banks, but what about the smaller, regional operations like NCNB? They ended up following the lead of archrival Wachovia Bank & Trust Co., which had introduced certificates in $1,000 denominations, something an individual could purchase. While some gave Arthur Roth, the aggressive marketing whiz of Franklin National, credit for creating the smaller-denomination CD market, he said he learned of the idea while attending a bankers' convention in the South. He learned well. In a month or so after his return, Franklin National Bank had raised $420 million from the sale of CDs.

Regulation Q was not going to go away, and it would present recurring problems for the banks. If NCNB was going to grow, it would have to find ways to accumulate funds to meet its customers' needs. If it couldn't, they would go somewhere else, either to another regional bank or to New York, which was becoming as much a competitor as the other banks in North Carolina. That was the case in the summer of 1966. As money-center banks raised their rates, regional banks like NCNB were frozen out. Large depositors like corporations began shifting their cash north.

What NCNB needed was a more reliable source of funds. Reese, Clark, and Storrs talked about spinning off the consumer credit business and then borrowing money to pay for it. The most appealing idea again was coming from First National City Bank.

In 1967 Tom Storrs organized a committee to study a whole new dimension of doing business. Two years earlier, CIT Financial Corp., a finance company, had purchased a bank. The transaction set bankers thinking. Why couldn't a bank own a finance company, or an insurance company, or a credit card company or anything else? Just across the street, First Union had restructured after it joined forces in 1964 with Cameron-Brown Co., a mortgage company. A new corporation was formed—a one-bank holding company—that owned the bank and the mortgage company. Storrs asked an NCNB team to investigate the one-bank holding company possibilities for NCNB.

One-bank holding companies were not new. Nonbanking companies such as Goodyear Tire and Rubber, Sears, and Montgomery Ward had owned banks for some time, though the law was designed primarily to accommodate banks in smaller communities that owned other businesses.

Storrs's committee came back with a resounding endorsement of creating a new entity, called NCNB Corp., that would own the bank and also own any other business that might meet the strategic objectives of the company. The holding company arrangement would permit the bank to issue bonds or other commercial paper to raise money, allow the bank to expand into other businesses, and also permit NCNB to conduct nonbank business in other states.

"As we talked about nonbank lines of business," Storrs recalled, "it seemed that we had the opportunity to provide sort of counterbalancing businesses that would not be subject to the same cyclical events that the banking business was, and therefore would help to hold up earnings for the corporation at times when the bank earnings were under pressure. This was one reason why we were very much interested in the consumer and sales-finance business."

In late spring the plan was presented to the bank's board of directors, which enthusiastically adopted it. On July 5, 1967, Storrs, Jim Sheridan, who was the funds management executive, and legal counsel Jim Kiser incorporated NCNB Corp. Eleven days later, the NCNB directors approved a plan of reorganization under which the bank became part of the corporation. Reese was named chairman of the board, Storrs was president of the corporation, and Julian Clark was elected vice chairman.

The new organization opened several opportunities to Reese, not the least of which was to create a new board of directors that reflected the plans for the future rather than the traditions of the antecedent banks. From the outset, NCNB had more people interested in board positions than there were seats available. To appease those left out when the original board was formed, advisory board positions were created. Now, with the holding company, Reese was not restricted by federal banking regulations limiting board membership to twenty-five. Both the bank board and the holding company board offered prestigious positions for potentially important members of the growing NCNB family.

Wachovia also had begun planning for conversion to a one-bank holding company. Wachovia actually beat NCNB to the Federal Reserve with its plans, but flaws in the proposal sent executives back to Winston-Salem to make revisions. (Wachovia Bank & Trust Co., the largest state-chartered bank in North Carolina, completed the conversion on January 1, 1969.) When NCNB's conversion took place on November 4, 1968, it became the largest one-bank holding company in the Southeast, with resources of $1.2 billion.

Reese moved quickly to consolidate the corporation's position. On October 15, the NCNB board approved a plan to acquire the Charlotte insurance firm American Commercial Agency, Inc., a company that had been the insurance department of American Commercial Bank, which had been sold in the 1960 merger. In November the board created NCNB Properties, Inc., which purchased much of the bank's real estate for $12 million and leased it back to the bank, thus freeing capital for use in acquiring earning assets. From this point on, NCNB and most other banks would carry real estate on its books only as long as necessary. In December, NCNB Mortgage Corp. was formed. Raising money through commercial paper sold on the New York market, NCNB Corp. financed the purchase of most of the mortgage and construction loan portfolio and all of the mortgage servicing agreements of NCNB.

Expansion continued into 1969. NCNB purchased Stephenson Finance Co., Inc., which gave the business sixty-five consumer lending and sales finance offices in the Carolinas and Georgia. The acquisition of Stephenson expanded NCNB into South Carolina and staked a claim to business in new markets. Late in the year, plans were completed for the acquisition of Factors, Inc., of High Point.

One-bank holding companies swept the nation. By the end of 1969, about 30 percent of the nation's bank deposits were in banks owned by one-bank holding companies, though few had taken their new authority as far as NCNB. Congressional hearings suggested that restrictions should apply, but NCNB's nesting of business in bank-related activities was never threatened by the new legislation.

Chapter 7 **Winning One for Reese**

When Addison Reese became a banker, iron bars still encaged the tellers, credit was something banks offered only to their best customers, and bankers were cast in the image of moviemaker Frank Capra's old Mr. Potter—grumbling, miserly beings whose delight was tight control of the community's capital.

As Reese prepared for the close of his career in the late 1960s, banking was a business no longer measured by how much money was in the vault, but by the number of dollars in the marketplace. It was an industry that attracted bright young college graduates with advanced degrees. In North Carolina's competitive market, NCNB, Wachovia, and First Union fought for depositors' dollars and businessmen's commercial loans with aggressive marketing and eye-catching promotions.

Banking was hot. And as the 1970s opened, NCNB was one of the hottest on the block. Its stock price was climbing, and people beyond North Carolina, inside and outside the world of finance, were taking notice. The number of stockholders increased by more than 80 percent in the five years after NCNB converted to a one-bank holding company.

NCNB people liked to refer to themselves as the Citibank of the South. Indeed, just as George S. Moore had turned First National City Bank into a multifaceted financial services company, so had Reese and Storrs transformed NCNB from an aggressive statewide bank into a competitor for the financial needs of businesses across the South.

The bank now spanned more of North Carolina than ever before. Mergers had extended it east to Greenville, home of East Carolina University, smack in the heart of tobacco country and at the front door of First Citizens Bank & Trust Co., the leading eastern North Carolina bank. The bank opened a new Hickory office, and NCNB was prepared to make a substantial investment in the state's western urban complex growing up along Interstate 40. At the end of its first decade of business, NCNB had more than $1.3 billion in total resources, with ninety-one offices in twenty-seven North Carolina communities. Every major urban area in the state, except Asheville, had an NCNB office. In 1969, the first foreign branch was opened in Nassau, the Bahamas.

Luther Hodges, Jr., who had been promoted from Chapel Hill to Charlotte city executive in 1968, was demonstrating that banks had a humanistic side. At his behest, NCNB started opening new lines of business in areas previously considered off-limits for major uptown banks. In Charlotte, the bank opened a branch on Beatties Ford Road, near Johnson C. Smith University, in the heart of one of the city's black neighborhoods, and put one of its young black officers in charge. The move drew criticism from the black-owned Mechanics and Farmers Bank. Hodges countered the black bankers who complained about the competition, asking, "How are you going to talk about black capitalism and how are you going to talk about our being more progressive and doing things if you criticize us?"

Later, in the eastern North Carolina town of Lumberton, NCNB helped Lumbee Indian leaders organize the Lumbee Bank of Pembroke and then trained without charge the employees needed to run it. In mid-1971, NCNB quietly began testing a program of loans to low-income borrowers referred to the bank by social agencies in six communities across the state.

The bank even developed a reputation in the arts. The bank's interest in North Carolina art, a project favored by Reese, won *Esquire* magazine's Business in the Arts award in 1968. Under the direction of an in-house curator, NCNB's collection of North Carolina art and crafts surpassed that held by the North Carolina Museum of Art in Raleigh and encouraged more local artists. Regional art competitions stimulated local interest, and the bank commissioned original works for its offices.

Sarah Toy, the bank's first full-time art coordinator, turned the lobby of the South Tryon Street headquarters into a gallery where more people saw art than at Charlotte's Mint Museum. A new sculpture, an expansive work of gold and silver wires extending eighty-eight feet, was commissioned for the lobby wall. Sculptor Richard Lippold's creation replaced the stiff models representing industry, education, and the arts that had hung there for a decade and were never Reese's favorites. The new piece was called *Homage to North Carolina*.

There was enough of an open, innovative spirit about the place to permit the bank's public relations chief, Ken Clark, to create a carnival atmosphere in the lobby from time to time. On the day of a space launch, passersby crowded around twenty-four-inch television sets positioned around the lobby near tables with coffee and cookies. The sets returned for the World Series. Cheers of excited viewers broke the quiet of Reese's mezzanine office. During the 1970 political campaign season, Clark arranged for a donkey and a baby elephant to pose in the lobby. The donkey ended up kicking a Republican county commissioner, Clark said, and the elephant was removed following a complaint from the local chapter of the Society for the Prevention of Cruelty to Animals. To mark the occasion of the opening of the Hickory branch, Reese cut a ribbon of dollar bills strung across the front door. Each of the dignitaries on hand received one of the bills in a handsome frame. The remaining cash was given to charity.

The image of banking was changing. Instead of activity in a stuffy mausoleum where people talked in hushed voices, customers at NCNB might be greeted by a banking staff decked out in outrageous clothing on something called Mayglomania Day. Even Reese, who was of the era when proper dress was as important as a balanced financial statement, got into the spirit by wearing a bright sport coat as part of Mayglomania. Reese's casual attire startled employees, who seldom saw the lighter side of their leader.

Marketing of the NCNB name, image, and, of course, services was a growing line item in the budget. One promotion featured pocket calculators that were given free to housewives from low-income families to use in grocery shopping. One of the country's earliest automatic teller units, a Docuteller that dispensed cash, was installed at the College Street Corporate Services Center in Charlotte. The bank sponsored tennis tournaments and won recognition for the branch offices with designs coming from avant-garde Charlotte architect Harry Wolf's drafting table. Southern Bell's North Carolina office installed its first picturephone, the short-lived Bell Labs invention, for use between the headquarters and NCNB's operations center. (It was removed a year later, having proved to be impractical.)

During the late sixties, recruiting continued, but with new vigor. Promotion Qualification was the name of a program designed to turn MBAs and new college graduates into officers as quickly as possible. The annual quota was thirty new recruits. Special attention was directed to black applicants, and the bank set goals to add more black bankers to its officer ranks. One article in *NCNB News*, the company magazine, was titled "The Best Man for the Job May Be a Woman." In it, Reese said, "Women can hold down any job in the bank, if they want to—in time. But it is going to be a little while before a woman can represent us in some jobs, not because of ability, but because she lacks acceptance by our customers." At the time, two-thirds of NCNB's employees were women; 6 percent were officers.

"There was little happening in Charlotte that NCNB was not involved in," Clark recalled. That included the redevelopment of Charlotte's central business district, where NCNB made its home and planned to expand. Reese became a strong supporter of the city's redevelopment plans and in September 1969 gave unqualified endorsement to a major bond package: "My banker's mind is enthused at the thought of transforming this area in the heart of Charlotte, now mainly unproductive and decidedly unsightly, into a generator of jobs and income and tax revenues. If we can't sell this package to the taxpayers as a good, sound, income-producing investment, then we are poor salesmen indeed." The bond issue passed.

It was a heady time. "The board thought that everything we did turned to gold," Hodges recalled.

Indeed, North Carolina was a place for an aggressive company to make money. Personal income in North Carolina was growing faster than the national average as manufacturing employment and manufacturing spending continued to outpace the rest of the nation. The state's population was increasing. After decades of net outmigration, North Carolina's population was growing faster than that of other states, and the new residents were better educated, better trained, and better consumers than those who had left in the decades before. The state was experiencing a boom in everything from textiles to tourism. The sounds of construction and heavy equipment building resort communities pumped new dollars into what had once been remote areas in the mountains and along the coast. Reese told an associate: "In this environment, in this climate, anybody can make a success. You'd have to work at it now in North Carolina to fail in banking. All we want to do is get our share of growth that's coming to North Carolina."

The conversion to a one-bank holding company provided the psychological boost that Reese needed to challenge the hungry corps of young officers led by Hodges, McColl, and Dougherty. It also opened the opportunities for much-needed capital for his second-in-command, Tom Storrs, to expand the reach of the banking operation during a period of rapid growth. In the remaining few years of Reese's administration, the bank would find new markets with innovative programs. First, however, NCNB needed the funds to take advantage of the expansion opportunities. The holding company was just the platform Reese needed to take the story of NCNB's phenomenal growth to a national audience of securities analysts, who, it turned out, were eager to receive him.

NCNB executives had learned in a survey of national securities analysts that the bank was well regarded by those who knew the company. But the bank's problem was that very few analysts knew NCNB at all. Reese and Storrs had appeared before New York analysts, but these visits had been too infrequent to breed familiarity. In early 1970, Clark arranged a series of sessions designed to introduce the Southeast's first one-bank holding company to a national audience of securities specialists. The trip was crucial. These were people who through their in-house reports and tips to investors could make or break a stock. Clark booked sessions in St. Louis, Chicago, San Francisco, Los Angeles, Atlanta, Baltimore, and, of course, New York.

On March 3, Reese, Storrs, Dougherty, and a small supporting cast of Clark's road show climbed the side steps of a DC-3 that NCNB leased from S&W Cafeterias. Quarters were cramped and travel uncomfortable in this sausage with wings as it headed for the first stop, Boston. The plane had some years on it. The S&W pilot, a Navy veteran, had flown the very same plane during World War II, twenty-five years earlier.

"Ours is a story of the future, rather than a story of the past," Reese said in opening his presentation to the Boston analysts. "This, we believe, is what you want to hear about." Then in a smooth, logical fashion, Reese told of the bank's record of growth, speaking from an outline that he had crafted personally and revised up to the time he stood before the group in a Boston hotel. Storrs and Dougherty joined him at the front of the room to sell both the bank and North Carolina, which was viewed by many outside the region as still only a few steps removed from a farm economy.

Reese emphasized the youth and vitality of NCNB's management. He pointed out that the average age of executive and senior vice presidents was forty-seven; the average age of profit center managers was forty-three. "Our emphasis on youthful management has been based on the belief that we can profitably substitute brains, education, and training for experience, if we provide them with strong staff and senior management support," Reese said.

Dougherty's computer-based management tools also were part of the program. Profit planning, responsibility reporting, measurement against plans, and work measurement studies had enabled NCNB to detect movement in the market well before such change might be reflected in annual or quarterly earnings reports. Reese told the analysts, "We are making management decisions today based on hard and timely facts, and that is an advantage I have not always had in my banking career.

"Truly NCNB Corporation is a story of the future; one comprised of the future of our holding company, our bank, and our region. We have one guiding financial goal—to grow at an annual rate of at least 10 percent in earnings before security gains and losses."

The DC-3 had not returned to Charlotte before the trip's results were in. During the three-day swing, NCNB stock jumped six points. "People were calling us from all over the country," Clark recalled, "and they said, 'What's happening to NCNB stock?' The word had started getting out that this was a unique bank with some innovative traits and a lot of aggressive people."

These meetings, and others that followed on a regular schedule, gave

NCNB the introduction it needed to a market eager for new investment opportunities. NCNB captured additional funds through the issuance of commercial paper, the first to come from a one-bank holding company. By the end of 1970, nearly $70 million had been raised this way, with $25 million set aside for anticipated growth of the bank.

The first three years of the new decade brought more expansion of the banking business into communities across the state. In addition to Hickory, near the North Carolina mountains, the bank was expanding in the east with a merger in Greenville in September 1969. Altogether, the bank added seventeen new cities to the NCNB roster between 1970 and 1973. Most were new offices in secondary markets or areas of the state experiencing new growth and development in both the mountains, where resort homes were being built and the new Southern ski industry was booming, and in the east, where new industry was locating in what once had been tobacco fields. Offices in Monroe, Spruce Pine, Boone, and Jacksonville opened in 1970 and 1971. Pinehurst, Wilson, Goldsboro, Lenoir, and Kinston opened in 1972 and 1973.

Expansion of NCNB operations also continued in existing markets. In September 1971, NCNB announced an $11 million, fourteen-story office building for Winston-Salem. It would be the company's largest building project outside of Charlotte, putting the NCNB name on the skyline of the hometown of the bank's principal competitor, Wachovia. By year end, the bank would be ranked among the top fifty banks in the United States in one-year and five-year earnings growth.

There were additional mergers. The Bank of Washington joined in 1971; Carolina Bank of Commerce—with offices in Eden, Reidsville, and Wentworth—came into NCNB in 1972; Farmers Bank of Woodland and the Bank of New Bern in 1972; and Citizens Bank & Trust Co. of Henderson in 1973. Like others, NCNB was finding fewer and fewer local banks available for sale. First Union and Wachovia also were expanding their bases through acquisition.

NCNB's top officers were all over the state, looking for merger possibilities. It was not uncommon for the company's pilot, Lee Noble, to fly seven or eight different hops per day. One day, he dropped into the Raleigh airport seven times.

The 1960s had indeed been a time not only of consolidation of management but also of expansion of business. As a result of mergers, consolidations, and a few conversions, the number of state banks had declined from 147 in 1960 to 86 at the end of 1969. By the end of 1970, the number had fallen to 76. At the same time, the number of branches operating had increased from 378 to 519.

At least once, the scramble for new acquisitions created some confusion between Storrs, who headed the banking operations, and Reese, who had his own agenda. In January 1970, Storrs dispatched Hugh McColl and the bank's legal counsel, Jim Kiser, to work out a merger with the State Commercial Bank in Thomasville. NCNB didn't have any branches in Davidson County, a furniture manufacturing center just south of Greensboro, and the merger would help fill in the gaps in the Piedmont corridor, Storrs believed. The two finally worked out a deal and returned to Charlotte feeling like hunters who had bagged big game.

They were called to Reese's office, where they thought they would receive their just praise. When they arrived, Storrs was already there. "What in the hell are you doing in Thomasville?" Reese demanded in an angry voice that set McColl back. He had never seen Reese deal with subordinates in an angry way. The courtly manner had given way to a steely command that would not be denied.

"I've got a merger agreement," McColl answered.

"On whose authority?" Reese snapped.

McColl searched for a response. He knew he wasn't going to pass the buck; his Marine Corps training prohibited that. Then Storrs spoke up.

"Addison, I told him to," Storrs said.

Reese turned to his chief lieutenant and said, "You don't have that authority. I am the chief executive around here. I'm the only person who has that authority."

Looking back at McColl, Reese issued his last command on the subject. "You get your ass up that road and break that merger because we are not going to do it."

McColl wasn't sure how he would do that, but he answered, "Yes, sir," turned on his heel, and left the office with Kiser. He was stunned. He couldn't figure out what had happened. Later, when Storrs emerged from Reese's office, McColl learned that at the same time Storrs had been pursuing the Thomasville bank, Reese had been negotiating a merger with a bank in Lexington, Thomasville's neighboring community in Davidson County. Reese had not told Storrs about his discussions until he had a deal arranged, and Storrs hadn't told Reese about his pending merger plans. It was a lapse that was unusual in their thirteen years together, but NCNB now had an interest in two banks in the same county, an arrangement that would never pass the review of regulatory authorities.

McColl, the loyal foot soldier, returned to Thomasville with Kiser for a ticklish confrontation with the bank's owner, George L. Hundley, an influential businessman and well-known Democratic party politician. McColl didn't outline the details of the problem but said simply that the deal could not go through because of regulatory problems. Hundley was furious, and the two NCNB messengers felt his wrath. Humbled by the entire experience, McColl and Kiser took their lumps and returned to Charlotte.

The next day Reese called for McColl again. To his surprise, McColl learned that the Lexington deal had gone sour and now Reese wanted the Thomasville bank.

"I told him that I'd already broken off the transaction," McColl recalled.

"He said, 'Well, that's not a problem. Just open it. Just do it again.' Well, back to Thomasville I went, worked out a deal with George, at the same price, and did a deal with him."

If nothing else, the episode underscored the continuing problem of managing the business from two locations. Storrs maintained an office in Charlotte just two doors down from Reese on the mezzanine, and was in the city two or three days a week, but the dual headquarters notion, weak at the outset, simply never proved an efficient way to run the business. The arrangement was awkward, but it kept peace in the family and honored the agreement hammered out years before with the Greensboro interests.

In early 1970, however, NCNB dropped the arrangement, and Storrs left Greensboro for Charlotte. The Charlotte headquarters building, where Storrs took up permanent quarters, was quickly becoming overcrowded. As NCNB continued to outstrip each year's projections for growth, Dougherty, who supervised the bank's real estate, would update his space requirements, which then always fell short. "Our needs were always 50 percent greater than the space studies would show," Dougherty recalled. "That's how fast NCNB was growing, and we just couldn't project that kind of growth. It became very evident to all of us that we had to do something."

Dougherty investigated expanding the bank on its current site. After all, the building was not even ten years old, the lobby was first-class, and the bank already owned some adjoining property. At the same time, a Washington, D.C., firm that he commissioned to study the development patterns of the city reported that growth would probably occur on the side of Tryon Street opposite the bank's location.

While this study was under way, Charlotte's mayor, John Belk, paid a call on Reese. Belk was the chief executive at the Belk department store operation, with four hundred stores across the Southeast. His company also had a major investment in downtown Charlotte. While Belk was a member of the board of Wachovia, his brother Tom was a member of the NCNB board. Another brother, Irwin, sat on the First Union board.

Belk outlined for Reese his vision of a first-class downtown business district, which would need a major investment to succeed. A top concern was the city's center, the Square, as the intersection of Trade and Tryon streets was called. At the time this intersection was a display of urban decay rather than dynamic growth. Small shops with ragged fronts were all that survived at the crossroads that was noted more as the major transfer point for the city's bus service than as anything else. The city's new civic center was planned for the corner one block east, and the shabby storefronts nearby did not make for an inviting front door to the new building.

Belk wanted a major corporate partner for this project. He had already been to Wachovia, whose building one block west was showing signs of age, but he had been turned down. Accounts of Belk's first meeting at NCNB differ: Dougherty recalled excitement among NCNB executives; Belk, cold indifference.

"Cold," Belk told a reporter later. "I've been to some cold luncheon meetings, but if we'd had had some cold cuts served at this one it would have seemed like a hot meal. Those folks at NCNB acted like I was a thief. Here was a director of Wachovia trying to tell them to move out of the finest office building in downtown and build a new one."

Belk did not know that Charlotte architect A. G. Odell, who had designed NCNB's operations center and had prepared the master downtown plan for the city, had already sold Reese and Storrs on the Square. They restrained their enthusiasm so as not to encourage Wachovia. Storrs thought it should be worth at least a half million dollars more in extra visibility to the out-of-town Wachovia than to NCNB.

NCNB executives were still nervous. Their present site was comfortable, and the project being discussed involved more than just erecting a building. NCNB didn't have the talent on board for a major urban development project. In addition, the bank would need special permission from the Comptroller of the Currency to proceed.

Dougherty also assumed that once the full scope of the city's development project—which included an office tower, a plaza, a retail mall, a parking garage, and a hotel, with at least 25 percent of the space open to the public—became known, then others would want a piece of the deal. When the Charlotte city council opened bids for the redevelopment project, which would involve local government funds as well as NCNB's private investment, NCNB was the only bidder.

NCNB was not the first major bank in Charlotte to expand its facilities. First Union's thirty-two-story tower was already under construction when the steel for NCNB's new building was going up. Odell wanted what he considered the number one location in the financial center of the Carolinas to be different. So did Reese. "We know that it will be the dominant structure in Charlotte when it is finished," he told the *Charlotte Observer*.

At the time, all of Charlotte's office buildings faced squarely onto the main street in front. First Union's new quarters were set back, with an open plaza in front, but it didn't break the patterns of right angles that had Tryon Street as their baseline. Odell wanted a building that not only would dominate the Square with its sheer size but also would present an imposing visual image and provide pedestrian movement through the block. Odell's designers proposed turning the building at an angle to the street so it would point to the center of Trade and Tryon streets.

In addition to the rotated front, Odell's designers proposed the trapezoidal hotel with its slanted roof and the sloping front for the building's main entrance. The project's design architects, Thompson, Ventulett, and Stainback, Inc., of Atlanta, objected to the Odell ideas, but NCNB turned down the TVS plans for a smaller, motel-type facility in a U shape that would contain an atrium and an ice rink. With the hotel moved to the north side of the site, the building had easy access to the civic center and open views from the lower floors to the southeast.

The early drawings of the building presented a tall, angular structure, a six-sided tower sheathed in glass. Public discussions of the size of the building included a reference to "at least thirty-six stories." The height of the tower, however, remained an open question. Dougherty's space estimates indicated that NCNB would need a minimum 300,000 to 400,000 square feet. If NCNB wanted half of the building for itself, then the mathematics for Odell's design called for forty stories. During one meeting, a boastful McColl suggested a fifty-story tower, tall enough for NCNB to block the sun from its competitors.

Once the fundamentals of the project were settled, decisions on the undertaking shifted from Reese to Storrs. Eighteen months before his official retirement date at the end of 1973, Reese began moving more and more responsibility to Storrs and the management team of younger executive vice presidents: Hodges at Banking Group I, the retail bank; McColl at Banking Group II, the commercial and international business; and Dougherty, whose responsibilities covered operations and the non-bank subsidiaries.

Reese's retirement was no secret. The bank required board members and bank officers to step down when they turned sixty-five, a policy that Reese joked was founded on "presumptive incompetence" but that he honored. Most observers inside and outside the bank had pegged Storrs as the most likely replacement. He was Reese's chief lieutenant, he had demonstrated management ability, and he was responsible for much of the bank's record of growth and success.

Reese had begun preparing Storrs even before he moved to Charlotte. Not long after James Farr began his management consulting with the bank in the early 1960s, Reese told him he believed Storrs was "the best man in the bank. He really looked ahead. He was a very long thinker, very patient."

As Reese's retirement date approached, NCNB moved closer to realizing his goal of matching Wachovia's dominance in the state. The gap between NCNB and Wachovia had closed to within striking distance.

At the time, NCNB included banking (North Carolina National Bank), insurance (American Commercial Agency, Inc.), home mortgages (NCNB Mortgage Corp. and C. Douglas Wilson & Co. of Greenville, S.C.), investments (Bullock-NCNB Co.), factoring (NCNB Financial Services, Inc.), an interest in a real estate investment trust (NCNB Tri-South Corp.), consumer finance (Stephenson Finance Co.), and trust business in North Carolina and Florida.

In late April 1972, the first quarter's earnings reports were published. The newspapers carried the news that Addison Reese had been waiting for almost from the day he arrived in North Carolina nearly twenty years earlier. For the first time, NCNB was larger than Wachovia. The margin wasn't great, but his bank now was the largest in the Southeast, with $2.9 billion in assets. Wachovia's assets stood at $2.7 billion.

Reese told his stockholders, "NCNB was formed for one basic reason—to increase banking competition in the state and the Southeast. At the time of its formation, there was one bank which dominated the state and a large part of the Southeast. We saw a need for increased competition and an opportunity for a large, well-managed banking company."

Capping Reese's final year by making NCNB larger than Wachovia wasn't in any formal plans, but it was a goal of his chief lieutenants. "That was the year we turned on all the faucets, driving up the volume," McColl recalled. "We used more and more borrowed money and more and more Eurodollars, pushing out more and more assets in order to make that plan and have Mr. Reese go out on top. Nobody ever said that, but that is what we were doing."

For the most part, NCNB let the media make the comparison with Wachovia. That didn't stop Bill Covington, city executive in Winston-Salem, from bearding the lion. He couldn't resist saying something when he spotted Wachovia board chairman John Watlington standing with a group of his executives at the annual Tanglewood Steeplechase in Winston-Salem. Covington, dressed in Bermuda shorts befitting the Saturday social outing, spotted the more formally dressed Watlington, who was standing with a couple of his board members. Covington walked up to him and needled, "How does it feel to be number two?"

Covington recalled that Watlington was momentarily taken aback, then quietly responded that his bank wouldn't be number two for long. In fact, the numbers did change before the end of the year, and the lead seesawed between the two competitors for several years.

In July, steelworker Butch Alsup moved the last piece of structural steel into position in NCNB's office tower high above the intersection of Trade and Tryon. Fifteen hundred people crowded Tryon Street to watch the beam, carrying the signatures of Charlotteans who accepted NCNB's invitation to be part of the occasion, move slowly, surely into place. Reese stood with NCNB dignitaries to see the symbolic evergreen blow in the summer wind 508 feet above. A steel band played "Up, Up, and Away," and the National Drum and Bugle Corps, flown into the city by the North Carolina Air National Guard, performed.

With its new building, the bank also adopted a new logo—a bright

Hugh McColl (left), William Dougherty (center), and Luther Hodges, Jr. (right), the three young, strong senior leaders around whom new NCNB chairman and CEO Thomas Storrs organized the business. Dougherty was the eldest of the group at age forty-three.

red "NCNB" closely set in heavy, blocky type, produced by the New York firm of Schecter and Luth.

On January 1, 1974, Tom Storrs became chairman of the corporation, chairman of the executive committee of the bank, and chief executive officer of both. Dougherty, formerly vice chairman of the corporation, became president of the corporation. He would supervise operations and the nonbank subsidiaries. Hodges, formerly a vice chairman of the bank, became chairman of the board of the bank. Hodges was to be responsible for all retail banking operations. McColl, formerly a vice chairman of the bank, became president of the bank, continuing to manage the corporate banking business.

Storrs's management arrangement immediately provoked speculation about which of the three would eventually succeed to the top job. It was a young team. Dougherty was the oldest, at forty-three. Hodges was thirty-seven, and McColl was thirty-eight. Storrs had intended not to set up some kind of artificial competition but to create a functional structure that apportioned responsibilities along the lines that these three had been working and to keep three good leaders in place at a time when he needed them.

Storrs recalled later: "Had any one of the three thought he had the job, then we would have been in imminent danger with the other two. I wasn't trying to stir up a horse race. Each one of them had a definite assignment."

The three remained competitors nonetheless.

Chapter 8 **The Party Was Over**

In early May 1974, Tom Storrs traveled to Washington for the quarterly meeting of the Federal Advisory Council, a small group representing the nation's leading banks that by statute meets with the board of governors of the Federal Reserve. Storrs had earned his seat on the council through his work with the Association of Reserve City Bankers, a prestigious group that limited its membership to about 440 bankers nationwide. NCNB was no longer simply an up-and-coming statewide bank in North Carolina. Wall Street counted it among the major regional banks and had widely touted the stock during the previous five years of explosive expansion in the financial industry.

NCNB had grown like kudzu in the hot summer sun. In a few short years, it seemed, NCNB was everywhere—and into everything. The bank's international operation had expanded from the Bahamas to London, where it was active in the Eurodollar market. NCNB Mortgage Corp. had moved beyond home mortgages to more speculative ventures in shopping malls and resort development, and the TranSouth Corp. (formerly Stephenson Finance Co.) was financing lots for second homes in the Carolina mountains and on the coast. The number of NCNB stockholders had doubled since 1969, and the price/earnings ratio was the highest in the industry. In October 1972, NCNB stock had sold at the rate of twenty-six times earnings, better than that of any other bank in the country.

Most of NCNB's growth had been financed primarily with borrowed money, but analysts and NCNB's own advisers said that was fine. It did help to expand NCNB's retail operation, but at a cost. The more conservative Wachovia, for example, operated more profitably than NCNB and had a larger, more dependable supply of cheap dollars in bank checking accounts.

At the May meeting, Tom Storrs knew his bank was balanced on the end of a long limb. As Arthur Burns, chairman of the Federal Reserve, began to talk to the bankers, Storrs thought he heard a crack. For some time, Burns, the tough-minded manager of the nation's financial system, had been discouraging banks from pumping more and more money into an overheated economy that was reeling from the OPEC cartel's hike in prices. "What do we have to do to make you fellows stop lending money?" Burns asked. By the time Storrs left this session, he knew the Fed was prepared to move even more decisively. Changes were afoot. He left Washington with a knot in his stomach.

Immediately upon his return to Charlotte, Storrs called a meeting of his management team. The team's chief lieutenants also joined the group to hear Storrs deliver his report from the council's session. Burns was serious, Storrs said. The price of money was going up. Burns was going to stanch the flow of loans from the nation's banks. The party was over.

The first to react to Storrs's message was McColl. He was not only in charge of the commercial and international business but also responsible for raising money for the bank. McColl's operations would be affected immediately. If the cost of money continued its climb, then NCNB would be hard-pressed to compete for more business. More important, the business that NCNB already had committed would bring less profit for the bank. Higher rates meant lower margins, or no margins, even losses. The news left McColl deeply concerned and nervous that the

Hugh L. McColl, Jr., Executive Vice President, and Robert M. Barker, Senior Vice President, announce the opening of North Carolina (Inter)National Bank. 93 Gresham Street, London. We're the only Southeastern bank with a full service branch over there. **NCNB**

NCNB executive vice president Hugh McColl (left) and senior vice president Robert M. Barker promoted the bank's new London office in advertisements placed in national financial magazines as the bank began expanding beyond its regional base in the early 1970s.

Fed's policies and NCNB's wobbly stock price would encumber his attempts to raise funds to operate the bank.

NCNB was highly leveraged, with about three-fourths of its funding dependent on the will and whim of brokers. Only 26 percent of the bank's portfolio was funded by direct deposits, which had never been promoted by management as strongly as had expansion of the bank through lending, with the cash coming from borrowed funds. In the good years, that strategy was not a problem. If NCNB's reputation began to erode, however, the result could be fatal.

It wasn't totally apparent yet, but the curtain was falling on what had come to be known as the "go-go years." In the previous decade, America's banks had increased their loan portfolios by 170 percent. Bank assets had climbed 143 percent. Now years of inflating business to boost price-earnings multiples, expansive growth, and an ever broader inventory of new ways to raise money to lend in the booming Southern market were about to take their toll. Two events that shook the world banking community were just a harbinger of the difficult days ahead.

In June, bankers around the world shuddered at news that the Bankhaus I. D. Herstatt in Cologne, West Germany, with $760 million in deposits, had closed its doors, facing losses of $190 million from currency deals. American bankers were already worried about the impact of the troubles at Franklin National in Philadelphia, which had announced a previously undisclosed loss of $39 million. Soon Franklin National was on the FDIC's operating table, consuming infusions of cash before eventually being declared insolvent in October. Troubles like this had not been seen since the Depression.

Storrs had less than two quarters of business behind him as NCNB's CEO when the clouds on the horizon billowed and darkened and spread to produce a major storm that would threaten some in the industry and demolish others. Instead of spending time planning for more dynamic years of growth, he found himself organizing damage control, a phrase that would become common in correspondence and in-house discussions. During the next three years, NCNB would be tested to its limits. Exactly how it would emerge from severe strains to its credit, and its credibility, depended on Storrs, a proper Southern gentleman whose background had prepared him more to survive esoteric discussions of banking economics than the threat of banking disaster.

Thomas Irwin Storrs was reared in Richmond, Virginia, where his father had a successful business brokering sales of equipment used in making cement. Business was good enough to send Irwin, as his mother called him, to St. Christopher's School, an Episcopal prep school with rigorous standards and strict discipline that reinforced his family's lessons on honesty and integrity. By 1934, however, the Depression had virtually wiped out the elder Storrs's business. That summer, just before he turned sixteen, Irwin, who had been given the nickname of Buddy, found a job as a runner at the Federal Reserve Bank in Richmond. Among other things, his job was to carry coded messages involving interbank transfers from one desk to another, racing from one floor to the other. Runners had strict orders to use the elevator only for trips of two flights or more.

At the end of the summer, Storrs learned of a permanent opening for an office boy at the Fed offices. He had slightly more than a year left at St. Christopher's, but the full-time job appealed to him. He quit school to take the job. The decision was not reached lightly, but the family simply needed the money. Yet the consequences of his decision didn't sink in until two years later, when, seeking something better than late nights in the mail room at the Federal Reserve, Storrs applied for a job selling office supplies for Remington-Rand. When he appeared for his job interview, he learned there were companies that didn't hire people without high school diplomas.

Storrs was stuck. He had picked up some credits in night school but not enough to qualify for entrance to college. Anyhow, he didn't have any money. He took his problem to an economics professor from the University of Virginia, E. A. Kincaid, whom the new president of the Federal Reserve bank in Richmond had hired as an adviser.

"Are you willing to work?" Kincaid asked the teenager. Storrs said he was. "Well, we'll work this out."

Kincaid steered Storrs through the admissions process at the University of Virginia and got him a National Youth Administration job in the library that paid $15 a month and another job as an 18-cent-per-hour cashier in the student cafeteria in the University Commons. Storrs prospered and, by accelerating his class load, graduated in three years. In 1940, he returned to the Federal Reserve to work with Kincaid in the research department. A year later, he left the job behind at the outbreak of World War II when he enlisted and reported to Midshipman's School.

His early duty was as an ordnance and gunnery instructor, and, Storrs confessed later, he learned as much from his students (trained as engineers and metallurgists) as he taught. He later landed an assignment on the U.S.S. *Nelson*, a destroyer that was scheduled to be part of the Normandy invasion sea screen until it was disabled during a docking accident. The ship was deployed anyhow, but with only one screw operational it was assigned to help escort a convoy that crept across the channel at a slow six knots the day after the initial landing. While anchored offshore, however, as part of a protective shield for the ships closer to the Normandy beaches, the *Nelson* suffered a torpedo hit that killed twenty-six of her crew and destroyed sixty-five feet of her stern.

Storrs came back from the war a commander and was welcomed back to his job at the Fed. His old mentor, Dr. Kincaid, encouraged him to return to school for graduate studies in economics. Just before he left for Harvard—the birthplace of true economists, according to Kincaid—he married Kitty Bird, whose father was the president of Citizens & Southern Bank in Columbia, South Carolina. Storrs spent two years in Cambridge, cramming to complete course work for his doctorate while Kitty worked at the Cambridge Savings Bank. He would finish his dissertation on the job, he told himself, and so he returned to Richmond, this time to run the research department. Six years later (one of which was spent in the Navy during the Korean War), Storrs's dissertation was still just an idea. The incomplete on his record nagged at him. Finally, in 1955, he finished the treatise that he titled "Credit Control Tools," took a special exam out of the normal sequence, and got his degree.

In 1959, the top branch position in Charlotte opened unexpectedly. The president of the Richmond Reserve Bank organized a committee to decide who would get the job. "I was late to a meeting of the committee," Storrs recalled later. "When I got there, they said, 'You're going to Charlotte.' I said, 'I have a job. I'm vice president in charge of research.' Well, they said it would do me good to go down and take over running an operation that had more attributes."

Storrs arrived in Charlotte just as the mergers that would create NCNB were in negotiation. When Neil Vanstory and Addison Reese put offers to him in 1960, he knew the inner workings of the nation's financial system, but he had no practical banking experience. He had never sat across from a businessman looking for a stake, much less chased after corporate accounts. He was a book banker, a theoretician with a vast understanding in economics that didn't amount to much on a loan platform. But Reese saw what he needed in Storrs. Here was a man with a keen mind and some management experience. Here, too, was someone with the experience of a large organization who could find his way around the inner workings of finance, a quality Reese would need if he were to grow a bank.

Appearances always have been important in banking. Reese and Vanstory were tall, distinguished men who made a statement with their mere presence. Storrs was shorter than most of his colleagues, but he still looked the part of a solid, reliable banker. The conservative venues of the Fed had trained him well. Though forty-two, he appeared older than his years, thanks to thinning hair that he combed from a precise part on the left side. His reserve was broken by an amused, almost mischievous smile. Unfailingly correct in his manners, Storrs made up for his stature with a powerful intellect that ran several clicks ahead of most in the crowd. The only problem he seemed to have in his early days was his name.

Storrs's childhood nickname, Buddy, had stuck with him through his career at the Federal Reserve, and it was with him one evening shortly after his arrival in Greensboro when he was presented to the wife of one of the bank's more influential board members. Without apology, she told Storrs that she didn't believe people would want to turn their financial affairs over to someone called Buddy. A few days later, Storrs and Reese were walking to lunch and about to cross the street in Charlotte when Storrs related the encounter and asked Reese's advice. Reese suggested that if "Irwin" wasn't satisfactory—Storrs believed it never did exactly roll off his tongue—then perhaps he should just stick with "Tom." From then on, "Buddy" was a name reserved only for his wife and old friends.

Reese's management consultant, James Farr, was probably one of the first to know just how serious Addison Reese was about grooming Storrs as a successor. Not long after Farr began working with NCNB, Reese called him aside during one of his weekly visits to the bank and asked him to begin paying special attention to Storrs. Reese liked his protégé, who was building an impressive record in Greensboro, and could find no fault with his precision planning, his structured and precise methods, his quick mind, and his ability to stay on top of difficult situations. But Reese believed Storrs was not as sensitive to the people about him as he should be. If Storrs was to command the NCNB legions, he would need better people skills.

"Smoothing off the rough edges" was what Reese called his assignment for Farr. To learn more about his subject, Farr began sitting in on Storrs's staff meetings. He found a man who was thinking so much faster than his subordinates that he often would interrupt a junior executive during the preliminaries of a discussion and impatiently move his speaker on to the point. Storrs's manner tended to stifle discussion. Farr recalled, "He dealt with people by being an absolutely courteous, kind gentleman, following all the rules and manners, but he didn't notice you were dying there behind your eyeballs.

"He was smart as the devil. That was the problem. He always wanted to get to the point four times as fast as somebody who thinks they are smart. They would feel interrupted and not heard. Addison said, 'That man ought to be my successor, but, with that quality, I'm not sure he will make it with the board.' "

Storrs was a quick learner and took Farr's counseling to heart. "He was just so number-oriented, logic-oriented, but he learned sensitivity just the same way he learned his economics."

Though not a natural diplomat like Reese, Storrs effectively negotiated difficult times in Greensboro and, later, in Charlotte. During his ten years in Greensboro, a city that he loved and that his family hated to leave when they moved to Charlotte in 1970, he had been more than a manager of a major operating side of the bank. He had also been Reese's liaison, his bridge to the Greensboro interests. Storrs enjoyed the trust of Reese's principal nemesis, Neil Vanstory, who credited Storrs with keeping Greensboro from falling off the map as far as the Charlotte headquarters was concerned. And he had represented the bank well as chairman or president of every major civic organization.

But the fact that Storrs was based in Greensboro also was looming as a liability. Six months before Storrs finally relocated to the headquarters on South Tryon Street in Charlotte, Addison Reese surprised many within the bank by hiring Elliott "Pete" Taylor from TransAmerica Financial Corp. in San Francisco, where he had been executive vice president and chief operating officer. Taylor was given responsibility for the nonbank subsidiaries, titles to compare with Storrs's, and a seat on the board.

Taylor's arrival caused a stir in the bank's inner circle. While Reese had been grooming Storrs to succeed him, he was bucking pressure from some members of the board who believed Storrs wasn't ready. Storrs was seen as a steady, loyal, and extremely intelligent executive, but he wasn't a "banker" in the traditional sense. He was still an economist. In the early days, even Reese had joked about his resident Ph.D.—"I suppose we could call him a reformed economist who decided to go straight and become a commercial banker," he quipped to New York analysts on one occasion. Now that was no longer a joke.

Taylor joined Reese on the mezzanine level of the headquarters building and decorated his office in desert hues with California-French accents. (Reese once said it looked like a "fornicatorium.") Taylor was urbane, a stylish dresser, but more important, some on the board thought, he brought experience, a touch of gray hair, to an uncommonly youthful management team. He was named executive vice president of the bank, vice chairman of the board, and, in September 1970, president of NCNB Tri-South Corp., a real estate investment trust (REIT) formed with First & Merchants Corp. of Richmond and First National Holding Corp. of Atlanta. REITs were the glamour business, and NCNB joined in in a big way, taking responsibility for its share of $50 million in first mortgage construction and development loans. The project was a particular favorite of Reese's.

Taylor's appointment particularly disturbed McColl, Hodges, and Dougherty. In their opinion, Taylor got in the way of their projects and stifled the growth of the bank. In addition, these ambitious young men had put their money on Storrs, and now the new horse in the race left their own futures in doubt. In time, after their level of frustration had risen sufficiently to overcome their trepidation before Reese, they voiced their complaints.

Even McColl was reluctant to approach the issue head-on. He knew he wasn't one of Reese's favorites; his brashness chafed at Reese's smooth diplomacy. But one day, as the two were returning from a visit with an important client in Fort Mill, South Carolina, Reese asked him what he thought of Taylor. McColl answered with his characteristic bluntness, telling his boss just what he thought, until Reese cut him off, saying, "You know, you and Luther can learn a lot from Pete Taylor."

"Yeah, what's that?" McColl rejoined, with what Reese heard as youthful sauciness.

"I should never have said that. Boy, he just worked me over," McColl recalled. "He started ticking off all the things that I wasn't, and I was sorry I had said anything."

Hodges, who considered himself a contender in the mold of Addison Reese, also voiced his objections about Taylor. And Dougherty, whom Reese had personally recruited, went to bat for Storrs. Finally, without any warning, Reese announced in December 1972, at the end of one of his weekly staff meetings, that Taylor was leaving the company. One who was there said Reese's report was brief, about three sentences long, and he left the clear impression with those present that he wasn't interested in a long explanation. To all but the careful observer, Taylor was just a blip on the screen. His name didn't appear in the corporation's 1972 annual report. Finally, Storrs's succession was secure.

In his farewell message a year later, Reese gave Storrs his unqualified support. He wrote to stockholders, saying, "Perhaps the most important part of my job has been finding the right people. I have had a few strike-outs—most of which are known to you—but the new management team that we have now fielded seems to indicate that my batting average has been pretty good." And he went on to give unqualified endorsement to Storrs and the management team poised to assume leadership of his bank.

On January 1, 1974, when Storrs officially took total command, NCNB Corp. included the nation's twenty-sixth-largest bank, with more than $3.6 billion in resources. The bank was the core business of the corporation, but NCNB's nonbank division of commercial and residential mortgages, consumer finance, and investment counseling included 250 offices in six states and two foreign countries. There were a few trouble spots, but the balance sheet for them looked good. Overall, earnings were up more than 13 percent over the previous year as Storrs prepared to move NCNB's Charlotte headquarters into the newest, and most impressive, corporate home in the Carolinas, the forty-story glass tower that commanded the city's skyline.

Storrs was confident about the future. In fact, NCNB's top management had grown downright cocky about the bank's position. Bankers from all over the country were calling on them to find out how they handled a particular kind of business or how they managed certain data. NCNB's management information systems were considered some of the best in the country, well ahead of what most banks had to offer. The company was constantly on the lookout for something new to attract customers. It was not only the first North Carolina bank to enter the credit card business, it also was the first in the Southeast, and one of only six in the country, to win approval for an automated bank branch, which it installed on the Duke University campus in Durham.

On May 5, just before his meeting with Burns in Washington, Storrs, his top managers, and the impressive new NCNB office tower were the subject of a front-page feature in the *New York Times* Sunday business section. The story was generally favorable and recounted the bank's rapid rise to fame. It also hinted at what lay ahead. "This is a success story," the article said, "but its luster has dimmed somewhat recently. Bank stocks have declined this year, about in line with the stock market in general, and Southern bank issues have been the hardest hit of all."

The markets were as volatile as Burns had predicted. Within sixty days, Storrs knew that NCNB was in for the toughest time of its existence. Each day produced a new round of challenges. The company already had begun to experience problems in selling NCNB's commercial paper or notes. Notes were coming due, and instead of rolling over for the long term, they were due in just a day or two. Even notes payable in thirty days had no market.

The crunch was hard and deep for banks, like NCNB, that were very market-driven. Over the years, the NCNB loan portfolio had grown, but a prime source of available cash—demand deposits—had not kept pace. As a result, the bank had become a large-scale participant in the money markets, backing loan judgments with projections that interest rates would either rise or fall. Operating in these markets required a heavy dependence on economic and interest-rate forecasting.

As the storm grew, Storrs agreed to go ahead with a May 23 meeting with New York securities analysts. The news would not be good— NCNB would report its first decline in earnings after forty-one straight quarters of increases—but Storrs and Dougherty, NCNB's point man in the stock market, believed it was better to deliver bad news than to avoid the issue and create suspicions that could be even more damaging.

NCNB had carefully cultivated securities analysts, and presentations in New York and elsewhere were generally pleasant affairs. Usually, the company delivered good news, and brokers helped their clients make money by translating these reports into stock purchases. This time, the show was different. Storrs disclosed NCNB's deteriorating position, and the NCNB team outlined what the bank was prepared to do about it. As Storrs talked, he heard the rattle of chairs and a commotion at the rear of the room. It didn't take long for him and the rest of the NCNB team to realize that the noise was coming from brokers scrambling for the door to contact their West Coast offices, where the market had not yet closed for the day. Sell orders were placed before Storrs had completed his presentation.

Ken Clark, the bank's public relations executive, prepared the texts for Storrs and others. "We were the first bank in the country," he recalled, "to tell the bank analysts that not only was the bloom off the banking rose, particularly in the Southeast, but there was a lot of root rot, too."

In the five trading days after the meeting, NCNB's stock fell 22 percent. It had been as high as $39.75 and now stood at just over $23. The *Wall Street Journal*'s Heard on the Street column said: "Analysts haven't any doubts about the soundness of the bank company. However, there's some concern in Wall Street that the growth impediment may be neither as temporary nor as superficial as the recent interest rate impact might indicate."

By June and July, the credit demands and pressure from the Federal Reserve had reached a crescendo. NCNB found the market for its notes drying up. Other regional banks were facing the same drought. NCNB had just been one of the first to air its bad news. Money was moving from these institutions back to the money centers, which were better credit risks because of their large size. Investors were running to quality, Storrs called it. NCNB finally heard from its investment banker, Salomon Brothers, which had taken on NCNB as its first major bank client, that it could no longer find a market for NCNB's commercial paper. McColl said, "It had really gotten to where Tom was sort of like the admiral of the fleet and on the deck every day, and he and I fought to cover ourselves."

Each day Storrs, McColl, and executives Rufus Land from balance sheet management, Bob Barker from the marketing division, Jim Sheridan from the investment division, and James W. Thompson, who was in charge of the bank's bond and funds management department, met to review the bank's balance sheet and assess activities to determine how the bank was going to operate that day. They gathered at 8:30 A.M. on the seventh floor of the new, unfinished NCNB tower, where a few departments had already moved into offices in the midst of workers com-

James W. Thompson, who ran the bank's bond and funds department, met daily with Thomas Storrs to review the bank's position as NCNB worked its way carefully through the 1973–74 recession.

pleting the building's interior. Their strategy room was the small, soon-to-be trading room, where bare wallboard and concrete floors added to the stark reality of the difficult situation in which NCNB found itself.

McColl would never forget that Fourth of July holiday. His schedule had developed into a carefully timed regimen. He spent the mornings scrambling for money, keeping lines of credit intact and managing funds, and the afternoons handling new developments and problem areas. When the bank closed on Wednesday for the holiday, it appeared that NCNB would be short by some $40 million when the bank opened for business on Thursday because of a chain of circumstances and quirks in the calendar that had dislocated money throughout the American banking system. Overnight, interest rates on the bank's short-term borrowings had skyrocketed to 25 percent, and fear was causing investors to hold on to cash. Regardless of the reasons, which were beyond the bank's control, the bank would be technically insolvent, unable to meet its payments on obligations that would come due July 5.

The holiday would close other financial institutions in the United States, so McColl turned to London, where NCNB had had an office since April 1972. The international business was a source of pride for McColl and Storrs, who had lobbied Reese for the expansion to keep money-center banks from luring away the business of North Carolina textile firms that needed help abroad. By 1971, the Nassau office had produced about $750,000 in profits to NCNB. The London office followed in 1972, when it became apparent that, if NCNB was to have any position in international finance, it would need a more visible base than Nassau. NCNB was not a veteran, but it had hired some good people from banks with longer residency.

On Tuesday, July 3, McColl placed a call to the bank's office at 93 Gresham Street, about two blocks down the street from the Bank of England. McColl reached Bernie Furlonger, who had been hired away from the Bank of America office. He was one of two men that NCNB had lured away from the financial giant, thus provoking a complaint to Storrs from Bank of America's chairman. McColl gave Furlonger his orders: raise $40 million in twenty-four hours.

While Americans celebrated a holiday, Furlonger succeeded in boosting the bank's Eurodollar holdings sufficiently to cover the amounts due on the fifth. Furlonger, McColl said some years later, became "bullet-proof" at NCNB, his position forever secure. And the London office, considered an expensive and questionable proposition by Reese, would become a permanent NCNB address. After McColl became CEO, he vowed that the London office would never be closed under his administration. "I needed it then, and I might need it again."

On July 11, NCNB got hit with what McColl called "a blow that was just blinding." NCNB had a $3 million short-term investment in the Israel-British Bank Ltd. in London, and the bank failed on the day before it was to pay off NCNB. "That was the straw that broke the camel's back as far as the market for our paper," McColl said.

Each day throughout the crisis, Jim Thompson left the morning strategy session not knowing just how NCNB's name would be regarded in the market. Each day was a test of the bank's resilience and the trading skill of Thompson and others in the department. A top priority was NCNB's image, which had suffered badly under the depressing news of the first quarter's earnings. "Just like any other type of borrower, you don't recover overnight," Thompson recalled. "You have to reestablish and rebuild your foundation and your position in the marketplace. Once you've lost it, there is nothing that has a higher priority."

For Thompson, who had joined the bank as a trainee in 1963 with no notion of building a career in banking, it was also a test of his skill in managing the bank's bond department, which he had seen grow and prosper, surpassing even NCNB's archrival Wachovia. He found that the bond department, once a backwater and largely taken for granted during years of easy money, was now a keystone of the operation, as NCNB scrambled to make it through the summer.

Dougherty, vacationing with his family in Pittsburgh, was lunching with friends when he got an urgent call from Storrs. Because NCNB's commercial paper wouldn't sell, Storrs said, the bank was turning to its lines of credit with other banks as a backup for the cash needs. Storrs had never particularly liked these reciprocal agreements in which one bank agrees to stand ready to lend money to another bank without any compensating balances or fees. But NCNB had established lines at the urging of board member Huger King of Greensboro, who had stressed the need for some safety net despite investment bankers' advice that such lines of credit were passé. In the days when the sun had shown a little brighter, King had braced Dougherty at a board meeting with the question "Dougherty, what are you going to do if your commercial paper won't sell someday?" The day that NCNB's New York advisers said five years earlier would never happen had arrived.

Storrs and McColl placed the calls to the major United States banks where NCNB's lines of credit were in place. When Storrs reached Bank of America chairman Chauncey Medberry, he was told that not only was the $10 million line in place but Medberry would double it. When another NCNB officer reached Chemical Bank, which had just sent Storrs a beautiful gold clock in honor of his election as chairman, he was told that the $10 million line there was available only in a proportionate share with other banks. This stipulation would have required NCNB to notify all its correspondent banks (those it did business with) of the company's plight, thus further damaging NCNB's position in the market.

Storrs subsequently spoke with the most senior officer available at Chemical and asked if the bank was unable to meet its commitments for the $10 million loan to NCNB.

"Of course not," he was told.

"Very well," replied Storrs, "our note for $10 million will be there tomorrow."

Chemical made the loan, but McColl and all other senior NCNB officers never forgot the episode. They resented the treatment the company had received when it needed help. An old and important relationship had now gone sour.

After all their work, NCNB was still $25 million short. Finally, Storrs put in a call to Walter Wriston, the chairman of Citicorp, and found him in Washington. Wriston and Storrs knew each other through the Association of Reserve City Bankers, and the relationship between Citibank and NCNB was solid. Storrs and Dougherty hastily arranged a flight to Washington for an impromptu meeting with Wriston, who told them he had just been instrumental in pushing through a Citibank policy not to make such loans. Wriston said that NCNB's request put him in a difficult position.

"In spite of this," Dougherty recalled later, "he looked us in the eye and said he would do it even though it would make him look bad back at the bank in New York. On a handshake, we had the remaining $25 million we needed to be fully covered. Walter gave us a ride in his limousine out to the airport, and Tom and I flew back, breathing a lot easier knowing we were fully covered."

Raising money was just the first step. Further drastic action appeared on NCNB's agenda. In a flying tour across North Carolina, Hodges and McColl visited every NCNB branch office with news never before heard on a NCNB loan platform: don't write any new consumer business and shut off any indirect loans. This directive effectively put NCNB out of the automobile financing business and severed ties that would take years to reestablish. The branch tour was an exhausting exercise; the two were in the air from one city to the next for about three weeks. At the same time, McColl began winding down the offshore business.

"All through the summer, I was fighting the funding and gave an order to reduce the Eurodollar placements," McColl recalled. "I got a lot of bitching and moaning from the troops that that was going to cause us problems. I actually had sheets, and I marked off each Eurodollar deposit as we collected. I had a list of maturities by dates. I'm not a very precise person, but when I get into the banking mode, I am very precise and very organized."

As Storrs assessed the damage, he found his bank was being battered on all fronts. When he had a chance to look around, he saw that other banks were in the same shape. An unexpected turn in late 1973 had pushed interest rates to 12 percent by mid-July, 50 percent higher than the 8 percent level of a year before.

A particularly troublesome area was home mortgages. In September 1973, NCNB had gambled heavily that the prime rate, which stood at 10.5 percent, was going to drop; consequently the bank announced that it would begin making home mortgage loans of 8 percent, well below the market rates. Hodges announced the program: "I know this is going to be successful in the long run because we're going to get new customers and new friends for the bank. Some people are giving away dishes and gold bars. They're not what the customer needs. This responds to consumer needs. We think the cost to us will go from 10.5 percent to 9.5 percent fairly soon, though it's not going to 8.5 percent for a while. But maybe it will by mid next year."

The program was aimed at eager middle-income home buyers who had pulled out of the market because of rising interest rates. North Carolina law set a limit of 8 percent on home mortgages, and the market had simply disappeared as the prime climbed above that. At NCNB, home mortgage customers now could get 80 to 90 percent financing on thirty-year loans up to $45,000. Hodges wasn't specific on how much money the bank would commit to the program but suggested in news reports that $10 million to $20 million a month would be available.

Immediately, the bank was overrun with applications. A week after the announcement—which a top First Union executive publicly called a "smart idea"—NCNB had loan applications for more than $6 million. Two Charlotte customers left $135 in loan application fees lying on the desk at a Wachovia branch office to take their business to NCNB. Six weeks after the announcement, more than $33 million in applications had been presented. The volume was nearly three times what NCNB Mortgage Corp. had ever accepted within one month.

The NCNB home mortgage program looked like it might work. In November the prime dropped a quarter of a point, to 10.25 percent, and builders who had had houses sitting vacant for months found a new market. Ed Tipton, a Greenville, North Carolina, builder, reported that he sold nine houses in the wake of the NCNB announcement.

Hodges closed the door on the home mortgage experiment on January 31, 1974. He said NCNB would have an investment of $55 million in the program when the more than two thousand loan applications had been processed. That was the good news for consumers. Within the bank, analysts reported that the predictions of a falling rate weren't holding. The prime had fallen further, to 9.5 percent—the price NCNB was paying for its money invested in these mortgages—but a week later it reversed course and crept up by another quarter point. By April, it was at 10.25 percent, and in July it peaked at 12 percent.

While the home mortgage program was draining cash out of the bank, other consumer ventures also were falling apart. Hodges had pushed an easy-credit consumer lending program, offering loans on a customer's signature. It took about a year for those loans to go bad. By the end of the year, losses in consumer loans alone would amount to $5.6 million, which was more than the bank would lose in this line of business during the next ten years.

In addition, the bank and its subsidiary, TranSouth Financial Corp., had aggressively marketed loans for mobile homes, recreation lots, and second mortgages. In the mobile home business, for example, the bank had extended long-term credit, financing the product like automobiles. When interest rates began to climb, and the state's economy began to sag because of layoffs and short work hours in textile mills and furniture plants, the bank found itself with a growing inventory of bad debt. Delinquency rates on consumer installment loans reached historic highs in mid-1974 and remained there for the balance of the year.

"When the textile industry started turning down, it started laying off the young ones, keeping the oldest and most experienced ones," McColl recounted later. "We were having an energy crisis, and when you got down to the low-income people, they were getting chewed up. And they went home to mama. Nobody ever thought about them going home to live with mama and daddy, but that is what happened. So they just abandoned their trailers, their mobile homes. They are immobile, I might add, and they are worthless when you try to pick them up and move them."

Nearly 20 percent of TranSouth's loan portfolio was tied up in mobile home loans. At the end of 1974, the company had nearly $30 million invested. At one point, NCNB had so many deserted mobile homes that it had to lease space on small airstrips to park them. "The situation was classic for depressions," McColl said. "I guess we weren't old enough, we hadn't lived enough, and we didn't understand that that's how people behaved."

Storrs and Reese had experienced the Depression of the 1930s, and because they should have known better, their embarrassment, frustration, and tension rose throughout the late summer and into fall as the problems mounted. They hadn't seen it coming; in fact, they had pushed the aggressive programs that were now collapsing around them with compounding consequences. Years later Storrs would wonder if, had the directors seen the problems ahead, they would have put someone without hard lending experience in charge.

Storrs kept directors advised of the problems facing the business. In fact, beginning in January, he increased the number of board meetings. During his last few years in office, Reese had cut the number of board sessions to a minimum after years of working with a board that overdirected his affairs. Storrs returned to monthly sessions, and in the fall of 1974 these meetings became increasingly tense, as each month he and his team reported more difficulties.

Finally, at one session in the early fall, the question that some had raised in their own minds was aired openly. Could the current administration handle the affairs of NCNB? After nearly ten years of steady gains, increasing stock value, and growth, the business was setting the stage for a decline in earnings of 38 percent in the fourth quarter. It became apparent to all around the table, as complaints from board members increased, that Storrs might leave the boardroom that day stripped of his position.

First Reese and then Jack Lindley of Greensboro, who had helped engineer the NCNB merger in 1960 and remained as chairman of the corporation's executive committee, spoke in defense of the management team. Among other things, Reese told the board that if he were still board chairman and not retired, NCNB would be facing the same problems. The tension eased.

Lindley later recalled the meeting and the consensus that developed. Board members decided "you might as well go ahead and bite the bullet," Lindley said. "Take the losses, write them off, and turn round and start out anew and not do the same things. If management wasn't able to do that, then there were going to have to be some changes. I think that was the sense of the meeting."

Directors remained edgy about the growing list of problem loans. At one meeting, after the board had reviewed the major items on the bank's problem-loan watch list, one director said, "What else?"

"We don't know what else," Storrs replied.

"Well, you're going to be back here next month with some more on there. You must know what they are," the board member said.

Recalled Storrs: "It was a very difficult time to keep in perspective. There were some directors who were very concerned about the company. There were some directors who were concerned about their own skin, as to whether they were going to get into some sort of problem or not. Nobody on the board or in management had any reference points. This was a more serious situation than any time in the business careers of those involved. And they didn't know where it was going."

The annual report that greeted shareholders with the account of business in 1974 was in sharp contrast to the bubbly and colorful presentations of previous years. The euphoria of 1973, when NCNB had passed Wachovia, was gone. In fact, NCNB had lost the lead to its archrival with the third-quarter reports. There were no elaborate descriptions of new programs and services. The business report reflected a North Carolina economy that was laboring under an almost 30 percent increase in business failures. To compound matters, the bank had to take over the South Tryon Street building after a proposed sale fell through. (NCNB had repurchased the building to get out of its sale-leaseback arrangement of 1967.) And the first of what would be a series of commercial loan failures was developing at the Erwin Company, Charlotte's largest home builder and one of several large customers whose business had been hit hard by the recession.

More specifically, NCNB's earnings had tumbled from $26 million in 1973 to $17.6 million, the lowest since 1970. The corporation set aside $15.7 million for loan losses, two and a half times the 1973 level. In addition to the more than $5 million in consumer loan losses, commercial loan losses had climbed to more than $3.7 million, double the experience of the previous year. Interest expense at the bank was 41 percent higher than in 1973. The holding company had used its lines of credit at a daily average of more than $813 million, up from $512 million the year before.

"This was a year of testing for a number of executives," Storrs wrote to the stockholders, "who found themselves in new roles, confronted by a rapidly changing environment that made unexpectedly severe demands on them."

What Storrs did not say—what he could not say—was that the previous six months were just the beginning of a period of workout that would provide even more severe tests and begin to prepare the management of NCNB for a period of further expansion that nobody had time to consider as the crises of 1974 passed into history.

Chapter 9 **Show Them No Mercy**

NCNB's $60 million downtown redevelopment project, with its forty-story towering glass office building, 450-car parking garage, 50,000-square-foot shopping arcade and full-service, 371-room hotel, began to look like quite an extravagance when viewed from the bottom of the balance sheet in 1974. Some critics complained that downtown Charlotte was woefully overbuilt when NCNB began moving its offices from South Tryon Street into the new quarters. At the time, even Tom Storrs thought he might have a hard time defending NCNB's long-term lease for 370,000 square feet in the new building. After all, office space was going for $3.50 per square foot, and NCNB had just signed a thirty-five-year lease for $6.50 per square foot.

From his office on the twenty-third floor, Storrs could look out on the city's new civic center, under construction just below. Beyond lay a major redevelopment area of downtown Charlotte, part of which would eventually be filled with parks and additional office buildings.

Storrs's office was well appointed, though not large by corporate standards. During the interior design stage, Storrs had directed Erwin Smith, one of the NCNB managers on the project, to allocate him an office of fifteen by twenty feet and to give the same space to Hodges, McColl, and Dougherty, whose offices were beside his own. The size of all other offices in the building scaled down from those in the executive suite. Storrs's modest-sized quarters allowed Smith to counter requests from middle-level executives who were expecting larger quarters. "You probably don't want an office larger than the chairman's, do you?" Smith would ask, effectively ending the discussion.

In the winter of 1974, Storrs was standing at his window, absorbed in the view from nearly 250 feet up in the Carolina sky. McColl was with him. It was late in the afternoon, and the two had just finished another day of dealing with problems that piled one upon the other, only to be replaced by even larger, more inconceivable difficulties.

"I never thought it would come like this," Storrs said, speaking more to himself than to McColl.

McColl didn't answer, but he was shaken by Storrs's words. Here was his leader, cool to the point of appearing emotionless, and McColl believed he had had just seen Storrs flinch. Did Storrs really believe the bank wouldn't survive? McColl didn't ask.

Others in the bank thought the unthinkable. Middle-level managers—experienced enough to know that things weren't going well and savvy enough to read the tension that was building in the executive suite—talked among themselves. Some called McColl, Hodges, and others and put the question directly. That experienced officers would even inquire was evidence of the growing doubt. People were nervous, but at the time Storrs was too busy fighting fires to read the minds of subordinates.

"He misunderstood me," Storrs recalled years later, when asked about his comment that McColl remembered from that day, "and I never did anything to correct it. What I was really talking about was what was happening in the credit market. I came to understand that he thought I was talking about what was imminent for the bank.

"You see, banking problems in the past have always come out of runs on banks because of lack of confidence, and bank illiquidity and banks trying to raise money from other banks. What was happening, though, was that the market was running to quality, and our concern every day was whether our name would slip below what the market would accept. I think, in retrospect, we never came close. But we didn't know that then."

By the end of 1974, NCNB was recovering from its first round of problems in funding the bank. Pressure on the interest rate mismatch was abating. Funds were available on a schedule that NCNB could more easily manage, rather than driven by market conditions or the whims of outside investors anxious about NCNB's commercial paper.

There was even some good news. The new office tower would come in about $1 million under the projected cost. Construction and outfitting of the new building were moving into the final stage of relocating the banking lobby, and Storrs was eager to get the project behind him. The joint venture was NCNB's first experience with a partner in a project like this, and the relationship had been rocky at times, but he was pleased with the result.

And the building accomplished its mission. While the tower didn't block the sun to South Tryon Street's other banks, it was the most commanding structure on the skyline. At one point, designers experimented with placing a crown of fluorescent lights that would outline the top at night. It would be NCNB's signature in lieu of the corporate logo. Storrs and Smith viewed different versions of lighting from a room atop the city's new Sheraton Hotel, several blocks away. Finally, Storrs scotched this ornament as a feature that would be misunderstood in the midst of the nation's concern for conserving energy.

Beyond the office tower, the rest of the development also loomed large in Storrs's concerns. Besides the Carolina horizon, Storrs also could see the unfinished portion of NCNB Plaza from his window. NCNB had committed to developing nearly the entire block, not just a single office building. Title to the property under the office tower was in jeopardy if NCNB backed out now, no matter what the conditions in the financial market. Storrs and Dougherty, who had supervised the project and represented NCNB's interests, questioned whether NCNB should proceed. It was a tough call. The two considered postponing further construction and planting grass in the vacant lot facing Trade Street where the $17 million Radisson Plaza Hotel was to go.

Finally, Storrs relied on numbers to help make the decision. NCNB was obligated to complete the project, and it would only cost more if it were postponed. He gave the order for construction to begin on the hotel, the first to be built in downtown Charlotte in about fifty years. The fifteen-story hotel also was to wear a glass skin and have a unique trapezoidal shape.

Storrs initiated action on another front as well. As soon as the annual report for 1974 was in his hands, he called a council of his management team. Together they divided the country into territories and took assignments to visit with the credit departments and chief executives of banks in each area that had lines of credit open to NCNB. Storrs believed it important to explain NCNB's situation and to find new lines that would be available when needed. It was plain and simple selling of the bank, its management skill, and its ability to rebound from a tough year. While none of NCNB's crises had reached the pages of the financial or daily newspapers, the figures on the 1974 balance sheet spoke for themselves.

Storrs and McColl already had experienced one such round of visits, and the trip had left them drained. In December they had covered five international banking capitals in five days. Rather than appear to be licking their wounds, the two told European bankers they were conducting a study to determine just how big a role NCNB should play in Europe and to express concern about the Eurobond market's replacing bank lending in London. Some bankers thought their visitors were over-concerned. Others lectured the two men on how to run a bank. Storrs and McColl were told that NCNB was too dependent on international markets, that the bank had bad loans, that they didn't know how to run their business!

As if the verbal abuse weren't bad enough, the two also had to meet a grueling schedule. Their itinerary called for meetings during the day, lift-off for the next city at dark in time to check into a hotel around ten or eleven o'clock for a short dinner, and then sleep. The weather was rough, and on the Zurich-to-Brussels leg their plane took off in a blinding snowstorm and landed short in Brussels, hitting the grass in front of the runway.

"We practically had to fight for a cab," McColl recalled. "We stood in the line very patiently waiting our turn. Finally, just as we got to a cab, this very tall, powerful-looking individual came up and set his two suitcases in the trunk. Tom was standing there, and I was, too, and Tom put down his bags, reached in and took this fellow's suitcases out of the trunk, and said, 'This is our cab,' and put his in.

"This large guy, who has yet to speak a word, reached in and took our bags out and puts his in again. And Tom repeats the process—at which point I'm thinking about where to hit this fellow, but I'm going to hit him before he hits Tom. The guy finally backed down, and we went to town."

With the European trip behind them, Storrs wanted to deal with his credit sources at home. The NCNB teams covered the country, stopping in New York, Chicago, San Francisco, Los Angeles, and Dallas. There were disappointments, and there were surprises. Chicago banker A. Robert Abboud delivered a lecture on the banking business and turned down a request for credit. On the West Coast, NCNB didn't have a line of credit with Crocker National Bank in California, but McColl arranged a courtesy call anyhow. He left with a new $20 million line of credit. At Republic National Bank in Dallas, the bank's management brought in twenty or more officers to hear the NCNB presentation. Dallas bankers were feeling prosperous. A downturn in banking business was something from another world when viewed from the Texas plains. Their position was improving daily, with oil prices setting the Texas economy afire. McColl and Hodges got a line of credit for $7.5 million.

The flying tour reaffirmed NCNB's position with its creditors and secured the lines of credit that Storrs believed were necessary to provide NCNB with an emergency reserve. "We did not find that our name was being associated with unusual differentials in the CD market or the commercial paper market," Storrs recalled. "We were in about the same relationship with New York banks that we'd previously been, and this was the way the market had of saying, 'We expect you to get through this all right.' "

Storrs also created a new structure to help guide the management of the balance sheet. The new Balance Sheet Management Division maintained ongoing evaluation of account and economic forecasts and balanced these against the possible impact of external changes that might affect the forecasts. These recommendations were forwarded to a new asset/liability management committee composed of NCNB's top management.

In the summer of 1975, *Business Week* magazine took a look back over the previous tumultuous year in banking. NCNB's problems were perhaps no worse than those of some other institutions. The business had been wracked by balance sheets suffering from "too much question-able lending, too much borrowed money, too little capital to support swollen losses, and monetary growth slowed to dead zero," the maga-zine reported. More than $1.8 billion in loans showed up as chargeoffs on the financial industry's annual report. One banker was quoted as saying, "Last summer scared the pants off some of these bankers. I don't mean the sixty-year-old bankers. I mean the thirty-five-year-old tigers."

The magazine's special banking report also included an article on NCNB, which, the reporter observed, was one of many banks that had changed from asset to liability management in its philosophy of busi-ness. Properly contrite, McColl assessed the bank's international busi-ness by saying, "We'll stick to things we know something about, like the exporting of textiles or the whole field of agribusiness, from tractors to tobacco."

Accompanying the article was a group photograph of Hodges, Storrs, Dougherty, and McColl. They all looked pleasant but weary; none wore a broad smile. In fact, the business was taking its toll. A few years after the crisis had passed, Storrs said Walter Wriston told him he thought his old friend had looked bad the day he and Dougherty had called for emergency assistance. Storrs would always wonder how he survived without getting an ulcer. But he remained in control, never showing what-ever fears he might have felt deep inside.

The stress and long hours fell heavy on McColl, whose hair began turning gray during this time. "We ran on adrenaline all the time," McColl recalls. "You would go home and slug down a couple of Scotches. It wouldn't have any effect on you, and then it would flatten you out until three or four in the morning. Then you would go back to work. We did that for two years."

McColl considered leaving it all behind at one point in early 1975. A corporate headhunter contacted him about taking the presidency of a bank in California. McColl visited the bank and considered the move, but decided to stay put.

"It was pretty tense there," Storrs recalled. "It's the sort of thing that you get your hands around something and all of a sudden another prob-lem of the same magnitude turns up."

Departmental operating budgets were reviewed closely, trimmed, and reviewed again, with the corporation's top management examining every line item. There were no major layoffs, which reflected NCNB's lean organization going into this period more than anything else. Hiring, except for critical positions, was curtailed. Actually, NCNB had always had much lower personnel costs than comparable banks. As a bank that traditionally had depended more on rented money, it had learned to hold down costs in other areas.

Programs not considered essential to the business were trimmed. One casualty was the art program. None of the collection was sold, but purchases stopped. The staff position was eliminated, which—even in the face of the budget restraints—prompted some complaints directly from board members to Storrs.

As NCNB was bringing its liquidity and consumer-loan problems under control, yet another boulder began rolling down the hill. When it hit in full force, it would shake the business to its very foundation once again. The number of items on the watch list (potentially problem loans) for commercial lending, in the mortgage banking business, and at the bank's real estate investment trust were about to peak simultaneously, increasing the drag on NCNB earnings. These difficulties would not be solved easily. Nor soon.

When NCNB Mortgage Corp. had been formed as part of the holding company reorganization, the company primarily served the residential market. At the end of its first year in business, in 1969, NCNB Mortgage was servicing about $5 million in loans. Three years later, NCNB Mortgage had expanded into South Carolina with the acquisition of C. Douglas Wilson & Co. of Greenville, and the next year NCNB acquired Blanchard & Calhoun, with offices in Georgia. NCNB Mortgage and C. Douglas Wilson produced a combined mortgage loan portfolio of more than $625 million. Blanchard and Calhoun took NCNB into the booming growth of Orlando, Florida, with offices there and in Jacksonville.

NCNB Mortgage's business was no longer limited to residences. The company was now underwriting the construction of office buildings, shopping centers, manufacturing plants, apartments, condominiums, residential developments—practically any kind of property that could produce income for an owner. The company also had an interest in resorts in the North Carolina mountains and along the Atlantic coast, golf courses, even a theme park at Myrtle Beach called Pirate Land.

NCNB Mortgage handled the construction financing and then placed the business with one or a group of major institutional investors. The company's list of thirty major investors included some of the biggest names in the business. Investors liked what they saw, as evidenced by the more than 100 percent increase in commitments for long-term financing that NCNB Mortgage placed between 1971 and 1972.

These were the boom years, when the Southeast was enjoying its most active period of development since immediately after World War II. Population was increasing, and new homes were going up in subdivisions and in resort developments across the land. At the end of 1972, the unemployment rate in North Carolina was 3 percent. By the close of 1973, NCNB Mortgage had extended more than $234 million in loan commitments during the year, bringing its total commitments to $387 million. The company was servicing mortgages amounting to more than $674 million.

In retrospect, Storrs called it the time of the "bigger fool theory." One investor would launch a project assuming that someone else would come along and take it off his hands at a nice increase. Then another buyer would take the same property at an inflated price, preparing to sell it to someone else.

The first crack in the dam appeared at C. Douglas Wilson & Co. in 1973. Storrs dispatched Bill Covington, NCNB's city executive in Winston-Salem, to assume the presidency of Wilson, where he immediately ran into trouble, including conflicts with the former Wilson management. Digging deeper, he found files of bad loans and other problems that should have been discovered during the normal due diligence involved in the purchase of a business. By year end, the loan loss reserve was boosted by 50 percent to cover losses from loans made to a construction company that had gone into bankruptcy.

Compounding Wilson's problems was a rapid deterioration of the mortgage market all across the Southeast. Consumers and developers alike were just beginning to comprehend the effects of the Arab oil embargo that would send the United States economy into disarray. By the end of 1974, the textile and furniture industries would have idled 50,000 workers in just twelve months. Overall unemployment in North Carolina more than doubled, reaching nearly 11 percent in February 1975. Resorts and travel-related businesses, which had begun to soften before the embargo, were dying now, as their customers conserved their meager resources and stayed home, rather than travel in cars that burned too much expensive gasoline. Bank deposits fell and retail sales declined sharply, stifling plans for more and larger shopping malls. Commercial loans dropped by 30 percent, and the mortgage company reported a loss of $1.4 million.

Covington's background was in the retail bank, and he was inexperienced in the commercial business. But he had proved himself an aggressive manager in assignments in Wilmington and Winston-Salem. "I didn't know how to spell mortgage when they asked me to go," he said. "I said sure. I learned quickly how to spell foreclosure. We foreclosed on half the damn state." Covington found that 40 to 50 percent of the business that Wilson had on its books was shaky and would eventually go into default, with more than $50 million in foreclosure. By the end of 1974, NCNB Mortgage had more than $37 million in nonperforming assets, with more than half of that in apartment projects, resort developments, and condominiums.

A feature in the corporate annual reports for years had been a standard glossary of terms, arranged alphabetically. In 1975, probably for reasons of design as much as anything else, this glossary appeared just inside the front cover, on a flap that readers could not miss. The first words a reader saw in 1975 were "Assets acquired through foreclosure." The placement was an unintentional warning of what was inside. NCNB Mortgage Corp.'s list of nonperforming assets was growing rapidly. By year end, the amount had doubled the 1974 figure.

In April 1975, NCNB hired Tom Woolwine as the chief financial officer for the mortgage company. What Woolwine found when he arrived was not one operating company but an amalgamation of three companies (NCNB Mortgage, C. Douglas Wilson, and Blanchard & Calhoun), each with its own computer system, its own style, and its own management. Loan procedures were either weak or nonexistent. The systems that Dougherty designed for performance reporting and management analysis in the bank had not made their way into the subsidiaries that now reported to him. In September, Dougherty asked Woolwine to inventory the construction loans and supply him with a report, rating each loan according to its threat to the business.

Woolwine hit the road, personally visiting sites of projects on the corporation's watch list. What he found was discouraging. Loan commitments had been made on projects that would never succeed. For example, further investigation by qualified appraisers and engineers would show that loan officers had not determined if property designated for development was worth the value proclaimed by developers or would qualify for the intended purpose. In one case, a major North Carolina home builder, with a solid reputation for construction and sale of residential projects, had failed to determine if property purchased for a housing development outside of the established metropolitan sewer system could support a septic system. At the same time, the lending officer had not asked to see if a percolation test had been performed. Woolwine's investigators found that the property would not handle septic tanks for the homes that the developer had said would be built.

Overeager loan officers with little or no experience beyond home mortgages, coupled with NCNB's own aggressive posture, had contributed to the problems. Lending officers had been so determined to make some deals that when contracts for major loans were signed, the borrower had little of his own money tied up in a project. When deals went sour, those borrowers often drove away leaving NCNB holding the bag, their personal property untouched because borrowers had not been required to tender personal guarantees.

Woolwine gathered his materials, put together his best estimate of the future viability of each project, and in January 1976 presented his report to NCNB's top management. "I think they were astounded. I don't think they showed their emotions in front of me as they later did. I think Mr. McColl knew the mortgage company had problems, but he never knew the magnitude because he was not involved in the day-to-day operations and did not sit on our board. From subsequent conversations with Mr. Storrs, I think he was astounded, too."

Some of the mortgage company's problems were obscured by the way payments from developers had been handled. On paper, construction loans for apartment buildings, condominiums, or other projects were considered to be performing if interest payments were being made on time. If a borrower was current on his interest, then the project looked sound, and further advances would be made against the initial commitment. What NCNB found, however, was that in some cases the developer was using money advanced for construction to pay the interest.

"The people in the mortgage company had the job of monitoring the progress of the thing and cutting off money if they got into trouble," Storrs recalled years later. "And they didn't do it as well as they should have. It took longer for the really bad situations to show up. There is no warning light flashing until certificate of occupancy is issued and nobody moves in."

The problem loans involving major real estate projects were consolidated into a single portfolio. Covington was recalled from Greenville and assigned to work out each one. Where he could, Covington looked for buyers. But at the time condos at Hilton Head Island that would one day sell for $300,000 each would not move at $40,000. In Myrtle Beach, where NCNB took over Pirate Land, the partially completed theme park that defaulted on a $1.9 million loan, NCNB agreed to find a buyer and operate the park for a year as Magic Harbor. Also in Covington's portfolio was a development and golf course near Calabash, North Carolina, houses and land at the North Carolina mountain resorts of Beech Mountain and Sugar Mountain, and a tract of land about thirty miles outside Cincinnati, Ohio.

When he found a buyer or had a way to resolve a problem, Covington could act quickly. He dealt directly with McColl, who had organized three teams of top executives—one headed by Francis "Buddy" Kemp, one headed by James Berry, and one that McColl took for his own—that were devoting more and more hours daily to workouts of problem loans. Storrs had given McColl and his lieutenants the authority necessary to resolve problems.

"I ran them all, but the three of us were what I called the principals," McColl recalled later. "We assigned key junior officers who had great skill in credit—Covington, Walker Lockett, Bill Vandiver, Ron Savas, Neil Trogden, Ed Spears, guys like that, and we had our outside lawyers. Harry Grim is one of our most important ones. He dealt with all the heavy workouts, as did Barney Stewart."

Storrs leaned heavily on McColl and his workout teams. "They not only had the background to handle our situation," he said, "but they really relished doing it. For either one of them, collecting a sorry loan was about as much fun as doing a good one. There was real money lying right there on the table. And he liked to pull that back in."

McColl said, "We had all the authority of the bank. Mr. Storrs had given us authority. There wasn't any question about it, and that was an important thing. We didn't meet with anybody to decide to do something. We had to have carte blanche. We were up against deadlines always, such as bankruptcy proceedings."

As these and other deals unraveled, Storrs also learned that, in addition to weak or limited investigation on specific projects, one part of NCNB's operation was not even checking with the other. Even Dougherty was caught off guard by the number of cases in which the bank's total exposure to an individual customer was not known until business from all NCNB subsidiaries was tallied. In one instance, the bank had lent money to a borrower believing that a finance company subsidiary was making sure that reserves were held to cover the loan. But the subsidiary had used the reserves for other loans. So when the borrower defaulted, there were no reserves to cover the loss to the bank.

Another deal, involving a loan to a construction company, amounted to more than $35 million. The company was sliding into bankruptcy, and the potential loss to NCNB was equal to more than the company's earnings the previous year.

"More important," McColl said, "the loan failure would have caused a market collapse of confidence in the company. It would have taken out the company. We would have been insolvent and taken over by the FDIC. It was that close."

This deal and others were dicey and required an understanding of finance as well as the provisions of the bankruptcy laws. McColl and Kemp found one subsidiary of the ailing construction company that was making some money. They shored that up to produce some cash and went in search of an investor who would join NCNB in underwriting the other parts of the business until it could recover. They scheduled a negotiating session for a Saturday in Charlotte with an insurance company that stood to lose if the company went into bankruptcy. They proposed a solution: NCNB would put up $5 million and the insurance company would put up $5 million. After hours of wrangling, they had gotten nowhere.

"Finally," McColl remembered, "I told them, 'Well, we're going to let it go bankrupt.' They got all upset and huddled, and finally Buddy and I went back in the room. They said, 'We're not going to match you, but we will guarantee your debt.' I was trying not to smile because that was better than dollar for dollar. Kemp never broke stride, and he said, 'Well, what about our interest?' And we got it.

"We went into the kitchen after they left—we had been there ten hours on a Saturday—and we got one of Mr. Storrs's bottles of wine and opened it and drank the whole damn thing. It was a great triumph."

Compounding NCNB's problems was the failure of the real estate investment trust to keep up its obligations. The downfall of the REITs, which were failing right and left, was a lesson that Storrs would recall from his childhood. The business was predicated on a never-ending increase in value, as projects rolled over from one owner to another. The notion was quite similar to some first mortgage bonds that someone had sold Storrs's father just before the stock market crash in 1929. By the fall of 1975, Tri-South Corp., NCNB's Atlanta-based REIT, had 65 percent of its portfolio of $240 million in a nonearning capacity. The European banks that had loaned Tri-South Corp. $15 million were calling their note. Tri-South won a reprieve in December after lender banks agreed to renew loans of $161 million.

Storrs fielded continuing concerns from his board. With the help of Addison Reese, he stalled the resignation of one longtime board member because he feared the departure would stir more rumors of NCNB problems. Other board members peppered Storrs with memos and letters containing questions and concerns over the growing list of nonperforming assets.

Also nagging at Storrs throughout this period was the fact that, while NCNB Corp. was plagued with problems, North Carolina National Bank remained strong. Thinking about the banking business would require some reorientation. At a meeting of the Charlotte bank's loan officers during the height of the crisis, when lending officers were stunned by what they saw before them, Storrs asked those gathered what their job was. "They said making loans," recalled Joe Claud, the Charlotte city executive at the time. "Storrs said, 'No, your job is to, every day, go out and manage risks.' That sort of turned us around in Charlotte. We knew there was no such thing as a risk-free situation."

Once the bank and the corporation's liquidity problems were solved in 1974, the remaining drag on NCNB's earnings was coming from the nonbank subsidiaries, primarily the mortgage company. Most insiders were aware of the bank's condition, but Storrs worried that the continuing difficulties and weak earnings reports of 1975 would eventually cause serious damage to the bank's credibility. In January 1976 his worst fear—a bad press report on the bank—hit as he answered his telephone one afternoon late in the month. On the line was a reporter with the *New York Times* who said he had inside information from the Federal Reserve Board showing that NCNB was on a Fed watch list. Did he have any comment? Storrs was asked. The question chilled him to the bone.

"It really came as a bolt out of the blue," Storrs recalled, "because, by this time, I felt that we had made a significant improvement in our situation, and certainly no one had ever told me that we were on the watch list of the Federal Reserve. I was startled and didn't give him a very good answer."

After he hung up the phone, Storrs called in Ken Clark and others for a hasty strategy session. Clark realized that news like this wouldn't appear just in a New York paper. He advised that the story would probably be in the *Charlotte Observer* the next day and Storrs ought to act to diminish the impact. Though the *Observer* was only a regional publication, most of NCNB's major stockholders would see the story there first. Clark put in calls to the *Observer*'s business editor, Roy Covington, and to David Lawrence, the paper's executive editor, inviting them up to talk with Storrs.

"We met with them for two hours, told them what we knew about what the Federal Reserve was doing, and then went into considerable depth about the strengths of the company and how they were reflected in the markets in which we did business," Storrs recalled.

About nine o'clock that evening, Covington found the *Wall Street Journal* story in the *Observer*'s computer system. He put together what he got from the New York paper (it was carried in both the *New York Times* and the *Journal*) and Storrs's explanation of the bank's situation and produced what Storrs called a "balanced piece of reporting that presented both sides."

The incident gnawed at Storrs's sense of fair play. With some digging, he found out that NCNB had indeed been on a list, but it was a list generated after a brief analysis done by someone preparing a report for the director of the Division of Banking Supervision and Regulation. He also found that the list had never been approved by the Federal Reserve. The report was an internal memorandum that also included the name of Chase Manhattan Bank, and it had no official standing. Storrs finally learned the contents of the report and said it contained incorrect as well as inadequate information.

Nonetheless, the damage was done. Storrs mounted his own offensive to counter the bad publicity. He prepared a response and sent it to his own board members as well as to the chief executive officer of each bank represented in the Association of Reserve City Bankers. He told them that this was the kind of thing that could happen to them, too. At one point, he read the company's response to a friend who was on the Federal Reserve Board.

"'I hope you didn't send that out,'" Storrs said he was told.

"I said, 'Well, the fact is I already have.' He said, 'You're going to lose a lot of friends here at the board for that.' And I said, 'Well, you've lost a lot of friends here at NCNB because of what you did.'"

Not long after the episode, Storrs was at a dinner meeting of the Federal Advisory Council, where he was being honored for his service as chairman. As he was entering the dining room, Fed chairman Arthur Burns caught up with him and apologized for the leak of the report. Later, during his impromptu remarks to the gathering of bankers from every leading financial institution in the country, Burns complimented Storrs and NCNB, calling the bank one of the outstanding institutions in the country.

Except for a significant drop in 1974, the bank's earnings increased steadily between 1972 and 1977, with a five-year compounded growth rate of 5.6 percent. The expansion of the bank into new markets had slowed to a crawl before the financial problems arose, but during 1974 Luther Hodges had opened new offices in Salisbury and Southern Pines, and the bank extended into the upper Piedmont with a merger in Mount Airy, a farming and manufacturing community north of Winston-Salem. Nearly every major North Carolina city now had the familiar red NCNB logo outside a branch office. The notable exception was Asheville, the anchor market in the western mountains.

In addition, the bank had regained its position as the largest bank in the Southeast. With 158 branches in fifty-eight North Carolina cities, its total assets were greater than Wachovia's, but the Winston-Salem institution outstripped NCNB on several significant measures, including total deposits, which made Wachovia a more attractive investment. That fact was not lost on Storrs or his board members.

Hodges had been an aggressive proponent of expansion of the NCNB banking system and was frustrated that NCNB had succeeded in every market except Asheville. A good merger opportunity there simply eluded him. As chairman of the board at the bank (as opposed to the holding company), Hodges enjoyed statewide prominence, and he did nothing to discourage talk in political circles that he was available for public office. Hodges said years later that he was considering a campaign for governor in 1976 when NCNB's problems erupted in 1974. He postponed his political plans to tend to banking business until NCNB was out of the cycle of bad business.

All told, Hodges was probably the best-known and most visible member of the NCNB management team. On more than one occasion, when Storrs was introduced as being with NCNB, someone had asked if he worked for Hodges. Even as a young officer, Hodges had talked about the day when he would run NCNB. He saw himself as the natural successor to the tradition of Addison Reese, a man he admired more than any person alive, and his career track seemed to be pointing that way. Hodges had ended up supervising every boss he had ever had, except one. Tom Storrs.

Hodges often found himself at odds with Storrs and his old friend McColl. "They didn't think I was sufficiently profit-oriented," Hodges recalled. "I thought they were obsessed with the numbers. I was being painted as a more public figure, a more political figure than a hands-on banker. I guess I sort of painted that picture myself, and I don't apologize for that."

The playing field for Hodges, McColl, and Dougherty changed in 1976. The proxy statement released in early 1977—about the same time that Hodges's decision to leave became known—showed that during the previous year, McColl and Dougherty had received raises higher than Hodges had. Those who read the change in their status as a shifting of power were right.

In January 1977 Hodges announced his plans to leave the bank in July, when he would begin putting together his campaign for the Democratic party's U.S. Senate nomination in the 1978 spring primaries. "He and I talked about his leaving at some length," Storrs recalled. "He didn't just come in one day and surprise me. I expect he decided to run for office when his father succeeded Governor Umstead. I believe that it was always in the back of his mind that he would pursue a career in business to a point of achieved position and recognition and then go into politics. And he achieved a higher position than his father did, and he did it at an earlier age."

The departure of Hodges simplified the management structure by narrowing the field, which lowered the tension level on the executive floor. During the three years that Storrs had his three competitive executives together, employees had joked about ducking the gunfire as they passed before the executive offices on the twenty-third floor of the NCNB tower. There were more serious consequences. Executives in the lower ranks had often found themselves in uncomfortable positions, feeling forced to choose sides and line up behind one of the three. Definite proposals, and even offhand comments, were sometimes taken as signals of hidden agendas or pet projects of one of the three.

When the management structure was reorganized, McColl assumed responsibility for NCNB's banking business, consolidated under him as president of the bank, while Dougherty continued to oversee the non-bank subsidiaries and the operations side of NCNB's affairs as president of NCNB Corp. There was still no clear signal as to which man would succeed Storrs, whose retirement was six years away, but the balance of power was tilted toward McColl. Of the two, he was the banker, and his battlefield experience in the credit and workout war of the previous years had impressed Storrs. While McColl may have thought Storrs identified with Dougherty, whose numbers and analytical approach were more his style, Storrs was impressed with McColl's prowess at the negotiating table, his skill in handling difficult loan problems, and his experience in the international markets, where Storrs believed opportunities awaited NCNB.

On September 1, 1977, Addison Reese succumbed to cancer. His illness had been diagnosed as terminal more than a year earlier, but he had continued to come to the NCNB offices as a consultant. In his last year, he devoted as much of his time to his two favorite projects, the University of North Carolina at Charlotte and Charlotte's Mercy Hospital, as he had before. Until he was bedridden shortly before his death, his routine varied little. He arrived, briefcase in hand, about 8:30 A.M. and often carried work home with him.

When he was no longer able to come to the office, his interest in the business did not wane. His secretary, Pat Hinson, carried work to him at home, took dictation, retrieved papers that needed Reese's signature, and delivered others for his review.

Shortly before Reese died, McColl paid a visit to his room at Mercy Hospital. A nurse told him her patient was resting. McColl was about to leave when he heard, "Is that Hugh McColl out there? Send him in here." McColl proceeded to tell Reese about the indiscretions of the head of North Carolina's Northwestern Bank, based in North Wilkesboro, who was the target of an investigation by the Internal Revenue Service and the Federal Bureau of Investigation. The difficulties at

Northwestern had stunned the North Carolina banking community, and the bank was in disarray.

"What are you doing about it?" Reese asked. McColl said account and loan officers were going after Northwestern's customers in markets where they felt NCNB could take advantage of the ailing bank's difficulties. When McColl finished, Reese reached over, patted McColl's hand, and rasped slowly, "Show them no mercy."

"I'll never forget it," McColl said years later, after he had achieved some reputation as an aggressive competitor. "It was a great line. That is the corporate culture. In a nutshell, that was it. He was that way, if it was the enemy. That's what I've always tried to explain to people. It's not me that's caused all that. It's my predecessors."

Chapter 10 **Cranking the Engines**

When NCNB was born in 1960, most of the bank's top management had either experienced the years of retreat by financial institutions brought on by the Depression or had learned the business from bankers who had. Some of the same excesses that produced the bank failures of the Depression returned in the 1970s to humble high-flyers. As before, a more conservative mood settled on banking in the aftermath and period of rebuilding. NCNB was a much quieter place as it recuperated and its troubles began to fade.

In 1978, Tom Storrs's correspondence and conversations no longer included references to "damage control," as he began to focus more attention on the future. The business was responding to a healthier economy. His decision to press forward with the development of NCNB Plaza had paid off. NCNB sold its 80 percent interest in the remainder of the project, the Radisson Hotel, for $22 million. The success with NCNB Plaza helped offset the $2 million in losses suffered a year earlier on the sale of the former headquarters building on South Tryon Street.

However, the trying experiences of the previous few years had produced two camps within NCNB. One favored a conservative, cautious approach to avoid a repeat of the problems that created the crises of the 1970s. The other championed a corporate culture of aggressive competition and pushing the limits of the market—the approach that had given NCNB prominence in banking in the Southeast. "We had a group of people who felt that the only kind of company they wanted to work for was one that would be ultraconservative so that this would never happen again," Storrs recalled. "And we also had a group of people [who said] that if that is the kind of company we are going to run then they didn't want to work here."

At one point, the old Information and Advisory Panel, the group of young NCNB officers created by Dr. James Farr in the 1960s, recommended that the company be dismantled and troubled divisions sold to protect the integrity of the bank.

Storrs responded by dissolving the Information and Advisory Panel.

Now, sinking morale among some of his most talented managers weighed heavily on Storrs. Angry frustration rose in Hugh McColl, Storrs's hard-charging bank president, who believed that it was taking too long to get "the engines cranking again." From time to time, Storrs simply absorbed emotional outbursts from McColl, who knew Storrs hated to be confronted with hostility and irrational behavior but delivered it right to his desk anyhow. "I probably made his life miserable," McColl recalled.

"We had so many people around here with bruises from the workouts," Storrs said, "that if we didn't do something we were going to sink down with mediocrity. We stood a chance of getting taken over or pushed down."

This new set of challenges tested Storrs's ability to manage personalities as well as numbers. He knew the bank had to find new markets and begin to move, and he also needed the management talent to keep NCNB on the road. It was as critical a time in NCNB's development as the previous period had been tumultuous.

In a way, the combined interests of Storrs and McColl led NCNB to take a look at Charlotte's Fourth Ward neighborhood, which is an easy stroll from NCNB Plaza, in the city's center. That is, the old Fourth Ward neighborhood was within walking distance of NCNB's gleaming office tower, if anyone actually wanted to go there in the mid-1970s. The inviting broad canopy of the neighborhood's old trees that could be seen from the NCNB tower disguised neglected houses and vacant lots. This was dangerous territory at night; Fourth Ward had made its contribution to Charlotte's distinction as the per capita murder capital of the United States in 1974. Among the few remaining structures were cheap boardinghouses, brothels, and drug dens.

In 1975, Charlotte attorney Dennis Rash called on McColl and reminded him of a conversation the two had had two years earlier, after Rash had returned from London, where he visited with his college roommate, George Campbell, who ran NCNB's London office. Rash and McColl talked about what they liked about London and other cities of the world, where the streets were alive at all hours of the day and where people didn't escape to the suburbs at the end of the day, leaving a deserted center city.

Although McColl had lived in Charlotte for nearly twenty years, he was not really a part of the city. Consumed by the business of the bank, which had required extensive travel, he had never bothered much with the affairs of Charlotte. When McColl thought about Charlotte, he saw it as the "countryest" of country towns, with a dying downtown.

Rash's return visit had more of a purpose than just a friendly chat. As the unelected head of a group of urban pioneers who believed they could convert Charlotte's Fourth Ward into a livable neighborhood, he was counting on NCNB's record of community involvement and corporate social responsibility to turn that vision into reality. He wanted two things from NCNB—a commitment for a source of nontraditional home mortgage and development money and a task force of bank people to help make it happen.

NCNB wasn't the only bank that Rash had approached for assistance. He also had called on First Union and found some interest. City National Bank was interested. Wachovia had rejected the notion out of hand. But, because of its reputation for community involvement, NCNB was the one Rash was counting on to come through.

In a sense, Rash was depending on the legacy of Addison Reese, who had preached that improving the quality of life in a community was important to a bank and its stockholders. NCNB's 1973 annual report,

published during Reese's last year as chairman, carried a forceful statement to that effect. NCNB's high profile as an involved corporate citizen
willing to look at new ideas and new ways of doing things for its customers and the communities where it did business also was consistent with
the kind of unconventional bank that Reese had tried to build. That
same philosophy had produced programs as broad as the low-income
lending program, support of a professional sports team in Charlotte,
low-interest loans to preserve historic buildings in Charleston, financial
assistance for an orphanage, and consideration of child care for bank
employees.

Rash also was counting on NCNB's obvious investment in Charlotte.
The bank had more money at stake in Charlotte's central city than any
other institution did. The parking garage and hotel were nearing completion. The hotel was due to open in 1977, and further commitment to
the city would enhance NCNB's position as a leader in the revitalization
of Charlotte's downtown, still a source of some embarrassment to the
city's leaders.

Despite all this impetus for NCNB's participation, Rash's timing was
not good. NCNB executives such as McColl had internal problems that
required all the manpower the bank could muster. In addition, real estate development, particularly risky ventures like this, was the source of
the bank's problems. Adding other less-than-solid projects didn't make
a lot of sense.

Nonetheless, McColl was ripe for a new challenge and liked Rash's
idea. He told Rash that NCNB would commit up to $3 million in mort-
gage money to help make Fourth Ward happen. In addition to the
money, McColl pledged the talents of Joe Martin, a scholar of medieval
English and former director of student activities at Duke University who
now coordinated NCNB's corporate social responsibility efforts.

McColl became an enthusiastic promoter of the Fourth Ward project.
He began raising money to renovate one existing historic structure,
called the Berryhill House, that would become Fourth Ward's first re-
claimed home. While work was under way on that building, Rash up-
rooted another Victorian house, relocated it next door, and became the
neighborhood's first new homeowner in years. One by one, additional
houses were moved and restored, creating an instant "historic" neighborhood around one central intersection.

Martin, Rash, and city officials were on the telephone almost daily trying to push and pull the project from dream to reality. When the project seemed to be all but stalled, Martin read in the *American Banker* that the Federal Reserve had approved a nonprofit subsidiary at the Bank of America to build a modest amount of low-income housing. Why couldn't NCNB develop the same idea in Fourth Ward? Working with city planners, who had put together plans for overall development of the area, and residents who already lived there, NCNB applied to Comptroller of the Currency John Heimann for broader authority to create a nonprofit corporation that could do what private developers wouldn't do in the general interest of urban development.

Heimann, who had been housing director of New York before taking his new job of regulating banks, liked the proposal. With his approval, in the fall of 1977, NCNB Community Development Corp. became the first venture of its kind in an American bank, authorized to undertake general real estate development "in the public interest." NCNB recruited Rash to become the corporation president and went into the inner-city development business.

Fourth Ward was taking shape, but slowly. After two years, about eighteen families had moved into the area, but they represented more an outpost of an urban settlement than a fully functional neighborhood. As yet, no major developer had taken an interest in investing in building homes, apartments, or condominiums. Most scoffed at the notion of urban, rather than suburban, living, and each was waiting for someone else to be first. Individual efforts were moving slowly, too. Even with the loan money available at below-market interest rates, the cost of mortgages was still too high to leave prospective homeowners with enough money to rehabilitate the houses they purchased. Of the $5 million pool of bank lending money available, only about $2 million had been used.

The Community Development Corp. was what the project needed. As one of its first undertakings in Fourth Ward, the corporation bought a stately old red-brick apartment building called the Poplar Apartments, restored it, and resold the units as condominiums. Next door, it built more than a dozen expensive townhouses in a joint venture with a private developer, Synco Corp. of Charlotte, which was owned by McColl's close friend Reitzel Snider. Profits from these buildings were reinvested in the community, which not only was becoming an appealing place to live but was gaining national attention for NCNB among city planners and others interested in reversing the trend of inner-city decay.

Not everyone shared NCNB's enthusiasm for the project, however. The early work drew complaints from private developers, who argued that NCNB's involvement presented unfair competition. Some employees and officers within the bank also questioned why NCNB should invest money and management time in such a risky project. The opposition died, however, as Fourth Ward blossomed and flourished.

Fourth Ward absorbed much of McColl's energy and attention, but the work was therapeutic. In addition to supervising the bank's community development effort, he became chairman of a new tax-supported group, the Charlotte Uptown Development Corp., that oversaw the development of downtown. The new focus in his life provided an outlet for pent-up energy that McColl would later concede he might have spent counterproductively at NCNB. He was impatient with the pace of the bank, which he believed was influenced by a cautious, conservative planning group overconcerned about avoiding a repeat of past sins. For example, expansion of the retail bank into new markets had virtually stopped after the Southern Pines branch opened in 1974.

McColl began to push in the area where he could make a difference, the international business whose growth was to become the most dynamic in the bank. In 1976, NCNB had upgraded the finance company that it had formed in Hong Kong in 1974 to a full-fledged international branch. An office was opened in Johannesburg, South Africa, in 1975 as part of a strategy to extend NCNB operations into the British Commonwealth. An office in Sydney, Australia, would follow in a few years. In 1977, the bank's merchant banking operations were expanded with the creation of NCNB Exports Ltd. Two years later, the London operations would be consolidated under one corporate structure, Carolina Bank Ltd. The focus of the business was on leasing and export services for corporate customers whose affairs abroad had originally led NCNB into business overseas.

The international banking business was particularly important to Storrs, who believed that NCNB should be a bank that provided service to a broad range of customers wherever they needed it. Since many of the bank's customers were in the export of textiles, tobacco, and other North Carolina commodities, it was natural to follow them to their foreign markets.

Storrs's early interest in expanding into international markets had run into resistance from Addison Reese. Though Reese was set on building a new kind of bank, his plans did not extend much beyond the borders of North Carolina. When the London office was proposed in 1971, he had objected, but finally he acquiesced, turning responsibility over to his successors. During a visit to London in the mid-1970s, while on his way to a meeting of the International Monetary Fund in Paris, Reese confided to George Campbell, NCNB's London office chief, that he finally consented to Storrs's insistence for an international presence in part because he was nearing retirement and he didn't believe he should inhibit his successor's plans for the future.

To keep track of NCNB's international exposure, Storrs created the Country Limits Committee, which met monthly to review situations in each of the nations where the bank was doing business. Later, an international economist would be added to the NCNB staff.

After opening its Johannesburg office in 1975, NCNB began to encounter public resistance to doing business with South African companies. Pickets marched in protest outside the Raleigh Civic Center when NCNB stockholders gathered in April 1978 for the annual meeting. In a statement before the meeting, a bank spokesman defended the bank's position, saying, "NCNB's loans in South Africa have helped to provide jobs and otherwise increase the economic well-being of blacks in that country."

Back home, the North Carolina base was strong. NCNB claimed about 20 percent of the North Carolina retail banking market and had offices in every major market except one. Asheville still eluded NCNB. Negotiations with the Bank of Asheville, the most likely partner, had begun under Hodges but had not come to fruition. After Hodges left NCNB in 1977, Storrs and McColl continued to talk with the Asheville bank, and finally a merger committee from Asheville met with them. These talks dissolved when Storrs and McColl decided the asking price was too high.

A short time after the Asheville merger talks cooled, Storrs reopened discussions with John Youngblood, a member of the Bank of Asheville board. In early 1979, he flew to Asheville to spend the day with Youngblood. The two talked at Youngblood's home, but after a couple of hours of give-and-take, they still had not reached agreement on a merger plan. Things appeared to be at an impasse, and the two men left for an automobile tour of the city to kill time before Storrs's return flight was due at the Asheville airport. As they rode, they talked about the city, its future and development and building projects underway. Finally, as Youngblood pulled into the airport entrance, Storrs raised the topic of merger again. "I turned to him, and said, 'What do you think you have to take to your board to make a deal?'" Storrs recalled. Youngblood named a figure, and Storrs quickly answered, "We'll do it."

The merger was effective December 3, 1979, and NCNB added $100 million in assets to its books and six new offices in the Asheville market. The Asheville merger boosted morale at NCNB and seemed to say to those eager to move ahead that the bank was back in action, so to speak, after more than five years of retrenching.

It was apparent to Storrs, even before the Asheville merger, that major growth similar to what he had seen in the first ten years of the bank's life would stop as soon as NCNB reached the boundaries of North Carolina. Even with the reinvigorated North Carolina banking group, now under the direction of Buddy Kemp, the bank's 20 percent of the state's market would be limited to what the bank could do by growing that business with new products and more efficient services. Growth would be limited largely to the amount of growth in North Carolina.

Stagnation was unacceptable to a company that had expanded from just slightly more than $450 million in assets less than twenty years earlier to become the twenty-fourth largest bank in the U.S. with more than $6 billion in assets. NCNB would need to create new opportunities if it was to continue to grow. Otherwise it stood to lose business to the new entrants in the financial industry, the large, nationwide brokerage houses that would soon be permitted to perform some banking services. The traditionally docile savings and loans also were beginning to intrude aggressively in new areas of banking. Most important, NCNB's deposit base must grow if it was to avoid the problems of the past, prompted in part by heavy dependence on borrowed funds.

The crisis of 1974 had produced a new attitude within the company about sources of funds. When the bank found itself in difficulty in the summer of 1974, NCNB began to shift from its traditional source of funds, such as the brokers in the major money centers, to gathering more consumer deposits. It took four years, but by 1978, the bank had reversed the ratio and only 23 percent of its money was from brokers. The bank had successfully negotiated itself into a position of reaching investors directly.

Recalled Jim Thompson, whose performance in the crisis set the stage for his eventual emergence into top management as vice chairman: "In my judgment, that was the best experience this company ever had. We were able to manage our way through a crisis in the market and in our own balance sheet, and we learned from that experience that we needed structure in the company, needed to have solid sources of funding on a diversified basis, and had to have well-coordinated functions in the company so we could turn on and turn off the flow of business in short order, based on analysis."

Yet to expand, the bank would need new sources of capital. The shortage of available funds already was being felt again as McColl started trying to expand beyond NCNB's traditional base. Before the 1974–75 recession, NCNB had aggressively sought corporate business but had limited its list of contacts to national companies that had facilities or conducted business in North Carolina. In 1977, McColl assigned NCNB's chief planner, Frank Gentry, to find new markets and new customers at home and abroad, regardless of their connection to the state. The strategy was successful, but the expansion was stymied by lack of capital.

Nothing brought NCNB's position home more painfully than an exchange Storrs had with one of his board members, Joseph F. Abely, the CFO and a vice chairman of R. J. Reynolds. RJR had announced its acquisition of Del Monte one day before an NCNB board meeting. When Storrs saw the RJR executive, he learned that RJR had lined up its financing for the deal without calling NCNB. "No," the RJR man said, "I needed $500 million. I called eight banks and I got the $500 million. I don't think you would have committed more than $5 million and I couldn't make a hundred phone calls just to get a half-billion dollars."

Storrs approached the bank's dilemma of where to go and how to get there the way he had been trained to—with facts, numbers, and analysis. In early 1980, Storrs organized the Executive Conference of top NCNB executives and gave them the tasks of looking at the changing environment for financial institutions and measuring NCNB's strengths and weaknesses. "That process," recalled Gentry, "came to focus on a set of factors like volatile interest rates and high inflation and competition, severely increased competition, and deregulation which would increase competition not only from other banks but from nonbanks getting into the banking business. It also focused on the limitations of state boundary restrictions on banks and bank holding companies."

Storrs had no doubt that NCNB's future involved some form of expansion of NCNB's interstate business even beyond mortgage banking and consumer finance offices in other states, principally South Carolina. NCNB also owned a nondeposit trust company in Orlando, Florida, and had corporate loan customers located in that state and others. Storrs, McColl, and others within NCNB had talked about interstate banking as early as 1973, when there appeared to be no limits to what NCNB could become. In typical fashion, McColl had boasted that when interstate banking was declared legal, NCNB would be across the state line by breakfast the next morning. In fact, NCNB had tried to establish a trust company in Camden, South Carolina, and had even received a charter for the American Trust Co. from the Federal Reserve, but never received approval from state authorities to open for business.

Perhaps no state expressed the protectionist attitude better than Florida, whose large deposits were envied by bankers across the state's borders. As well established as the protectionist view was in Florida, interstate bank expansion had at least one prominent advocate there. Storrs had heard the case for interstate banking from his friend and fellow banker, Guy Botts of Jacksonville, chief executive officer of the Barnett Banks of Florida, who had first advanced it in a speech at the Association of Bank Holding Companies annual meeting in Colorado in 1976. As head of Barnett, Botts had championed development in Florida of a network of banks that had brought the benefits of statewide banking to a state where banks had never done business outside their main-office locations. Botts said the time of interstate banking would come, but he conceded that he was not certain what shape it would be in when it arrived.

If smaller independent banks were concerned about being swallowed by larger regional banks, the regionals did not want to become a meal for the money-center banks either. All feared the power and resources of banks from New York, Chicago, and large West Coast institutions. Botts suggested some sort of regional interstate compact that would permit banks within a region to expand across state lines but not permit banks from outside the region to enter.

In 1978, when Storrs saw Botts at a meeting of the Association of Reserve City Bankers in Palm Springs, California, he had asked his friend to tell him more about his idea on interstate banking. Their talk began as a poolside chat but continued into a meeting room and an expanded afternoon session, when Storrs learned that Botts, a skilled corporate lawyer, had researched the law and found that there was nothing to prevent states from organizing compacts to allow interstate banking within the region. Storrs gathered the NCNB delegation for an impromptu session to hear Botts's ideas. Before they returned home, Storrs and Botts had agreed to see what they could do to change state laws to permit banking across state lines.

When the North Carolina General Assembly convened in January 1979, NCNB was ready with proposed legislation to permit regional banking. Under the bill, banks from one state would be permitted to do business in other states if reciprocal legislation was in place there. The legislation got nowhere. It even failed to gain the approval of the North Carolina Bankers Association, and Storrs couldn't interest the larger banks in the state, Wachovia and First Union, in the bill. It never got out of committee. Botts met the same resistance in Florida. A similar bill introduced there also failed to gain support.

Storrs continued to talk about interstate banking at home. It became one of the speeches he delivered to civic clubs. He cornered politicians, made a tour of the state to meet with bank chief executives, and talked with them about his idea. Some smaller banks liked the notion because it would give them a bigger market if their bank was put up for sale, but most were skeptical. For the most part, regional interstate banking remained NCNB's cause alone. The issue appeared to be at a standstill, adding to the frustration at NCNB, where on a clear day executives could see from their office windows into the next state.

A plan for growth drafted by the Executive Conference was presented to the board of directors, which endorsed it. In early 1980, in the annual report for the previous year, Storrs presented his case to NCNB shareholders in a two-page statement of the case for interstate banking. America already had forms of interstate banking, Storrs wrote, with money-center banks using multistate solicitation of bank credit cards. Bank holding companies already engaged in mortgage banking and other nondeposit business across state lines. "The question of interstate banking is no longer 'Should it be permitted?' Instead, the relevant question is, 'What is the way that will have greatest public benefits?' "

Storrs argued in favor of a change in national laws to permit bank holding companies to acquire banks or other bank holding companies in other states "within a logical market," such as the Southeast. "Such a change would create a stronger and more versatile banking system throughout the country. It would eventually end the present concentration of banking market power in the ten or fifteen largest banks in the United States by providing fully competitive alternatives in regional financial centers across the country. Gradually a network of strong regional banking companies, capable of providing the whole range of services to consumers and business, would emerge. As they evolved they would strengthen the U.S. banking system and make our nation more competitive in world banking."

As the incoming president of the Association of Reserve City Bankers, Storrs was speaking as more than just a regional banker. He had a much larger forum from which to reach a broad and influential audience of bankers across the land.

In Florida, Botts was even bolder, with a similar statement published for his shareholders. Botts's special report said, "Nationwide banking, in my opinion, is inevitable. But if we had a transition period of ten or fifteen years during which we could form several large regional institutions, we could create a banking system capable of meeting our nation's expanding economic needs, while avoiding the dangers of concentrating that power in a few monolithic banking institutions."

The banking establishment was not moved. As the topic gained prominence, largely through NCNB's agitation, banking analysts who kept track of such things ironically gave Wachovia, not NCNB, the best chance at gaining from interstate banking. They argued that because Wachovia was less dependent on borrowed capital and had fewer long-term debt obligations, it was the most logical bank to be in the vanguard.

What analysts could not see on the balance sheets was the commitment that NCNB had to the idea. In late 1980, Storrs had asked heads of NCNB departments to look at ways their individual areas could increase business out of state. A staff team, called the Interstate Banking Group, was organized to push the process. The group included Ken Reynolds, a marketing specialist who had recently returned to the bank; bank attorney Paul Polking; government relations officer Mark Leggett; marketing vice president Winton Poole; corporate affairs vice president Joe Martin; and Frank Gentry, the corporation's chief planning officer.

Storrs's charge to the group was to find ways for NCNB to expand business across state lines immediately, rather than wait for new laws and regulations. Gentry had earlier prepared a draft of assumptions on interstate banking that eventually became the foundation of NCNB's interstate strategy.

Gentry's view of the future assumed some form of interstate banking by 1984. When that happened, NCNB would restrict its base to the Southeast and look for targets of merger opportunity in the $100 million-plus size range. Investments in nonbank subsidiaries would continue. When mergers presented themselves, NCNB would seek the dominant role and avoid being acquired by larger institutions.

Various options made the Interstate Banking Group list. Extending installation of automated teller machines in other states, the acquisition of savings and loans, testing regulatory limits on activities of TranSouth's consumer finance offices, creating industrial banks, opening Edge Act Banks (whose business is limited to foreign operations), and relocating the credit card business to other states all were suggested, as was the founding of new state-chartered banks that would be owned in whole or in part by NCNB. Increasing the size and volume from out-of-state loan production offices also was considered.

In addition to types of business, the task force also looked for the most promising markets. By almost any measure, the most tempting was Florida. It was growing faster than North Carolina and already was one of the richest financial markets south of New York. Total bank deposits had grown from less than $2 billion in 1950 to nearly $35 billion in 1980 and were expected to increase to more than $60 billion by the end of the 1980s. Florida also appeared to be a market where competition would be slack. The banking industry was fragmented and dominated by a host of small, independent banks; state laws gave a virtual monopoly to local institutions.

Florida was one of the most underbanked states in the nation. It had consistently ranked as the state with the largest number of citizens per bank. Florida's laws not only prohibited banks from out of state but protected the franchise of local, small-town banks. Banks found it difficult to expand and only recently had received approval to open drive-in "facilities," as long as they were within one mile of the main bank. Branching, approved in 1977, was still difficult. Only two new branches were permitted within any single year.

Outside of the bank, Storrs continued his campaign for interstate expansion. In early 1981, NCNB joined with seven other banks across the nation, from Citicorp in New York to Security Pacific in California, to monitor and promote the interstate banking issue in Congress. At home, Storrs tried to get NCNB's friends in the state legislature to revive a reciprocity bill. The new law would permit banks in other states to do business in North Carolina if their home states permitted North Carolina banks to operate there. NCNB lobbyist Mark Leggett enlisted the support of North Carolina governor Jim Hunt, who appointed Storrs to the economics task force of the Southern Growth Policies Board. Together they maneuvered a recommendation through the board's Commission on the Future of the South, whose report was the first endorsement of the idea by an official body outside of the financial industry.

Politicians were particularly receptive to the NCNB argument that without regional cooperation a nationwide banking system was inevitable and would result in a system controlled by interests outside the South. "Our banks," Storrs argued, "have to be able to gain size and strength before the New York and California banks get in here." North Carolina's lieutenant governor, Jimmy Green, a tobacco warehouseman from the rural eastern part of the state, accepted Storrs's thesis quickly. "It's simple," he later reported to his colleagues after a visit by NCNB executives. "Hugh McColl returns my calls. [Citicorp CEO] Walter Wriston will never even know who I am."

Storrs found it tough to win other converts within the banking community. CEOs at other large banks publicly acquiesced to the notion of interstate banking, but never vigorously joined the effort to make a change. On one occasion, when Storrs raised the subject among his peers in a chance meeting with North Carolina governor Jim Hunt, the other chief banking executives simply walked away. In April 1981, Joe Martin wrote Storrs, "Our momentum is stymied by the Wachovia–First Union stance, although both say they're favorable." In fact, in May, Wachovia opened a commercial loan production office in Tampa. It already had a mortgage loan office in Pensacola. Martin recommended that NCNB press forward with its cause, although he could not get the legislative committee of the North Carolina Bankers Association to even put the topic on the agenda.

One of the expansion options on the bank's own list was the purchase or creation of industrial banks in other states. At the first meeting of the Interstate Banking Group, bank attorney Paul Polking, who had handled many of the bank's mergers and acquisitions during the 1970s, was assigned the job of investigating legal issues surrounding this option. Polking also was asked to determine if Florida law would permit expansion of the business of the Trust Company of Florida, a small nondeposit trust operation that NCNB owned in Orlando.

Few people within NCNB even knew that the bank owned the Trust Company of Florida. Addison Reese had bought it in October 1972 when friends he knew from his summer retreats to Nantucket told him it was available. It was a one-office operation with about $35 million in assets that had been established to serve the interests of the founders and their friends. Throughout the 1970s, it had been lost in the press of other matters and had gone through a series of managers and management problems. Frankly, early marketing projections had never been proven, and the business had languished and become little more than an after-thought in Charlotte. In fact, during the height of the bank's problems in 1974 and 1975, some executives, Frank Gentry among them, had recommended that NCNB sell the Florida trust operation. Storrs resisted because he liked the idea of having an NCNB office in Florida, if only for possible competitive advantage.

Polking, a careful, studious lawyer who had joined the bank in 1970, was aware that Florida law prohibited out-of-state ownership of banks, but he also was aware of NCNB's unusual status in Florida. Within weeks after NCNB had purchased the trust business in Orlando, the Florida legislature had passed a law prohibiting out-of-state ownership of banks, a move designed to head off New York institutions that wanted to follow their customers into retirement. Because the legislature could not force banks to sell any Florida operations they already owned, the legislature wrote an exception to the law to allow NCNB and two other companies, Royal Trust Co. of Canada and Northern Trust Co. of Chicago, to retain their subsidiaries in the state. Rereading the amendment, Polking realized that the language could be interpreted to permit the three grandfathered banking operations to own more than the nondeposit trust operations. If Polking was correct, NCNB was not barred from owning Florida banks.

"The legislation was somewhat similar to and almost identical in language to a statute enacted by the legislature in Iowa several years earlier," Polking recalled. That legislation was "designed to allow a Minnesota bank holding company to acquire additional banks in Iowa. The facts were a little different because they already had banks in Iowa. We were talking about a trust company and piggybacking on the ownership of a trust company to acquire banks, [but] the Fed had already determined that the statute had provided the authority required for a Minnesota bank holding company to acquire a bank in Iowa."

The morning after Polking's discovery, he encountered Storrs at the elevator on his way to his office. "What are you so downcast about?" Storrs asked.

Polking, who had stayed up late researching his new find, replied, "Well, I'm not really downcast at all. I've just been thinking about something and believe I have a way for us to go to Florida."

"What are we going to establish in Florida?" Storrs asked.

"A bank," Polking replied.

Chapter 11 **A Hole Big Enough to Drive a Bank Through**

The old Holiday Inn City Center in downtown Jacksonville, Florida, had seen better days. In the early 1960s, when it opened as the Robert Meyer Hotel, it was the finest the city had to offer. VIPs visiting the busy north Florida city stayed there, and one of Florida's richest and most powerful men, Ed Ball, kept a suite there. Twenty years later, in June 1981, however, it was clearly worn around the edges and was not the kind of place the leading bank in the Southeast would choose to put up its top executives. An advance team of two NCNB officers, G. Patrick Phillips and Margaret Winstead Rainey, had their reasons for selecting the Holiday Inn for a base of operations.

From the windows of his suite on the twentieth floor, NCNB chairman Tom Storrs could look directly across the street into the offices of the headquarters of Florida National Bank, a conservative, cash-rich bank. Up the street, he could see the signs of other large Florida banks, Barnett and Atlantic. The view was as clear as Storrs's determination was strong that before he left the state of Florida one of those banks would be owned by NCNB.

Phillips and Rainey had collected marketing information on the Florida banks while posing as newcomers to the city out to open accounts. They also made arrangements for the eventual landing team. To confuse inquiries about their mission, they reserved rooms and equipment in their own names. When they were through, they had contracted for two private phone lines to the Holiday Inn suites and office equipment such as a copier and Mag Card II memory typing systems.

Had Storrs's peers at the Florida banks known he was on their doorstep, they would have called his plans preposterous. Florida law clearly prohibited out-of-state ownership of its banks. And the Florida legislature had demonstrated that it was in no mood to change that. The balance of power in Tallahassee was on the side of Florida's comfortably rich independent banks, most of them relatively small, one-city institutions that operated at a pace and with a style much more relaxed than that found at NCNB.

What the Florida bankers believed mattered little to Storrs at this point. Tucked in his satchel was a legal brief from NCNB legal counsel Paul Polking, confirmed by two of the most-well-respected law firms in Florida and Washington, stating that because NCNB owned a trust company in Florida before the prohibition against out-of-state ownership became effective in December 1972, it could expand into the banking business there. The interpretation had not been tested in court, but the opinions were evidence enough for Storrs to mount NCNB's most ambitious venture, a move that would change the shape of banking in the Southeast. Before NCNB was through, it would nearly double its size through Florida acquisitions and accelerate legislative action on breaking through barriers to interstate banking.

NCNB's target, Florida National Bank, was a tempting prize. With $2.5 billion in assets, the bank was just the right size and offered NCNB an opportunity to move into many lucrative markets with one purchase. The bank was already "in play," with Florida National's management involved in complicated, and often devious, warfare to fend off an unwanted takeover move from Venezuelan financial interests. Just which way the bank would go was further clouded by the influence of ninety-three-year-old Ed Ball, who lay dying in a New Orleans nursing center.

Ball, whose style and power had shaped Florida banking for a generation or more, was the stuff of legends. Some said he was a man of another age, a perfect Southern gentleman who would rise and bow when a lady entered a room, who addressed all men as "sir," and who wouldn't tolerate off-color jokes in conversation. He also was regarded by his enemies as a ruthless competitor who was quoted as saying, "You can't expect to win if you follow Marquis of Queensbury rules in a bar-room fight." He was in almost constant litigation for forty-five years. One court fight lasted twenty-one years; his divorce took more than five years to settle. He didn't mince words or worry about their impact. During his divorce proceedings, his wife complained that Ball didn't attend church. Given his opportunity to speak, Ball explained, "I didn't go much because there were so many sinners, and I didn't want to keep them out by occupying a seat."

He was the last of the nineteenth-century robber barons, a notorious power in business and Florida politics. Prohibition hadn't deterred his daily regimen of two drinks of bourbon and water and the familiar toast "Confusion to the enemy." The story goes that he continued his ritual, drawing on a boxcar filled with liquor to supply his needs until the Volstead Act was repealed. He often invited legislators and politicians to his home outside Tallahassee, known as Highwayman's Roost, to extract their promises for pet projects. His power in the capital formed around politicians from mostly rural counties in northern Florida, where Ball's holdings were greatest. These politicians were known as the Pork Chop Gang, and they dominated Florida politics until the 1960s.

Ball's power was founded on the vast wealth in the Alfred I. DuPont estate, over which Ball assumed near-total control in 1935. Ball's sister was DuPont's third wife, and DuPont had taken a liking to his new brother-in-law. Ball had only a fifth-grade education, but DuPont had hired him in the 1920s to acquire forest lands in north Florida. Ball bought millions of acres of pine forests that later became the foundation of the St. Joe Paper Co. He pursued his boss's interest in banks, forming one of the state's earliest bank holding companies. When DuPont died, there were seven banks in the Florida National family. In time, Ball's power extended over 43,000 acres of sugarcane land in south Florida, three rural phone companies, the paper company, the Florida East Coast

Railway, and the network of about forty banks that formed Florida National Bank.

Ball's control over his empire was absolute and precise. He believed that his banks, which had survived the Depression with a pledge of faith from the DuPont fortune, should be the perfect image of stability and security. So he built them from granite and marble, most of it mined from quarries he owned in Georgia. The banks were run conservatively and cautiously, lending to blue-chip customers who were treated well, with Ball taking whatever steps were necessary to restrict outsiders from his territory. By 1960, the Florida National network dominated the state with $670 million in assets in cities from Jacksonville to Miami.

Competitors in Florida were scared of Ball's power and control, but in the summer of 1959, the chief executives of major banks from Miami, Orlando, Tampa, and Jacksonville had met in secret at isolated beach homes and ranch houses to organize a merger that, if successful, would produce a bank of combined resources larger than Florida National. While their methods were different, their ambition was not that different from what Addison Reese was attempting to achieve in North Carolina at the same time. After the details were worked out, they announced their plan; they had issued a preliminary prospectus before the Federal Reserve Board ruled against them. The plan died.

What other Florida bankers could not achieve was accomplished about fifteen years later, when the Federal Reserve Board declared the estate a holding company and ordered it to divest itself of either the banks or the St. Joe Paper Co. and Florida East Coast Railway. The banks were sold, but Ball personally retained ownership of 10.5 percent of the Florida National stock and remained a significant factor in Florida National affairs. Ball's interests were closely managed by Fred Kent, a Jacksonville lawyer who looked after Ball's legal business and was Florida National's legal counsel.

When the NCNB contingent arrived in Jacksonville in early June 1981, Tom Storrs and Hugh McColl, who had been promoted to vice chairman and chief operating officer of NCNB Corp. in April, believed that Kent was prepared to arrange a sale of Florida National to NCNB. NCNB had been keenly interested in Florida National since early April, when McColl was approached by a Chilean businessman, Guillermo Carey, who had told him about growing turmoil over stock ownership at Florida National and enlisted NCNB's aid in helping him acquire more stock to exploit a takeover attempt by a South American–based banking interest, C. A. Cavendes Sociedad Financiera of Caracas, Venezuela. The prospects looked ripe. McColl and Storrs believed that if NCNB had a legal loophole large enough to drive into Florida, Florida National Bank would be their perfect point of entry.

Storrs and his team were well versed in Florida banking politics. Their preparations for this exercise had begun in April when McColl and Joe Martin had met with Raymond Mason of Jacksonville. Mason was a protégé of Ed Ball, who owned a large portion of Mason's Charter Company, though they were at opposite ends of the spectrum in terms of style. For example, while Ball drove an old Chevrolet, the flamboyant Mason had a fleet of jets, including his own personal Boeing 727. Mason, McColl said later, "had a pirate's mind" and was one of many wheelers and dealers who had been attracted to NCNB over the years because of its reputation for aggressive lending policies.

During their meeting, Mason filled McColl in on the intrigue and maneuvering at Florida National. Much of the bank's future hinged on the health of Ed Ball, who, though weak and confined to bed, remained alert. His nurse read the *Wall Street Journal* to him daily. The key man at the bank was Fred Kent, an attorney who would assume control of all Ball's interests if the old man became incapacitated. And, Mason suggested, if NCNB was interested in Florida National and doing business in the state, it would need help. He recommended that McColl and Mason see retired state Supreme Court chief justice B. K. Roberts of Tallahassee, who was now in private practice, and he called to arrange an appointment for the following morning.

When they arrived in Tallahassee to meet Roberts, McColl and Martin found a quiet, courtly man with an easy smile and impeccable Southern manners. Despite the understated atmosphere and furnishings at Roberts's law offices, the firm's credentials gave attorneys easy access to the governor's mansion and legislative offices located just a few blocks away. The only evidence of the range of Roberts's long and powerful career were old photographs taken during his three terms as chief justice of the Florida Supreme Court. But this quiet, nonconfrontational lawyer—"I taught these boys constantly that court is the last resort," he says of his younger partners—had known every governor, every speaker of the Florida House, and every president of the Florida Senate for about as many years as McColl had been alive.

Roberts had first met Ball when he was a college student and boldly appeared unannounced at Ball's Jacksonville office to inquire about a loan for his fraternity. Ball took time to see his young visitor, then told him the bank didn't make long-term investments but he would arrange for the fraternity to get its money. He was as good as his word; the loan was negotiated through an insurance company. A few years later, Roberts's uncle, a county sheriff hired by Ball to ride with him while he bought up Florida pine forests, recommended his nephew, now graduated from law school, if Ball ever needed a lawyer in Tallahassee.

Ball looked up the young lawyer, and the two established a friendship that continued in Jacksonville, where Roberts, now a lawyer in the U.S. Navy, later was stationed. After one evening meal, while strolling in the garden of Ball's riverside home, Ball's wife remarked to the Robertses that there was trouble in the household. The next day she moved out. Ball came to Roberts and asked him to handle his divorce. Because he was in the Navy, Roberts said, he was unable to maintain a private practice and would have to decline.

After World War II , Roberts was discharged and had returned to his law practice in Tallahassee when Ball called on him. Again, he asked Roberts to handle his divorce. The case had been through a battalion of lawyers before a judge had thrown it out of court. All Ball had were big legal bills and no resolution of the matter. Roberts was reluctant to take Ball's side against his wife, who remained a friend to the Robertses, but he agreed to see what he could do.

When Mrs. Ball learned Roberts was involved, she called and asked if he would represent her, too. Roberts demurred but asked her what she wanted as a settlement. He suggested she get an attorney and have him call with that figure. Within a few months, Roberts had resolved the entire affair. In addition to the divorce, Roberts also was able to have returned to Ball all the stock that he had given his wife during their marriage. Most of the stock was in closely held corporations, and Ball had offered a price that was equal to the value of the stock at the time it was issued. When he had the stock back on his books, Ball found that the present value was more than what he had paid his wife as a divorce settlement. Roberts not only got Ball his divorce, but helped him make money too.

Pleased with his legal work, Ball asked Roberts for a bill. Roberts refused to charge his friend. "I told him," Roberts recalled years later, "that if I charged what I thought it was worth, then I would lose a friendship, and if I charged what he thought it was worth I would lose the respect of my peers." Ball let the matter drop. Two months later, Roberts was appointed to the state Supreme Court, where he remained until his retirement in the 1970s.

Roberts was prepared for his guests from North Carolina. After talking with Mason the night before, Roberts had called one of his law partners, Fred Baggett, and asked him to take a close look at what the Florida banking laws said about out-of-state ownership. When McColl and Martin arrived in the morning, Baggett told them what they already knew: the only way an out-of-state bank could do business in Florida was if it happened to own a trust company before December 1972. McColl asked Baggett to continue his research, to see if there were other changes since 1972, and asked him to put his findings in writing. They would be back in a week to see what he had.

On the return trip, Storrs traveled with McColl to Tallahassee. Baggett, an energetic and savvy lawyer and a former state legislator with a quick wit, remembers the chemistry of that meeting. His introduction to NCNB had been the bustling, direct style of McColl. When he met Storrs, he wondered how these two NCNB executives could work together.

"I mean, this was the gentleman of gentlemen," Baggett recalled of his first encounter with Storrs. "He was polished, chivalrous, and yet firm. He knew exactly what he wanted, but he didn't press you. Judge Roberts also is a gentleman of the old school, and he and Mr. Storrs sat there and they talked. You wouldn't think that any business was being discussed within the first twenty minutes. That was a time for gentlemen to be gentlemen, and Mr. Storrs and the judge hit it off right away."

When NCNB engaged the Roberts firm, it got more than a group of skilled lawyers. Roberts was well placed to counsel Storrs and McColl on their dealings with Florida National and the complicated battle for control that was building among interests in Jacksonville, Miami, and South America. Roberts knew many of the players, particularly Ball's representatives in Jacksonville, and he began negotiating with Kent on NCNB's behalf, without disclosing the identity of his client.

Roberts also offered some important advice that shaped the NCNB strategy. He believed the Florida National purchase would be complicated, even messy, with potential for the deal to slip off course at any stage. What NCNB needed, Roberts advised, was a clean, quick purchase of a bank in Florida with which it could test its interpretation of the law. He recommended that NCNB test its entry to Florida by first purchasing a small bank that was located in a county where NCNB wasn't presently doing business (to avoid antitrust considerations); that was controlled by a limited number of stockholders (to facilitate a quick sale); and that was in need of rehabilitation (to win the interests of regulators). NCNB also would need a national bank. Purchase of a state bank would require approval in Tallahassee rather than Washington, where local politics would matter less. If NCNB could find such a bank, it would present the Florida Bankers Association with the weakest ground on which to oppose NCNB's action.

That made sense to Storrs, and NCNB hired the investment banking firm of Robinson-Humphrey to scout the roster of Florida banks for a suitable candidate or candidates and make blind calls to determine if the troubled banks were for sale. It did not take long to compile a list of about a dozen prospects. The banks were in small country towns. Most just had one office. The smallest was the First National Bank of Jefferson County, with not quite $4 million in deposits, and the largest was the Citizens First National Bank of Citrus County, with $42 million in deposits.

Once potential candidates were identified, NCNB began preparing for its invasion of Florida. NCNB would need to move fast to complete its purchase and win necessary regulatory approval between the time the legislature adjourned the first week in June and the date it reconvened in January of the following year. Storrs did not want to move while the legislature was in Tallahassee for fear that a hastily drafted law would preempt NCNB's move. When McColl looked at his calendar, the code name for the project was inescapable. The first day after the legislature's scheduled Friday adjournment was June 6, the anniversary of the Normandy invasion in World War II. McColl dubbed the project Operation Overlord.

Martin also had requested that a code list be prepared. Jacksonville became Northport in memos and telephone conversations. Miami was Southport. Tallahassee was Main Street. Florida National Bank was First Company. The DuPont interests were The Lady's Estate, and Carey was Fiddler. Raymond Mason was Robin. One of the principals repre-

Storrs's "troops" in the march on Florida enjoyed the military metaphor. Posing victoriously with the flag of the state of Florida are (left to right) Hugh McColl, Paul Polking, Joe Martin, Mark Leggett, and Frank Gentry.

senting the Venezuelan interests was Dr. V.C. Martin's personal favorite was the name he gave Ed Ball: Jar Man (as in Ball brand jars).

In addition, the NCNB executives tapped for the landing team were instructed to leave word at their offices simply that they would be out of town. Pressing business calls were referred to legal counsel Jim Kiser, who would screen them before passing them on.

On Monday, June 8, NCNB's William Dougherty, Frank Gentry, and Paul Polking boarded an NCNB plane in Charlotte and headed to Florida. Their first destination was Clewiston, a small town on the south shore of Lake Okeechobee, about midway between Fort Myers and West Palm Beach in the heart of Florida's sugarcane fields. Their mission was to buy the Clewiston National Bank, which had a modest $8.2 million in deposits. In a memo to Dougherty, the senior officer of the team, McColl's instructions were to come home with a prize. "Our job," Gentry recalled, "was to find a bank and buy it, as quick as possible, no fuss, no feathers."

When the bank's KingAir prop jet rolled to a stop at the small Clewiston airport, the NCNB executives were met by the bank's board chairman, a pleasant man who was casually dressed in a pullover with his name stitched over the left breast. He didn't know who it was that he was meeting; the Robinson-Humphrey contact had told him only that he was bringing guests who wanted to buy his bank.

After introductions, the NCNB team rode to the bank's office, where board members had already assembled. Dougherty explained their mission and immediately ran into the first arguments that Florida law didn't permit what NCNB proposed. That didn't bother Dougherty, but when he asked for a short recess to talk with his colleagues he learned that the bank's stock was not as closely held as they had been led to believe. Even with agreement by the board, the deal could not be closed quickly. When they returned to the boardroom, Dougherty thanked the board members for their time and prepared to leave. Board members eager to sell—NCNB was offering two times the book value of their stock—asked that they not be so hasty. Dougherty, Gentry, and Polking had already decided, however. "They couldn't deliver on a handshake," recalled Gentry, "so we thanked them and left."

The trio flew north to Jacksonville, where they met the main body of the NCNB landing party. Though NCNB had shown its hand in Clewiston, secrecy prevailed. Martin, who was coordinating logistics and communications strategy, had learned that the legislature would not adjourn as scheduled and was continuing to meet in Tallahassee. Concern rose that if word of NCNB's plans reached the capitol, a last-minute change in the law could close the bank's loophole. As the NCNB executives checked into the hotel, each registered only as part of the "Martin Group." Rooms were assigned to Mr. Martin One, Mr. Martin Two, and so on. The cover was so good that it even frustrated NCNB's own chairman. Once when Storrs called the hotel and asked for Joseph B. Martin, the night operator told him, "I have a Martin in room 1901, one in 1903, 1906, 1908, and more—ain't none of them got no first name or middle initial."

The first day was not off to a great start. Dougherty arrived without a sales contract in hand. Gentry's scouts contacted a second bank, whose board members wanted a couple of days to think things over. Finally, late in the day, an evening meeting was arranged with three Iowa businessmen who owned 81.5 percent of the stock in the First National Bank of Lake City.

Located on the southeast corner of the Osceola National Forest about an hour's drive west of Jacksonville on Interstate 10, Lake City is an old north Florida community. During the Civil War, the area produced much of the food to sustain the Confederacy, and the town still depends on agriculture for most of its income. Lake City retains a quaint, country flavor. The Columbia County courthouse overlooks a small, picturesque lake, where in the spring, ducks hatch and waddle near the water's edge in search of food. Two blocks west, the aging Hotel Blanche is testament to vacation travelers who once stopped on their way south. Florida's booming growth passed Lake City by almost as quickly as Interstate 75, just a few miles west, could carry it.

The First National Bank of Lake City, which had about $22 million in deposits, had a rich history. It had issued its own gold certificates during the Civil War. Now, however, it was on the FDIC list of ailing banks. The Iowa investors were interested and could be in Jacksonville that night. After dinner, and about two hours of negotiating, NCNB had a deal and its key to the deposits of Florida's banking business. The bank was one of the smallest and hastiest purchases NCNB had ever arranged. Not a single NCNB person had set foot on the property, yet it would be one of the most important acquisitions in the bank's history.

The next morning, as Storrs and McColl prepared to push their case with Florida National, Gentry called from the Jacksonville airport. He and Polking had met the Iowa investors to deliver the contract and collect the necessary signatures. Gentry also was to ride with the owners to Lake City to meet the bank's president, K. C. Trowell, who knew nothing about the negotiations. Together they would return to Jacksonville for lunch with Storrs. When Gentry arrived at the airport, however, he found that the sellers wanted to modify the contract. They wanted a "no lose" deal, as Gentry later described it, that would pay them interest on the purchase price if the Federal Reserve Board turned down NCNB's bid to purchase the bank.

Storrs was furious. NCNB already was paying a premium—$19 million—for a bank that had a limited future and was still recovering from problem commercial and industrial loans. But he agreed to the changes. That created another delay. The contract had been initialed and changed in so many places that a new copy had to be typed. Although Martin had arranged for almost every detail, he did not have a typist handy. Gentry flew on to Lake City to pick up the bank president as Martin and Executive Vice President Buddy Kemp pecked their way through the new contract—and also through lunch and into the afternoon. By the end of the day, the paperwork was complete.

Kemp had prepared the detailed research on NCNB's prime target, Florida National Bank, and was tentatively scheduled to take over the operation if NCNB was successful in its bid. Though he had been reduced to clerk typist, he and Martin, a former classmate and fraternity brother at Davidson College, prided themselves on their dexterity at the keyboard. McColl was not impressed. The next morning, his secretary, Pat Hinson, and legal secretary Melva Hanna arrived to take charge of the office.

On Wednesday, Polking and Storrs headed to Washington to alert Federal Reserve Board officials and the Comptroller of the Currency to NCNB's plans. In Washington, they were told, "You can't do that," Polking recalled. "We said, 'Now, wait just a minute and let us explain it to you.'" The two spent several hours at each office outlining NCNB's position.

"They were very pessimistic and very doubtful that it would fly," Polking recalled. "But they said, 'If you think you want to try it, file it and submit your application and proposal and we'll consider it.'"

While the Lake City bank would form the test of NCNB's challenge to the Florida banking laws, the prize remained Florida National Bank. Immediately after the Lake City deal was made, the NCNB team swelled from six or seven to nearly twenty. McColl led the negotiations with Florida National officials.

The center of the NCNB operation was a suite on the Holiday Inn's nineteenth floor. McColl had one adjoining room; Martin, the other. Martin's job was coordinating logistics, including arranging a comprehensive Overlord notebook complete with daily locations of the principals and travel times to airports. Martin also was an observer and recorder for negotiating sessions at Florida National. Grounded more in academe than business, he was fascinated with the process, taking detailed notes of the negotiating sessions and noting body language and subtle signals for review later with the strategy team.

The pace of the effort at NCNB was never in sync with that found in the bank offices across the street. Florida National's chief negotiator and power broker, eighty-year-old Fred Kent, complained to Martin about NCNB's full-court press to buy Florida National. "We might be able to reach an agreement," Martin recalled Kent's saying at one point, "if you could get that boy McColl to calm down and quit making new proposals while we're still thinking about the previous one."

By the middle of June, and within two weeks after signing a contract for the Lake City bank, Storrs and McColl thought they had worked out an arrangement with Kent. Storrs, McColl, and Kemp had met with Florida National's executive committee, and based on what they heard there and from Kent, they felt good about NCNB's position. Rather than take a joint position with someone else, the NCNB executives believed that NCNB could have its own deal with Florida National if they could take the South American interests out of the picture. Finally, McColl negotiated an agreement with the Cavendes financial interests, which controlled about 33 percent of Florida National stock, and made arrangements to stall takeover efforts there. On Friday, June 19, McColl and Storrs laid out their plan in a meeting with Kent.

Despite the significance of the Lake City deal, the local newspapers had paid scant attention to NCNB's purchase of the small-town bank, and NCNB was not eager to stir up public discussion. When Martin called the *Wall Street Journal* and read the press release about Lake City, the reporter commented that a $21 million bank was not very large. "Well, we're a North Carolina bank, and the bank we're buying is in

Florida," Martin hinted. Nevertheless, the story was short and appeared deep inside the nation's leading business newspaper.

The most complete account of the Lake City action appeared in the *American Banker*, a trade publication, a week after the contract was signed. Storrs declined to outline the NCNB strategy and said the details could be found in NCNB's 184-page application that would be submitted in about a week to the Federal Reserve. Storrs said NCNB was relying on its interpretation of Florida banking laws. The story carried speculation by others that NCNB would use its exemption to the 1972 law as authority for the purchase.

On Monday, June 22, the story broke in earnest after NCNB released information about the offer to Florida National. Florida and North Carolina newspapers finally caught the import of NCNB's actions. So had others. "If this passes, hell, NCNB is going to own half of Florida," a Federal Reserve official was quoted in one account. "The whole country is looking at this one."

Florida bankers were caught off guard. Their initial reaction, according to John Milstead, executive director of the Florida Bankers Association, was, "Can they do that? Isn't that against the law?" Even after meeting privately to discuss strategy, the association was equivocal in what action it would take. Some owners of independent banks wanted to fight the move at every step. Others were concerned, but didn't want to thoroughly antagonize NCNB. After all, it was clear that NCNB would be buying banks, and they might want to negotiate a sale of their own some day. Phil Searle, the chairman of Flagship Banks, the fifth-largest in Florida, said, "If I were in Tom Storrs's shoes, I would try to do the same thing. They are wisely taking advantage of an unusual opportunity."

Donald Senterfitt, a vice chairman of Sun Banks of Florida, was legal counsel for the association in 1972 when the amendment was drawn. He was adamant and told the *Greensboro* (N.C.) *News & Record*, "I know first hand that out-of-state acquisition was not the intention. Perhaps the statute was inartfully drawn," he said, but it "was meant to 'grandfather' the types of activity that each was engaged in."

Bankers elsewhere cheered NCNB's move. "NCNB is taking a leadership role I applaud," Thomas G. Labrecque, president of Chase Manhattan Corp. said in a published quote. "Hooray for them," Paul L. Smith, vice chairman of Security Pacific Corp., told the *American*

Banker. The Independent Bankers Association of America restated its opposition to interstate banking.

At Florida National, reaction was cool. George Whitner, president and chief executive officer, declined comment on the bid offer. Robert M. Ulsch, executive vice president, said, "This offer was not invited by us. They made a couple of contacts just to express their interest."

At midweek, the stakes changed. After having recovered some of his health during recent weeks, Ed Ball died on Thursday, June 25. The following evening, Florida's rich and powerful gathered in Jacksonville for Ball's funeral. In an evening meeting, as some of Ball's old friends met for a final toast with Ball's favorite bourbon, Old Forester, McColl was stunned to learn that the deal with Kent was dead. Later in the evening, well after midnight, McColl was still boiling with anger. He paced the hotel room swinging a tennis racket and cursing. "He would have taken their heads off," recalled Roberts's law partner, Fred Baggett. "His bottom line was, 'We haven't left this town yet.'"

The irony of the evening was not lost on those who knew Ball. "I remember sitting there in that meeting," Baggett said, "and the Judge [Roberts] was there because next to him in spirit was Mr. Ball—sitting up there really enjoying it. It was his kind of wake."

NCNB pressed the matter further, but in July publicly withdrew its offer, worth about $210 million to Florida National stockholders, after Florida National announced that it would not respond until the legality of the Lake City purchase was established. Privately, negotiations continued as Florida National interests searched for a safe harbor and NCNB kept looking for an opening. Others entered the fray, including Florida's largest bank holding company, Southeast Banking Corp. of Miami.

As events unfolded, McColl and Storrs learned that they had been used effectively by Kent and the Florida National interests to stall the efforts of the South American investors. This gave Florida National time to work out a "white knight" deal with Chemical Bank of New York, which purchased an option to buy the bank when Florida passed legislation permitting interstate banking. (In 1989, Florida National sold to North Carolina's First Union, but not before giving NCNB a chance to make another offer—an opportunity that McColl declined.)

Some time later, McColl said, "I would have to say Mr. Kent beat us. The first time I went to see him, he told us I would have to solve his Venezuelan problem. So I went and solved the damn Venezuelan problem. I spent a ton of time negotiating with the Venezuelans. Finally, we got the Venezuelan position where we could buy it. And I went back, and he said, 'I can't do business with you; you are on the side of the Venezuelans.'

"He manipulated us beautifully. He beat us, and he did it in sort of an old-boy type of deal. I don't know that his motives were money as much as power. It is very interesting in that when you are dealing with power as a motive, it is much more difficult to deal with. If money is the motivation, you can buy people. You keep stacking money until they say yes.

"In his case, he had the power of the DuPont Trust and the ostensible power of running the Florida National Bank, and if he merged it, he would lose that power, no matter what we paid him. Looking back on it, it is now clear that it was a power issue. He was keeping his power, and he did a hell of a good job."

Formal opposition to NCNB's proposal finally formed around the Florida Bankers Association. The association's government relations committee began preparing its case against the merger that it would carry to the Federal Reserve. The association's John Milstead said the group believed NCNB's actions violated the intent of Florida law, that the exemption was written to permit existing companies to expand only in their present operations, not into other types of banking.

Part of the research that Fred Baggett and others in the Roberts law firm had conducted for NCNB included the question of legislative intent. The legislator who offered the amendment was Robert Hartnett, a Democrat from Miami, who had been chairman of the committee that handled the bill. Early on, Baggett had contacted Hartnett, who signed an affidavit that the intent of the amendment was not to restrict those who owned trust companies to that particular style of banking. Such institutions could expand their services.

The Roberts firm also arranged visits with bankers and business interests who were enthusiastic about NCNB's plans to expand into Florida. Among Roberts's closest friends were former presidents of the Florida Bankers Association. And in late July, shortly after the Florida National bid was publicly withdrawn, Storrs was given a helicopter tour of Tampa, breakfast with George Steinbrenner, the New York Yankees owner and a Tampa booster, lunch with civic leaders, and an introduction to the directors of Exchange Bank of Tampa, one of the oldest banks in the city. Storrs's host for the day was H. Lee Moffitt, an attorney and influential state legislator, who was promoting his city, rather than Jacksonville, as NCNB's eventual base.

In early October, as NCNB prepared for its Federal Reserve Board hearing on the Lake City application, Martin proposed a "post-approval" communications effort for Florida. Martin was worried that since NCNB's entry into Florida, the bank had gained a reputation as "gun-slinging attackers and raiders." In short, Martin said, NCNB was beginning to look more hostile than competitive.

Indeed, NCNB had done little to soften its image. The Overlord reference was sheer poetry to McColl, who prided himself on military tactics, and to Storrs, who had been on hand at the Normandy invasion in 1944. At one point, when the NCNB executives were in a clowning mood, they posed for a photograph, holding up a Florida state flag in Iwo Jima fashion. McColl looked on, grinning broadly from beneath a soldier's steel helmet with general's stars on the front. *Florida Trend*, the state's leading business publication, illustrated its main story on the NCNB incursion into Florida with an illustration that characterized NCNB as a rolling armored car flying a rebel flag and with large guns pointed south.

Speaking to a group of college students in Tallahassee, McColl further stiffened the spines of Florida bankers angry with NCNB's moves when he quipped: "You have a good number of banks in Florida with assets of $40 and $50 million. We call them drive-in branches in North Carolina." The article quoting McColl said the Florida bankers would certainly appeal the Federal Reserve Board's decision if it allowed the purchase of the Lake City bank. To that, McColl responded that NCNB would welcome a court challenge and the bank would "fight it with every dollar and every resource available to us."

Storrs remained clear of such posturing. He was as aggressive as McColl at the negotiating table, but in public he took a calm, reasoned approach. He also appeared more scholarly, with his horn-rimmed glasses and gracious, unhurried manner. He argued that NCNB's expansion into Florida was a natural move and part of the changing environment of banking. His bank might be pushing the schedule a bit. "Our strategy is to build up a very powerful, Southern-based bank," he said. "We don't rule out Cleveland, for example, if we can find a partner that makes sense. What we want to do is build a powerful banking organization that can compete worldwide."

Events beyond the immediate issue reinforced NCNB's contention that interstate banking was indeed on the way. The Commission on the Future of the South formally released its report in September, endorsing its subcommittee's recommendations, aired earlier in the year, that reciprocal agreements should be enacted by the state legislatures to permit interstate banking. In October, a congressional moratorium that prohibited out-of-state banks from opening bona fide trust offices in Florida expired. The moratorium was imposed to give Congress time to study a federal court reversal of the 1972 law blocking out-of-state trust departments. Seventeen banks had applications pending; the majority wanted to locate in Palm Beach County, with its $250 billion in trust assets.

If NCNB needed further incentive to succeed in Florida, it was getting it in its own headquarters city of Charlotte. While it was focusing on Florida, out-of-state banks had discovered the growing economy of North Carolina. By the fall of 1981, Manufacturers Hanover and Wells Fargo, two of the largest banks in the nation, had opened loan production offices there. Citicorp and Bank of America also had subsidiaries in the city, with bankers looking for the high-dollar loans that generate profits from fees and interest.

The threat of a court challenge by Florida bankers added to the anxious anticipation with which NCNB awaited the Fed's decision. Even if the regulators approved, the Florida bankers could take the case to court. In an effort to head off any local opposition, Martin courted leaders of the two other banks doing business in Columbia County. One was the State Exchange Bank, which included sports announcer Pat Summeral as one of its directors. "We made the point," Martin recalled, "that the bank was for sale in any event. If we couldn't buy it, somebody else would, maybe the Venezuelans they had heard about. They had a choice of letting it be sold to nice people from North Carolina or to some strange foreigners." NCNB arranged a reception in Lake City so that the directors of the State Exchange Bank could meet Storrs and McColl and size them up as prospective banking neighbors.

Roberts also contacted his close friends in the banking community, including an influential independent banker who was a former president of the association. His message: Don't be foolish. It's better to have someone besides Florida bankers in the marketplace bidding for your bank should you decide it's time to sell.

Late on the Wednesday afternoon of December 9, NCNB received the call it had been waiting for. Its application to purchase the First National Bank of Lake City was approved. Champagne purchased in advance poured into the glasses of employees at Lake City. Storrs issued a measured, even bland, statement that expressed NCNB's pleasure over the ruling. It endorsed Paul Polking's initial reading of the law.

The court challenge to the ruling never materialized. The Florida Bankers Association's John Milstead said later that some of the association's members pushed for the organization to carry the fight, but they were overruled in the absence of a request from any Lake City bank. Some interested in a court test contacted the State Exchange Bank and offered to pay legal fees if the bank would sue. The offer was declined.

Storrs wanted the closing scheduled as soon as possible, to avoid conflict with the Florida legislature's opening in January. The earliest date that would work was January 8. The formalities were concluded with all speed, and the event was scheduled early in the day. At 8:30 A.M., following a breakfast meeting with directors and officers and a group of dignitaries that included Governor Bob Graham, NCNB assumed ownership of the bank. By 10:30 A.M., Storrs was in the air, headed for Miami to talk with other prospects. Other NCNB officers remained behind for a perfunctory board meeting, but they were on their way to Charlotte by 2:00 P.M. Storrs had not succeeded in securing Florida National, but NCNB's toehold as the largest bank holding company doing business in one of the nation's golden states of banking was firmly established.

McColl put it this way: "We have stolen a march on the world into one of the fastest-growing banking markets."

Chapter 12 **Got Any Banks for Sale?**

When Tom Storrs signed the closing documents for the First National Bank of Lake City on the morning of January 8, 1982, NCNB had accomplished what many had considered an impossible feat. But the corporation's work in the state of Florida was just beginning. Storrs's challenge now was to make the most of the chance of a lifetime.

Storrs was sure that competitive forces would never permit NCNB to roam Florida indefinitely to pick and choose markets while all other out-of-state banks were barred by current law. Florida had tripled total bank deposits in the previous five years, and no banker in the nation could ignore a market like that. Northern Trust Co. of Chicago, which, like NCNB, was grandfathered under the 1972 legislation, followed NCNB's lead, applying to convert one of its trust companies to a full commercial bank and constructing an eleven-story office·headquarters building in

Sarasota. Royal Trust, the other company in the favored trio, was bidding for ownership of a commercial bank. And major New York banks were poised for an assault on the legislature to win entry to the state. If NCNB was to expand its base, it would have to move quickly, before other out-of-state banks—with far greater resources—appeared in the market bidding for business.

"NCNB is doing great things for the banking industry," regional banking analyst Buck Jones of J. C. Bradford & Co. in Nashville was quoted as saying in March 1981. "As NCNB pushes on this foothold in Florida, it can eventually help provoke a change, which is in everybody's interest."

Bill Hackney, regional research director for E. F. Hutton, said, "As Piedmont [Airlines] has helped put Charlotte on the transportation map, NCNB certainly is helping put Charlotte on the banking and financial map."

Events were moving more rapidly than anyone could have imagined just six months earlier. When Frank Gentry prepared his memo on Florida in December 1980, before Polking's discovery, he had predicted that interstate banking would be possible by 1984 and that the "necessary legislative action will be triggered by some unpredictable event." The "unpredictable event" had occurred, and now all were on a steep learning curve. For example, at NCNB's Trust Company of Florida, the once-neglected resource that had proved valuable beyond anyone's expectations, employees were confused and a bit bewildered over NCNB's new status. Since Trust Company was now part of a Florida bank holding company, they assumed, incorrectly, that they needed to be prepared to act like a bank. When employees first had learned of the Fed's decision, one of them purchased a small metal cash box at a nearby office supply store and cashed a $500 check at the savings and loan next door to have a little ready money in the till, recalled Trust Company officer Georgia Foster. "God help us if someone wanted to cash a check."

Storrs also knew that once NCNB had established itself through merger or acquisition beyond the one lonely country bank in Lake City, it would have a major challenge in assimilating the newly acquired Florida banks into the NCNB system. Storrs was not interested in a confederation of businesses. He wanted one strong, unified operation with consolidated interests that would build on NCNB's position as the dominant banking operation in the Southeast.

The expansion beyond its traditional base in North Carolina was founded on a strategy whose first phase included amassing the necessary capital to finance acquisitions. By the end of 1981, on the eve of the Lake City closing, NCNB shareholder equity had increased from $331 million in 1978 to $432 million. Part of the money was raised by the first-ever swap of long-term debt for new shares of stock in a bank. The additional equity increased NCNB's borrowing power and gave the company flexibility to carry additional assets. Within a few months, NCNB had an additional $200 million line of credit with a New York bank to further finance its Florida expansion.

The second phase included improving NCNB's market share in North Carolina and finding new markets. The Bank of Asheville acquisition, and a subsequent merger with Carolina First National Bank of Lincolnton, had filled major holes in the North Carolina market. While Storrs was scouting acquisitions in Florida, NCNB was preparing to close on its last significant merger in North Carolina.

On a Saturday morning in late January, two businessmen dressed in sport coats sat talking in a large, otherwise empty room just off the lobby of the famed Greenbrier resort in the West Virginia mountains. They looked a lonely pair, huddled close in the elaborately decorated space designed to accommodate up to three hundred persons. Neither was registered at the exclusive hotel, and whenever someone would walk through the room, the two wondered if they would be asked to leave.

The two men were Hugh McColl and C. D. "Dick" Spangler, Jr., of Charlotte, chairman of the Bank of North Carolina. They had known each other for some time. Both lived in Charlotte and moved in much the same financial and social circles. For nearly six years, their banks had shared a similar, close relationship. NCNB had loaned money and executive talent to help Spangler revive the Bank of North Carolina after it had fallen on hard times in the mid-1970s. Now, in 1982, with the bank sufficiently recovered, Spangler had let the word spread that the Bank of North Carolina was for sale.

Spangler's bank, with $425 million in assets, had its headquarters in Raleigh and seventy branch offices located primarily in eastern North Carolina, where the bank had been organized, in Jacksonville just after World War II. Spangler's father, whose construction company had built much of the Marine Corps' Camp Lejeune, started the bank after he became frustrated with banks in the area whose service left much to be desired. When the bank ran into problems in the 1970s, his son assumed direct control and appealed to NCNB for help. NCNB had forwarded cash and some of its executive officers, who for several months advised on management and operations until a new president could be found.

As the recovery developed, Spangler had talked with NCNB about merger, but NCNB's regulatory attorneys in Washington had advised that while the Bank of North Carolina would fill in some markets, there was too much overlap with existing NCNB offices in others. NCNB would have to spin off too many of its nonbank businesses, such as finance and mortgage company offices, in the Bank of North Carolina cities. The deal just did not look like it would benefit either bank after all the duplicate offices were sold. In the few intervening years, Spangler had held out hope for a deal with NCNB, but he also had not closed out talks with other potential partners. Though he was a builder like his father, not a banker, he had become a student of bank mergers and acquisitions around the nation and knew what price his bank should bring. He held out for a good price.

In January 1982, two things happened to revive NCNB's interest. Storrs, who closely monitored the mood shifts of regulators, saw a news article that led him to believe the regulatory climate had changed sufficiently so that if NCNB and the Bank of North Carolina merged, NCNB would not have to dispose of many offices. In addition, he heard that Spangler might be making a deal with a competitor. If a merger could be accomplished without the previously considered conflicts, the Bank of North Carolina was one he didn't want to let get away. Storrs discussed his thoughts with McColl and asked him to contact Spangler. When McColl reached Spangler's office, it was a Friday, and he learned that Spangler had already left for a long weekend. McColl left word for Spangler to call him or Storrs whenever he got the message.

Spangler was on his way to Snowshoe, a ski resort in the West Virginia mountains, where he planned to meet his wife, Meredith, and their two daughters. He arrived at the lodge at 1:00 A.M. on Saturday after driving from Charlotte and found a message waiting from his secretary that he should contact either Storrs or McColl. Thirty minutes later the telephone rang in Storrs's home in Charlotte and the NCNB chairman told Spangler that McColl was awaiting his call to arrange a time to talk about a merger. Spangler told Storrs that he was close to accepting another offer, but if NCNB would match it he was interested. When Spangler reached McColl, the two agreed to meet at an airport near White Sulphur Springs, West Virginia.

McColl talked with Spangler by phone from Miami, where he was continuing his work on developing the Florida market. When he hung up, McColl rousted NCNB's pilot, Lee Noble, out of bed, and the two headed for the airport. In a few hours, Noble was searching through the dark for the airport nestled in the West Virginia hills.

Spangler met McColl, and the two drove to the Greenbrier, which they knew would provide a quiet place to talk. Within about twenty minutes after they arrived, the largest bank merger to that point in North Carolina history was arranged—NCNB would exchange just more than 2.1 million NCNB shares worth about $32.2 million for the Bank of North Carolina. There really wasn't much reason to haggle. Spangler already had his price, and McColl knew as much about Spangler's bank as he needed to know. The two sealed the deal with a handshake, then talked for another forty minutes before going to lunch at one of the Greenbrier grills, where Spangler had to pick up the $10 tab. McColl had left home without any cash.

"When we walked out into the parking lot to drive him back to the bank's plane, I had a flat tire on my car," recalled Spangler, a tall, distinguished man with horn-rimmed glasses and sandy hair that he wears combed straight back over his head. "There was nothing to do but roll up our sleeves and change the tire."

The following Tuesday, when Spangler returned from his ski trip, the two met again to talk further. Finally, without lawyers or investment bankers, McColl scratched out details of the merger on a sheet of his personal stationery, recorded the time as "1824 hours," and dated it. The agreement bearing both signatures later joined other merger trophies on the wall of McColl's small conference room.

Regulators approved the fit. "As it turned out, we had to spin off practically nothing," Storrs said. Later, when he saw the attorney who had warned of problems at earlier merger talks, Storrs learned that he may have misunderstood the attorney's earlier advice. What had been presented was the worst case that could arise from the merger. "Well," Storrs responded, "we just assumed you thought we were going to have a worst case."

The merger required the sale of either NCNB's Goldsboro office or disposal of the much larger and better-established Bank of North Caro-

NCNB's merger with the Bank of North Carolina in 1982 completed the bank's coverage of its home state. With BNC chairman C. D. Spangler, Jr. (second from right), are (left to right) Hugh McColl, William Dougherty, and Thomas Storrs.

lina office located there. Storrs chose to close the NCNB branch, which presented him with a new situation. NCNB had never closed a branch, and Storrs faced some local board members who were upset and angry at their predicament. A half dozen or so had broken other banking relationships to get the Goldsboro office started fewer than ten years earlier. Some wanted to buy the bank, but Storrs wasn't in a position to get into a protracted period of approval. Their interest was set aside. "That was a bad day," Storrs recalled of his visit to make the announcement. "It wasn't much fun."

The Bank of North Carolina merger virtually completed NCNB's North Carolina network. With the seventy Bank of North Carolina branches wearing the familiar red and white NCNB logo, Storrs now had added $666 million to NCNB's assets and put an NCNB branch office within easy reach of most of North Carolina's six million residents.

As Storrs looked to Florida, he held out hope of a merger with one of the top-tier Florida banks. A large bank would allow NCNB to immediately penetrate major Florida banking markets. Such a merger also offered the greatest promise of acquiring better executive talent that would be available to help with further expansion.

Even before the formal closing on the Lake City acquisition, Storrs had talked with the chief executives of every major banking operation in the state. In early January, he pressed NCNB's interest at the offices of chief executives of Barnett Banks in Jacksonville, Southeast Banking Corp. in Miami, Atlantic National Banks, Flagship Banks, Inc., and Landmark Banking Corp. On one day's tour, Storrs's assistant, Mary Covington, arranged for him to meet personally with three different CEOs in cities more than four hundred miles apart.

In Miami, Storrs talked with Charles J. Zwick, chairman of the Southeast Banking Corp., the state's largest bank, with $6.4 billion in assets. Storrs asked about joining forces and reentering the chase for Florida National. After NCNB had withdrawn its bid for Florida National, Southeast had taken its place as an aggressive suitor. If a Southeast merger was out, Storrs also told Zwick, NCNB would be interested in any Florida National banks that Southeast might sell if Southeast was successful in its fight for control of the company. Two hours later, Storrs was in Jacksonville with his old friend and fellow warrior on behalf of interstate banking, Guy Botts, chairman of the Barnett Banks, a $4 billion multibank holding company. The two talked about combining forces. Botts said he would communicate NCNB's interest to his board, but the prospects looked dim.

Management and headquarters location were near the top of the list of Botts's concerns. Both Botts and Storrs were nearing retirement. "Were you and I in our fifties, we'd do it," Botts told his friend. "Since we're not, we have management questions to consider." Botts said he would discuss merger with his board and his apparent successor, Charles Rice, and get back to him. Storrs indicated that he would be talking to other bankers in the meantime but wouldn't do anything conclusive without checking with Botts.

In some cases, NCNB had done more than just talk. When Storrs met for lunch with Phil Searle, chairman of the Flagship Banks, on the day of the Lake City closing, he told Searle that NCNB had acquired 360,000 shares of stock in his company. Storrs also told him that NCNB wasn't interested in a merger with unfriendly overtones. The stock purchase simply meant that NCNB would have less stock to acquire if a merger were arranged, or that NCNB could profit if the bank were sold to someone else.

The top-tier banks were wary, and the delay in signing a merger agreement began to bother NCNB's top executives, who felt pressed to expand out of their embarrassingly small Lake City base. NCNB did have some interest from bankers at the medium-sized banks in the state. Two likely prospects were Gulfstream Banks, Inc., based in Boca Raton, a cash-rich resort and retirement community on the east coast north of Miami, and Exchange Bank & Trust Co., the old, established bank in Tampa, whose chief executive, Gordon Campbell, had first talked merger with Storrs while the two were attending the American Bankers Association meeting in San Francisco several months earlier.

The first to join was Gulfstream. On March 16, while sitting in for McColl at a meeting of a community development group in Charlotte's Third Ward, Joe Martin received a cryptic message from his boss, who was negotiating with Gulfstream owners in Florida. "The martin has found a nest," the note read, paraphrasing the memorable moon-landing announcement, "The *Eagle* has landed." That was Martin's signal to announce the purchase of Gulfstream, a deal originally structured as a stock trade but recast later to a straight cash sale worth $92 million. The change saved NCNB from diluting its stock so early in a period of mergers and acquisitions. With assets of more than $787 million, the Gulfstream bank was not at the top of NCNB's list, but it offered a good place to start. The bank had twenty branches in Broward (Fort Lauderdale) and Palm Beach counties, two of the better banking markets in the state. And it was close to Miami, a major market that NCNB strategists believed critical to exploit the bank's bid for international business.

The Gulfstream merger was not the "big, simple, and quick" acquisition that Storrs wanted. But the major players were moving slowly, and Storrs was not going to wait. He did not want to risk a loss of NCNB's advantage in the market. "Our unique authority had a very short shelf life, and we had to get on with it," corporate strategist Frank Gentry recalled. "We didn't have time to fool around."

Two months later, Storrs took the bank's next big step and established an anchor on Florida's booming Gulf coast. On the afternoon of May 28, Storrs announced that NCNB would buy the Exchange Bancorporation, Inc., for $135 million. The price was a premium, nearly twice the book value of the stock, but Exchange was a fair catch with assets of $1.6 billion and forty-four branches in ten Florida counties, including the fast-growing Clearwater–Saint Petersburg retirement communities.

With the Lake City, Exchange, and Gulfstream purchases, NCNB pushed past $10 billion in total assets, extending its lead as the largest bank holding company in the Southeast. In announcing the deal, a Tampa Bay–area reporter recalled an earlier quote from Storrs, who had recited NCNB's advertising slogan—"We want to be the best bank in the neighborhood"—and then added, "We want the neighborhood to include Florida, and that's only for starters."

By the time the Exchange merger plans were announced, nearly every Florida banker had had an opportunity to meet Tom Storrs and NCNB. Just three weeks earlier, Storrs had been a featured speaker at the eighty-eighth annual meeting of the Florida Bankers Association, at the Fountainbleau Hotel on Miami Beach. He hadn't exactly been given top billing. His session on interstate banking was scheduled for a Friday afternoon, and the perfect weather promoted golf, tennis, or swimming rather than a business meeting. When Storrs arrived, however, the meeting room was packed.

In the audience were a few bankers who believed that their banks might make good merger partners with NCNB and thus were eager to make friends. Most Florida bankers resented NCNB's preferred position in their state. The Florida Bankers Association's endorsement earlier in the year of a modified interstate banking proposal had followed total rejection by a majority of the association's members just a few months earlier. Storrs knew he wouldn't be meeting an entirely receptive audience, and he attempted to ease the tension when he quipped during his introduction that NCNB valued its FBA membership, "especially considering how hard it was for us to join."

He countered the image of NCNB as a raider from the north with his own cartoon depicting NCNB as Santa Claus benignly flying south with a bagful of benefits for Florida. Later, referring to the Santa Claus cartoon, banker Bill Price from the small town of Immokalee was skeptical of Storrs's characterization. "I'm a great believer in fairy tales," Price said, "and I think I've just been listening to 'Little Red Riding Hood.' "

When Storrs finished his speech, his first question came from Richard Ehlis, chairman of Florida National, whose future now was tied to a sale to Chemical Bank of New York. Chemical's option to buy Florida National would be exercised when legislation allowing out-of-state banks into Florida was passed. Why, Ehlis asked, should interstate banking be restricted within regions, as Storrs argued, and not opened to banks nationwide? Storrs responded that economic dominance by a handful of money-center banks from New York, Chicago, or San Francisco was not a good idea. Regional banking would prevent concentration of power outside the area and would provide an opportunity for regional banks to compete more effectively with money-center banks.

Storrs's argument was not convincing for some owners and presidents of small banks. Hjalma Johnson, president of the $121 million Bank of Pasco County, responded by saying, "Dr. Tom, it seems like you have an idea what the right size of a bank is and how many there should be. A lot of community bankers think they know what the right size is. It seems to me that what size is right all depends on where you are in the food chain."

By the time of the association's meeting, two things were clear: NCNB was not going away, and there was little that Florida bankers could do about it. Some legislators had made a vain attempt to head NCNB off in Tallahassee, but lobbying by the Roberts firm and Storrs's visits to newspaper editorial boards stalled those efforts. At the end of the year, NCNB had a Miami address, after the $6 million purchase of the Downtown National Bank, with $9 million in assets. Though a small bank, virtually invisible in the busy Miami market, it offered a base on which to build. NCNB's $200 million in purchases in Florida and North Carolina set a new record for bank acquisitions in one year.

On January 4, 1983, Hugh McColl passed a symbolic check for $60 million to Tampa mayor George Pennington in ceremonies in the lobby of the Exchange Bank & Trust Co. in downtown Tampa. Several hundred business people and community leaders joined Exchange and NCNB to mark the start of business for NCNB's newest subsidiary. The check represented the amount that a single customer now could borrow from NCNB. It also represented $10 million more than any bank in Florida could offer in a single deal. "Our corporate customers will no longer have to leave the local market for financing," a proud McColl told those gathered around the lobby.

In just four days short of a year, NCNB had grown from an interloper with a toehold in the small farm community of Lake City to a banking group with more than $2 billion in assets, offices along both Florida coasts, and a major presence in the state's largest industrial city. Storrs still did not have the major bank that he had set as his prize eighteen months earlier, but he had made good on his pledge to position NCNB as a contender in the Florida market.

A month later, in an interview with the *Florida Times-Union* in Jacksonville, Storrs sounded pleased with the results, but he suggested it was time for a breather. "We won't be making any major acquisitions over the next few years," he said. "We'd like to rebuild our equity. We're at the stage where we'd like to settle down a little and make some money." Then he chuckled and said, "We'll probably start to look around again after that."

Storrs spelled out NCNB's strategy. It was the same that had been successful in North Carolina from the early days of Addison Reese. With its added financial horsepower, NCNB would court large accounts, but it also would be calling on the smaller businesses, just like the ones that onetime corporate account executive Hugh McColl had chased in his early years. "There are two thousand middle-market companies in Dade, Broward, and Palm Beach counties alone," Storrs said. "That's more than in the entire state of North Carolina. These companies expect to use their bankers as experts in financial planning, for cash management, for all-around banking services. We can fill that niche."

The man Storrs assigned to run the Florida operations was Donald D. Buchanan, an experienced banker in his mid-forties who was a relative newcomer to NCNB's top management. Dougherty had recruited Buchanan in 1975 from a Denver bank to oversee NCNB's operations and trust groups. Among the NCNB brass, Buchanan had spent more time in Florida than most because his duties had included supervision of the Trust Company of Florida.

Buchanan's assignment loomed large. Storrs was under pressure to make the Florida purchases profitable, to "build equity," as he said, and he looked to Buchanan to accomplish that. At the same time, Buchanan was faced with integrating the Florida banks into NCNB's operations. It would prove to be a learning experience that the bank would look back on later when it turned its attention to Texas. In Florida, the testing ground, there would be some casualties.

Buchanan was faced with a banking environment that was conservative, fragmented, and colored by de facto territorial limits that had been encouraged through the years by established banking operations. As late as the 1950s, a time when North Carolina banks like NCNB and First Union were launching their expansion, Florida bank regulators took months to approve charters for new operations and warned that too many banks would create another catastrophe such as the state had seen in the 1920s, when the Florida economy collapsed under the weight of speculation in real estate. During the next twenty years, Florida law discouraged mergers and growth of large banking institutions. Branching was new, and management was unaccustomed to the centralized operation that had been in place at NCNB for more than a decade.

Florida law not only inhibited new banks, it also discouraged branching. As a result, most Florida banks had relatively low lending limits. If a developer, builder, or businessman needed large amounts of cash, he did business at loan production offices operated by large banking concerns outside the state. Few Florida banks handled foreign business. By 1981, the state had the highest concentration of Edge Act banks (special-purpose banks for overseas business) outside of New York City. Thirty-two out-of-state banks had such offices in the state.

To further complicate a nice fit, the retail end of Florida banking operated at a slower pace than NCNB was accustomed to. In Florida, Buchanan found that, to be successful, a banker needed connections at the country club or the yacht club. When he moved to Tampa, Buchanan was told by Florida contacts that the most important thing for him to do was become a member of the Gasparilla crew, a select club of businessmen who each year dressed as pirates and invaded the city of Tampa. Banking was as much an avocation as a career.

"That was the lure of going to Florida, if you were a banker," Buchanan recalled. "All you needed was to have a charter, open your door, and people brought you money. The loan-to-deposit ratio among the principal banks in Florida was like 50 or 55 percent. The banks down here were deal banks. There was much more sensitivity about the network, the social network. We had loan officers, business-development officers who carried out the culture and said they had to spend time at the club. You didn't let anything interfere with a good, sunny weekend on the beach."

This relaxed approach to banking was just the opposite of the NCNB culture, which—after more than a dozen years of work—had perfected Dougherty's management reporting systems. If anything, the quantitative approach had intensified at NCNB during the 1970s, when the results determined whether the bank would survive that difficult period intact. By the time NCNB reached Florida, the competitive spirit of its corporate culture was visible in the daily management reports. Corporate perquisites such as golf each Wednesday and country club memberships were out of the question. NCNB had never held out for such frills. Only a few top executives even got company cars, and users were expected to keep them for years. When an executive's car was turned in, it was often placed at airports frequented by NCNB executives, who were expected to drive it, dents and all, rather than pay a rental agency for something new.

A clash of corporate styles was inevitable and quick in coming. Two weeks after the smiles and applause that greeted Storrs at the formal opening of NCNB's operations at Exchange, *Tampa Tribune* business editor Harry Costello asked in his weekly column, "Has the bloodletting begun among the ranks of senior managers at Exchange Bank in Tampa, newest acquisition of North Carolina's NCNB Corp.?" The article recounted the dismissal of two top executives who had handled much of Exchange's community and political affairs in Tampa. Both were hired by Exchange's principal competitor, First Florida Banks, Inc. The same article named four other Exchange officers who had left recently.

Over the next few months, Buchanan watched as half the Exchange officers left for other banks or other jobs and Gulfstream went through an almost complete turnover in its officer ranks. NCNB had anticipated about 30 percent turnover, the average annual change in banking; it experienced 70 percent. "The banking industry was a game of musical chairs," Buchanan said, describing the situation years later.

Some left because their jobs were judged unnecessary and eliminated by NCNB. Others chafed at finding themselves in jobs where decisions once left to a local office were now shifted to Charlotte. One former Exchange officer, who left to join Florida National Banks, was quoted as saying, "Decisions you made on your own, like hiring a secretary, now had to be cleared by headquarters. I'd already been in the Army."

Operations problems were equally vexing. Exchange Banks, for example, had nine separate general ledger systems that had to be merged into one. Exchange Banks was in the midst of a change in its computer operations when the merger took place, but Buchanan found that the system was not adequate to handle even the needs of Exchange, much less the expanding NCNB business in Florida. In time, an entirely new operations center, designed and brought on-line in record time by NCNB executives Darwin Smith and Bedford Boyce, was opened to handle all the Florida banking business.

Compounding Buchanan's difficulties was the well-intentioned but misplaced assistance of numerous NCNB officials in Charlotte, who were eager to "help" get the Florida operations going. NCNB people from Charlotte-based departments poured into Florida during the transition. Rather than promote goodwill and speed the changeover, their presence sometimes further aggravated tensions within the Florida banking offices.

"So here was the scenario," Buchanan recalled. "Here's the troops, McColl and Buchanan, with one instruction: Don't make anyone angry or mad. Don't get them upset, but we've got to have 30 percent improvement. It began to set up the inevitable. Create the change to produce the result, but don't let any change really happen."

NCNB's newspaper and publication clip files began to bulge with news stories about its problems. In fact, the bank appeared to be getting more coverage in Florida than in its home state of North Carolina. Competitors made sure that reporters knew about the flight of NCNB's loan officers to other banks, its confusion over a name, and the general rough water through which the bank was passing. Because banking beyond checking accounts and routine savings is primarily a personal, one-to-one relationship, the internal troubles were costing money, as loan officers and others with strong ties to the community left the bank.

Buchanan was constantly fighting management brushfires. One day he drove to a branch office of a newly acquired bank after he received more than a dozen telephone calls from customers who were concerned about a recently announced merger. The office was near the Gulf shore, in an area that had become a retirement mecca for people from the Midwest. He parked and entered the bank unannounced just so he could look around and figure out why he had been bombarded with complaints. While standing near the teller line, he overheard a teller giving a customer his telephone number. "You know this NCNB has come in here, and you probably ain't going to like some of this stuff," Buchanan heard the teller say. "And you know it might be helpful if you'd call the president."

While Buchanan was trying to make the pieces fit, others were trying to look at a new name for NCNB that would accommodate Florida customers as well as those in the bank's primary market in North Carolina. The multistate operation wasn't the only reason to consider a change. NCNB corporate account officers, especially national and international account executives, had for some time been encountering customers' confusion over their bank's name. The problem was particularly acute abroad. "NCNB" does not translate in many languages, and "North Carolina National Bank" often didn't translate into initials that were the same as "NCNB."

After looking at thousands of possible names, picking through those that might apply in markets nationwide, NCNB executives finally settled on the word "Nova" as a name that would retain the N from "NCNB" and at the same time be short and catchy. Because it is a word that is both Teutonic and Latin in origin, "Nova" was also one of the few words that means the same in the major languages of the world, from Sanskrit to English.

It did have some problems. The dictionary definition of "nova" is not only "new" but "a dazzling burst of a star in the heavens that consumes itself and dies out very quickly." Joe Martin was aware that critics could seize on that to characterize NCNB's flashy, aggressive style. Martin also was told that General Motors had encountered problems with its Chevrolet Nova models in Spain, where the name was misinterpreted to mean "*no va*," or "it doesn't go." If these reports were true, "Nova" would not be appropriate in the Florida market, with its large Hispanic population.

Martin found, however, that General Motors had sold more of its Nova models in Spain than any other GM car. Research in South Florida revealed that residents there didn't divide the word. "They thought it was a good name for a bank," Martin recalled. "The name they thought was funny was 'Wachovia.' Some thought it was a collection agency pronounced 'watch ovuh ya.' Some thought it was some sort of Polish word. Honest."

The NCNB board liked the new name and formally approved Martin's recommendation changing "NCNB" to "NovaCorp," whose banks would be known as "NovaBank" around the world. Before new stationery was printed, however, NCNB learned that a California bank had created a new product they intended to call "Nova." They had invested heavily in the launch, and a fight over the name was guaranteed.

"It turned out they had such an investment in it that we knew they would outspend us to beat us in the courts," Martin recalled. "At best, there would be such a delay involved that we would not get the name changed before we had to consolidate Florida, and we didn't want to go through the double problem and expense of putting up NCNB signs and then having to take them down to put up Nova signs.

"So 'NovaBank' was blown away. I had to go back to the board of directors and say, 'That wonderful decision you made last month, we need to unmake.' Instead, we decided to drop the words from North Carolina National Bank and make it NCNB National Bank, as it had been NCNB Corporation."

Market research showed that NCNB was not generally recognized as a North Carolina corporation, any more than the NCR company was. "Besides," said Martin, "the public image of Florida banks was so bad that an out-of-state identity could actually be a benefit."

Midway through 1983, the Florida banks were all united under one corporate banner, NCNB National Bank of Florida. The consolidation not only brought them all together on the balance sheet but also produced a common identity. In March 1983, the orange and yellow X that had shown brightly across Tampa Bay from the top of the Exchange Bank building in heart of Tampa was replaced with the red NCNB logo. Elsewhere around the state, at the Gulfstream offices in Boca Raton, at Downtown Bank in Miami, and at Exchange offices on Florida's west coast, the red-and-white logo familiar in North Carolina went up on buildings, to be followed by an advertising fanfare that introduced NCNB to customers.

About the same time, the Florida legislature closed another chapter in the continuing battle over interstate banking. In late May, the state house and senate both voted down bills that would have admitted New York banks into the Florida deposit banking market. Citicorp and Chemical Bank were the leading proponents of the bills and spent more than $25,000 in campaign contributions to Florida legislators. Barnett Banks made contributions of three times that amount. That didn't settle the issue, but it gave NCNB at least another year before other out-of-state banks would be allowed into the marketplace.

About two weeks before the Florida legislation was defeated, the Florida Bankers Association suffered an irony that none could have expected. At its annual meeting, Gordon Campbell, former chief executive of Exchange Bank who had stayed on after his bank's merger with

NCNB, was inducted as the association's president. With coincidental good timing, NCNB had a spokesman at the top of the very group that had fought to keep it out of the state. (The irony was not lost on the association. At a private dinner following his induction, one of the association directors presented Campbell with a carpetbag.)

Campbell's position with the association gave NCNB an opportunity to promote its answer to the turmoil over interstate banking. It was clear that state barriers would fall; the questions were when and what would replace them. Storrs's regional approach appeared to be gaining favor, particularly with Florida governor Bob Graham, who had previously supported opening Florida to banks from anywhere in the nation. During his term as chairman of the Southern Growth Policies Board, Graham picked up the arguments of Storrs's economic task force and began promoting a "Southern Common Market."

Shortly after he became Florida Bankers Association president, Campbell joined forces with a Miami attorney, John Edward Smith, whose firm was counsel to Southeast Banking Corporation and who had the ear of Governor Graham. Together they lined up support from Graham, who agreed to contact chief executives in the other Southern states, and from other bankers. NCNB government relations specialist Mark Leggett cultivated the interests of state banking association executives, who agreed that the only way to prevent internal warfare was to promote consensus. Leggett and Paul Polking began building an agenda. Their efforts culminated in a two-day symposium in late August at the Marriott Hotel in Atlanta.

For two days, speakers presented the case for regional interstate banking agreements. It was a simple concept that required each state to pass legislation to permit banks from states that allowed out-of-state ownership to do business in their states. The advocates' chief witness was Roderick M. MacDougal, chairman of the Bank of New England Corp. of Boston, who told about the efforts of New England banks to fend off expansion by large financial houses in New York City.

After the speakers had presented the case for a reciprocal regional agreement, those attending the session broke into small groups and discussed the attitudes toward regional banking and their vision of the future of banking in their states. Robert M. Freeman, the president and chief operating officer of Signet Banking Corporation in Virginia, told

William Hoffer for an article in *Southern* magazine: "The concept of interstate banking was all kind of new to me. I didn't know what to expect. The way it was set up, I could tell it was carefully orchestrated. I can remember the Texas bankers saying, 'Over my dead body.' Bankers from Alabama and Mississippi were also adamant. Business was going well at the time. It was a typical parochial attitude."

Buddy Kemp, who led the NCNB delegation to the meeting, recalled that NCNB and other bankers were nervous about the attitude of the Texas bankers. In fact, the regional compact they envisioned would not include Texas because it was believed that the size of Texas banks might overwhelm other banks in the South if the Texas managements decided to cross the Mississippi.

The shift of interest to regional interstate banking, away from a nationwide system, was a point in NCNB's favor. At least New York banks, with three and four times the buying power of NCNB and other regional superbanks, would be precluded from competing in mergers in Florida and other states. But the shift also sent a message to NCNB that its favored position would be gone soon. With a consensus developing to a regional solution, appropriate legislation would not be far behind.

NCNB was about to improve its position in the Florida west coast market, which was bulging with development. Small, quiet coastal communities had turned into meccas for retirees from the Midwest. Retirement villages, from elaborate complexes with multiple golf courses and marinas to smaller mobile home communities, were consuming every available square foot of empty acreage. Serving much of this area was the Ellis Banking Corp., a $1.8 billion banking firm with seventy offices, managed and controlled by A. L. Ellis, who was nearly eighty years old and a protégé of Ed Ball's.

On a late spring morning, Mary Toth, Ellis's secretary for more than thirty years, showed Storrs and McColl into the boardroom adjacent to Ellis's office in his bank building in Tarpon Springs, a picturesque sponge-fishing village just north of Clearwater. His office was on a mezzanine that overlooked the main lobby, which was designed in a Spanish style, complete with a gurgling fountain near the rear entrance. A large oil painting of Florida's banker baron, Ed Ball, hung across the foyer from Ellis's office door. Like Ball, Ellis prided himself on his reputation as an ultraconservative country banker. During one thirty-year span of business, he claimed to have lost less than $9,000 to bad loans. "You can't just loan money to ANYbody—or you'll wind up in the hole," he once told an interviewer for the *Tampa Tribune*.

Ellis was interested in merger. He wanted to retire and had no family to carry on the business. NCNB's overtures interested him more than those he might receive from Florida banks. "I saw no point in merging with another Florida bank," Ellis said later. "I could put a bank anywhere they had one."

Storrs and McColl also liked the Ellis connections to the Ball-DuPont interests in the state. Ellis even had a bank in Jacksonville. As part of Ball's divestiture of the Florida National Bank's operations, Ball had sold Jacksonville National Bank to Ellis, and the Ellis banks were named the corporate trustee of the tremendous wealth of the DuPont Estate Trust.

Ellis liked his North Carolina visitors, but he didn't swoon. "I told them I wouldn't give up what I already had. I wanted to stay in the banking business, but I did not want day-to-day line responsibilities. I wanted a voice in management, and everything I asked for they gave me. In fact, the entire trade was made on my offers."

Ellis became the largest single shareholder in NCNB after the four million shares were exchanged for his banking business, and he became senior chairman of NCNB National Bank of Florida.

The Ellis Banking negotiations were Storrs's final assignment. With that acquisition complete, NCNB controlled assets of $11.6 billion, almost three times the amount that Storrs had been entrusted with ten years earlier when he succeeded Reese.

By now, McColl had emerged as Storrs's obvious choice for a successor. In April 1981, the board of directors had named McColl to a new position of vice chairman and chief operating officer. The move caught some analysts off guard because they still considered Dougherty, who was five years older than McColl, to be the leading candidate. "I understood him to be promised the job," one analyst told the *Greensboro* (N.C.) *News & Record*. That was not the case. Dougherty left NCNB about a year later to take a top position with Southeast Bank in Miami.

On August 31, 1983, the eve of his retirement, Storrs was on the NCNB plane with McColl as the two returned to Charlotte from Florida. It was late, and they had just finished another round of talks with a possible merger candidate. Storrs, the reserved and distinguished Ph.D., and McColl, the impetuous ex-Marine, had become an unlikely pair with their competing personalities. The two had been working mergers together for so long, however, that each anticipated the other's moves.

McColl had assumed more and more responsibility during Storrs's countdown to retirement, but Storrs remained firmly in command to the last. "You know, in the Navy," McColl said later, "if you are the captain of the ship, you are captain of a ship right up until the minute the next captain comes on board to relieve you. Then that's it. You are out of there.

"He was literally the CEO until the day he retired. He never handed me the reins. Never. In fact, on the night we were coming home, he gave the pilot an order about scheduling and then said, as an aside, 'Of course, someone can change that Monday.' And I said, 'I will.' "

Chapter 13 **The Tactics of Sun Tzu**

In late 1982 a writer for *Southern Banker* magazine described NCNB as "a mean, lean greyhound tearing up the track and threatening to end the deregulated race to size dominance in the Southeast before it even gets started." Indeed, the bank that Chairman Tom Storrs was about to turn over to Hugh McColl in the summer of 1983 was well positioned to build upon its success in Florida and challenge new territory under a new commander.

Storrs had set NCNB on its course with a strategy that ran counter to that professed in most banking houses. Banking was an industry of change that required fast reflexes and risk, he said. "If we lived in a static world," Storrs told the magazine, "and we knew that tomorrow would be just like today, then we ought to try to maximize today's earnings because that would maximize tomorrow's and the next day's and so on.

But we don't live in a static world, and this means that bank managements concerned only with maximizing today's earnings are doing it at
the expense of stockholders' earnings in future years.

"We have tried to take account of the world's changes, change with it
and find in the changes opportunities for the long-term advantage of our
stockholders, instead of trying to milk the situation for top returns
today."

The cool logic behind Storrs's philosophy was played out behind the
scenes in NCNB's raising of capital and its negotiations for future acquisitions. The foundation was laid in the planning period of the late
1970s and early 1980s, and the execution following the opening in Florida had gone smoothly. "We had prepared for expansion without knowing exactly what direction we should take, but that prepared us to seize
the Florida opportunity when it appeared on the horizon," Storrs said.

When McColl took over in September 1983, he was not moving into
a new job as much as he was expanding the one that he already had.
McColl may have chafed at the restraints that came with being number
two in the organization, but he had been the chief operating officer for
more than two years. He just kept operating.

The most immediate challenge was consolidating acquisitions in Florida. The Ellis merger was not complete and wouldn't have the final
agreement for several months after Storrs turned over command. In fact,
McColl recalled Storrs to duty when problems arose in the closing hours
of the Ellis merger. McColl had to pull the former chairman off his sail-
boat on the South Carolina coast and fly him to Tarpon Springs to work
out the last details with Ellis.

Storrs had succeeded in bringing interstate banking to the Southeast.
By the time he left office, it was clear that legislation providing for regional interstate banking would be introduced in most of the eleven
states of the old Confederacy. The Atlanta meeting had shaped a consensus that produced bills ready for introduction when state legislatures
convened in early 1984. Georgia, Florida, North Carolina, and South
Carolina acted immediately on legislation that established a one-year
waiting period. As the clock ran on the moratorium, other large banks,
particularly First Union and Wachovia in North Carolina and Citizens
& Southern in Georgia, began to pick their targets, waiting for the
proper time to move.

While the competitors began preparing for cross-state expansion,

NCNB was consolidating its gains in Florida. The Ellis banks were merged into the system, this time with a bit more sensitivity than had been shown when Exchange and Gulfstream were brought into the NCNB corporate culture. By the end of 1985, McColl had engineered another merger to bolster NCNB's position in south Florida. In December, a merger with Pan American Banks, Inc., with $1.6 billion in assets and fifty branches in six counties, was completed. As its competitors from across the South were just getting started, NCNB already had a Florida bank with $7 billion in assets and 205 branches in the state's prime markets.

In less than three years, NCNB had created a bank in Florida that was as large as the North Carolina business had been when NCNB acquired that first small bank in Lake City. The company had followed the advice in a book given to McColl by his friend C. D. Spangler. Sun Tzu, in his ancient treatise on Chinese military tactics, *The Art of War*, had written: "The value of time, that is, being ahead of your opponent, can be counted for more than either numerical superiority or the nicest calculations." Actually, NCNB had improved on Sun Tzu. It had not only time but the resources and calculations to move toward its goal.

As if to punctuate NCNB's dominance in the Florida market, McColl announced in early 1985 that NCNB would build a thirty-story headquarters building on the banks of the Hillsborough River overlooking Tampa Bay. The $100 million structure, to be designed by Charlotte architect Harry Wolf, would be constructed on the site of a city parking garage, which would be demolished and then rebuilt underground. McColl personally recruited Wolf, who had designed unusual and award-winning buildings for NCNB in Charlotte. In picking Wolf, McColl was fulfilling a commitment he had made more than ten years earlier, after the Charlotte headquarters was awarded to Odell Associates rather than Wolf's firm. The two walked the streets of Tampa together looking for just the right place for NCNB. They chose the riverfront because of its prominence and because it would recapture the access to the river that had been lost to the nondescript parking structure. Convincing the city officials of Tampa to make room for one of its first new major buildings in years was simple. The tall tower, round like a lighthouse, would become Tampa's new beacon on the bay, with the searchlights on the roof piercing upward into the nighttime sky.

McColl and NCNB appeared to be unbeatable, and McColl clearly enjoyed NCNB's dominant position. No bland chief executive, he made good copy. McColl told reporters in Florida that he was good for the banking business. "Everywhere my airplane lands, bank stocks go up." He had targeted Georgia as a natural state for expansion in a news conference in Miami, but he said he wasn't "going down every pig path" to achieve the mission. Colorful, boastful, McColl livened up the otherwise dour scenery of the bankers' clubs around the Southeast.

McColl's comments on banking kept media coverage of NCNB interesting. At the same time he was chasing new acquisitions elsewhere in the Southeast, he became the center of the controversy as he defended NCNB's policy of investment in business in South Africa. In an interview with the *Charlotte Observer* in early 1985, he was quoted as saying, "I love it. I think it's one of the most wonderful countries in the world." The quotation omitted reference to the context of the remark, which was about the country's natural beauty.

In 1983 and 1984, NCNB shareholders had rejected a policy restricting South African loans, after the bank's exposure had reached a peak of $249 million in 1982. The issue continued to build until 1985, when Citicorp and other major banking powers decided to eliminate all loans to the South African government.

McColl, who had visited South Africa four times, argued that American interests would actually force the South African government to abandon apartheid faster than pulling all United States investment out of the country. "I think it will be just like America," he was quoted as saying in the newspaper article. "As you raise the standard of living for more people and improve their education . . . they educate their children better. And I think you get a new class of people emerging, a middle-class black."

The newspaper article also highlighted other McColl quotes in bold letters: "My position is that investment in South Africa is good for black people, little black people, big black people, children, mothers, fathers, everybody. Even revolutionaries." And "I've lived in a segregated society, and that doesn't kill people." McColl said this remark also was taken out of context. He was actually criticizing conditions such as poverty and oppression that have brought about deaths in South Africa. The resultant publicity infuriated McColl, who considered it an attack on his and NCNB's morality.

McColl and others at NCNB believed the company had to make

no apology for the degree of its commitment to social responsibility. NCNB's Community Development Corporation had exported its Fourth Ward concept to other communities. The effort to rehabilitate neighborhoods that other lenders had ignored was recognized as innovative and bold by black leaders around the country. This record at home helped to mitigate local criticism. Community groups from minority neighborhoods in Charlotte, which had worked with NCNB in developing the inner-city areas, never vigorously joined those objecting to the bank's investment policy, although the Reverend Jesse Jackson led a marching crowd of protesters directly into the bank's main lobby in Greensboro, where he picked up a telephone and demanded an audience. Ironically, throughout the entire affair Jackson and NCNB's Dennis Rash, who organized the bank's community investment efforts, attended meetings of the board of trustees at North Carolina A&T State University in Greensboro, Jackson's alma mater, without exchanging a word about NCNB's South Africa investments. The bank's reputation for relations with community groups was an asset later in Florida, when many bank mergers were being stalled by challenges from minority groups concerned about commitment to low- and moderate-income borrowers.

In June 1985, the last possible barrier to interstate activity by NCNB's competitors fell as the U.S. Supreme Court upheld the state legislative regional banking compacts. Throughout the waiting period, NCNB and others had been working on mergers. A really large acquisition had eluded McColl's predecessor, Tom Storrs. McColl hoped that he would land a major merger that would catapult NCNB past its competitors. At the same time, however, other North Carolina bankers were back and forth between Georgia and Florida, two prime states. The court's decision opened the floodgates.

On the morning of June 18, a Tuesday, McColl picked up his copy of the *Charlotte Observer* and read news that ruined his fiftieth birthday plans. Two large banks that McColl had courted heavily had gone to competitors. The day before, First Union had announced it would acquire Atlantic Banks in Jacksonville and increase its assets to $14.4 billion. On the same day, Wachovia CEO John Medlin announced that a new company, First Wachovia Corp., would be created by the merger of Wachovia Corporation and First Atlanta Corp. in Georgia, a $7 billion bank with 104 branches throughout the state. The new company would have $15.5 billion in assets, which would edge NCNB into the number three position among Southeastern banks.

McColl was stunned. To lose First Atlanta cut to the quick. To lose to Wachovia made the defeat all the more bitter. "The biggest tactical error I ever made and, perhaps you could argue, strategic error, was when I had reached agreement with Atlantic Banks on what I thought were social issues like the name and location of the headquarters," McColl said later. "They then wanted fifteen times earnings, and my chief financial officer thought that was way too much. We went to New York, met with their investment bankers thinking we could talk them down, and they essentially broke off with us. We diverted and tried to take over First Atlanta and failed at that. And while we failed at that, First Union bought Atlantic. I consider that to be my biggest tactical error since I've been chairman."

McColl went after First Atlanta because "Atlanta is an important Southern city and we're not well represented there," he recalled. "From a market standpoint, it would make us so powerful in the Southeast that a company with any substance would find it difficult not to do business with us. We would increase the number of individual consumers we do business with by a staggering margin, so it has huge value to us."

For McColl, the merger made imminently good sense. The two banks shared similar philosophies and traditions. First Atlanta was known for its hard-charging commercial lending programs. It was a leading lender to Fortune 500 companies and was the seventh-largest issuer of VISA cards. Like NCNB in its home state, the bank was the first Georgia bank to introduce BankAmericard and had developed a large credit card operation because of its early entry into the business.

McColl approached First Atlanta as a takeover target after the bank's largest single shareholder, Mack Robinson, indicated through an investment banking house that he liked the idea of a merger. McColl met with Robinson and First Atlanta's investment banker at the Sea Island resort in Georgia, then later with First Atlanta's chief executive officer, Thomas Williams, at National Airport in Washington. "Vintage McColl," McColl said, recalling the meeting. "I probably told him I was going to buy his bank. I didn't tell him I wanted to; I told him I was going to."

First Atlanta's leaders were not flattered by McColl's invitation to dance. "What they were afraid of was that we would rationalize the company and take out a lot of people that weren't necessary and make even more money, which was a probability—not only a possibility—but a probability," McColl recalled. Personalities of the two corporate leaders clashed.

"Here was Hugh L. McColl Jr.," the *Wall Street Journal* said in a story about egos and mergers, "the ex-Marine chairman of NCNB Corp., trying to take over First Atlanta Corp. the way troops took Iwo Jima. There sat Thomas R. Williams, the genteel First Atlanta chairman, listening impassively. Using military jargon and Anglo-Saxon expletives, Mr. McColl of North Carolina pressed for surrender to his buyout offer until Mr. Williams of Georgia finally interjected, 'Hugh, you're not being very friendly.' Through clenched teeth, according to a witness, Mr. McColl replied, 'I *am* being friendly, damn it.'"

NCNB was offering $855 million, or $33.50 per share, but it wasn't enough to overcome Williams's tension and fears of the aftermath of a merger. He needed help, and he turned to his old friend John Medlin, Wachovia's chief executive. The deal was signed. Discreet and diplomatic, Medlin never referred directly to NCNB's role in driving First Atlanta into Wachovia's friendly harbor, but he told reporters at the announcement that First Atlanta would be a comfortable fit because "they have a culture and a philosophy that we found over time to be very similar to ours at Wachovia."

McColl's recollection of Williams's strategy was more pointed: "If he couldn't get anything else, with his last gasp at least he would get to deliver the company to whomever he wanted. He never wanted to sell it and since he didn't want to, he took his football and went home."

McColl said he could identify with Williams's reluctance, but that Williams refused to face facts. "We expected him to resist, but we didn't expect him to get away," McColl said with regret. "No one wants their company taken over. It's more fun running your own company. But the facts are that his bank did get bought. That's why people were so afraid of us. We could put anybody in play. Now the truth is we weren't into that, but the fear factor was there."

Whatever the reason, once again, for all their efforts, neither Storrs nor McColl had been able to snag the really large banks. In Florida, all the top-tier banks had turned down Storrs's offers to merge. Storrs had subsequently moved to smaller banks with which to build NCNB National Bank of Florida. Multiple mergers were more complicated, but the strategy had worked. NCNB had more than doubled in size by early 1985, but the quantum leaps that come with a big merger had escaped McColl, as they had Storrs.

The loss of First Atlanta was a blow, but McColl and NCNB were back in the news about two weeks later with a boost to their lead in regional expansion. On July 3, 1985, McColl signed an agreement for NCNB to acquire Bankers Trust of South Carolina, which gave NCNB the distinction of being the first regional banking company to establish connections in three states in the Southeast. By the end of the month, a merger was announced with a small bank in the Atlanta suburbs, the Southern National Bank, with $93 million in assets. The Atlanta deal was worked out within two weeks after SNB president Jerry Thompson contacted NCNB, offering his bank for sale. The two mergers would make NCNB the first Southeastern bank holding company to top $20 billion in assets.

If there was any satisfaction at NCNB, it was that Wachovia's prospective lead in assets had never materialized. The mergers and consolidation of business in Florida and North Carolina were a shot in the arm for NCNB's balance sheet. From 1982 through 1986, NCNB's assets grew at a compound rate of 25.5 percent, net income rose at 22.4 percent, and earnings per share increased at 13.2 percent.

Wachovia's expansion in the 1980s began and ended with First Atlanta. "Wachovia was the beneficiary of our aggressiveness," McColl said. "They've never actually negotiated an interstate merger. They just got one delivered to them." Wachovia did not make another out-of-state acquisition until seven years later, when it merged with South Carolina National Bank.

Meanwhile, the merger of First Union with the Jacksonville-based Atlantic Bancorporation, with $3.8 billion in assets, and a subsequent deal with the Central Florida Bank Corp., with $181 million in assets, gave the bank a strong position in Florida. By September, First Union, now headed by Edward E. Crutchfield, Jr., who as a young college graduate had been courted by NCNB, also had purchased the Northwestern Financial Corp., a $2.8 billion North Carolina banking group—the same bank that Addison Reese had spoken of in his last meeting with McColl. These purchases pushed First Union beyond Wachovia in total assets. "I like to come from behind," Crutchfield told the *Miami Herald*. "I wanted to spend my career overcoming and passing these other banks. But now, I actually worry about being larger than Wachovia."

In Georgia, Citizens & Southern Georgia Corp. (C&S Banks) bought the $4 billion Landmark Banking Corp. in Florida, which had spurned NCNB's earlier invitation. The acquisition included the Southwest Florida Banks, Inc., which had merged with Landmark in 1983. Like NCNB, the Georgia bank worried about its name and faced its own problems of integrating the slower pace of Florida banking into its operation.

When McColl tallied the results of his brief tenure as chief executive of NCNB, the numbers at the end of 1985 looked good. The corporation's return on equity had regained the levels prevalent just before Storrs's invasion of Florida and the bank's expansion outside its traditional borders. Earnings per share had climbed to their highest level in five years. In May, NCNB had sold TranSouth Financial Corp., the consumer finance company, for a handsome profit.

McColl also had begun to build a management team that reflected his own style of energy and determination. Buddy Kemp was elected president of NCNB Corp., and James W. Thompson moved up to vice chairman. Kemp had spent most of his career in the wholesale banking business, including time in the trenches with McColl during the workouts of the mid-1970s. Thompson was from the funding side of the bank; he too had won his stripes during the crises of the 1970s. Kenneth D. Lewis, an NCNB senior executive who had been developing service to middle market companies in the Southeast, moved to Florida to replace Buchanan, who had left the bank. W. W. "Hootie" Johnson, formerly the chairman of Bankers Trust of South Carolina, became chairman of the corporation's executive committee.

The Bankers Trust merger was the boost that pushed NCNB well past its competitors for recognition as the largest banking group in the Southeast. The largest merger during the flurry of activity in the previous four years, Bankers Trust added $4 billion in assets.

"When looking south from its Charlotte headquarters," said NCNB's 1985 annual report, "NCNB has never seen a state line, only opportunity. The merger with Bankers Trust at last gives NCNB full-service banking capabilities in a market that it has served for years with corporate lending officers—South Carolina."

It was familiar territory for McColl, a South Carolina native. He had traveled the state in his early days with NCNB, drumming up business for American Commercial's correspondent banking portfolio and corporate lending. From time to time, he had even butted heads with Johnson's bank in competition for clients. The two later became close friends, and the relationship between Bankers Trust and NCNB was strong at the time of the merger. By adding Bankers Trust, McColl's NCNB now had a 355-branch Carolinas network.

McColl turned the job of integrating the Bankers Trust operation over to Kemp, who also assumed responsibility for the Florida operations. Kemp was well aware of the problems NCNB had encountered in Florida, where, he believed, the bank had moved too quickly to achieve its goals. "We did not understand how unable they were to do what we needed them to do. We were trying to do overnight what it took me two or three years to do in North Carolina." Kemp moved deliberately but carefully. Personnel considerations were given high priority under the direction of Harris A. "Rusty" Rainey, NCNB's merger coordinator, and the attention paid off. Unlike Florida, where turnover in top-level executives stymied NCNB's plans, Bankers Trust was brought into the family with little turmoil, and NCNB retrained 95 percent of the former Bankers Trust officers.

By the end of 1987, forty states and the District of Columbia provided for cross-border regional banking arrangements. NCNB had expanded further up the East Coast by acquiring the CentraBank of Baltimore, Maryland, and the Prince William Bank in northern Virginia. These additions brought to six the number of states where the red NCNB logo could be found.

The CentraBank merger was announced in May 1986, just two weeks after McColl announced at the NCNB stockholder meeting that he would like NCNB to expand into the Washington-Baltimore market and west into Tennessee. NCNB agreed to pay $8.7 million, plus common-stock warrants valued at about $3.5 million, for CentraBank, a mutual savings bank with assets of more than $225 million. CentraBank had 30,000 accounts and eight branches in the Baltimore metropolitan area.

Expansion focused more and more attention on the need to recruit and retain talented officers. NCNB had been aggressively recruiting new officers from its early days. To constantly replenish the supply of executives, the company stepped up its management recruiting program in the early 1970s and moved away from what Senior Vice President C. J. "Chuck" Cooley called the "sheep-dip method," where management trainees moved from department to department for eighteen months as part of an orientation to the company. Instead, NCNB started hiring college graduates for specific divisions, at the time a radical departure from routine recruiting procedure among banks. The name of the company's program was changed from Promotional Qualification to Management Associates. From 1976 through 1989, NCNB hired 2,300 persons through the program, retaining 1,572 of them.

By 1987, McColl had expanded NCNB into six important Southern states, all of them experiencing greater growth than the national average. First Union had pushed closer and almost gained the number one position with the acquisition of First Railroad and Banking Corp., a Georgia bank with $3.6 billion in assets. First Wachovia was well behind and encountering problems in the consumer portfolio with its First Atlanta acquisition.

Wachovia had moved "completely off our screen," McColl later said. Having achieved a position as the largest bank in the Southeast, NCNB—and Hugh McColl—were looking elsewhere for a challenge.

Chapter 14 **Predatory Instincts**

Tim Hartman was anxious in the spring of 1988. Things were just too slow.

Hartman had joined NCNB as its chief financial officer six years earlier because he liked the energy and competitive atmosphere of the company. "The folks here don't have contracts, they own stock in the company, and they work," he recalled later. "It is very seldom that you find those three characteristics in management." The mergers in Florida had occupied much of his time since he had come to NCNB from Baldwin-United Corp., a former piano manufacturer that he had seen grow through mergers and acquisitions to become a $7.5 billion conglomerate. Until lately, the pace of life at NCNB had confirmed what he had first liked about the bank's corporate culture. This organization was going somewhere.

Now, in 1988, the plate was clean. There were no mergers in sight. In fact, he had spent much of the past year working through some credit problems with a Virginia finance company that had gone bust.

Hartman told his wife early in 1988 that if something didn't happen soon the bank was going to begin losing some of its promising young recruits who were eager to make their mark. The issue was of sufficient gravity that it was on the agenda at a directors' conference.

Hartman had looked around for expansion opportunities and had even run the numbers on a few banks in Texas, where he and Frank Gentry, NCNB's chief planner, had been spending some time together lately. In 1986, NCNB had invested $6 million in the Charter Bank of Houston, whose controlling stockholder, Jerry Finger, was a friend of Hugh McColl's. NCNB's position at Charter gave the bank a window on the Texas economy, which was in real trouble. Despite the obvious problems, Hartman and Gentry believed that Texas offered opportunities for NCNB. They discounted doomsayers who told them that many had gone broke underestimating the extent of the Texas financial disaster.

The Charter investment "allowed us to realize that Houston really didn't have grass growing in the streets," recalled Gentry, an experienced corporate planner who had come to NCNB from Exxon Corp. in 1973. He was named NCNB's principal contact with Charter shortly after returning to the Charlotte headquarters from Florida, where he had handled marketing of NCNB's Florida operations. There he had gotten to know officials of the Federal Deposit Insurance Corp. when NCNB had acquired the County Bank of Bradenton, its first purchase of a failed bank from the FDIC.

In early 1987, Hartman and Gentry had looked hard at the large Texas bank InterFirst, before its merger with RepublicBank, but they thought the $600 million price tag was too high. Later that same year, McColl, NCNB president Buddy Kemp, and Hartman made several trips to Houston to look at the $9 billion Allied Bancshares, Inc., which they believed offered merger opportunities. NCNB and Allied could not agree on price, however, and banking laws prohibited such a large acquisition outside the Southeast banking compact region, which stopped at the Mississippi River and did not include Texas.

"It turned out to be the right answer," McColl recalled later. "We had underestimated the depth of their losses. We still were talking about paying them $18 a share for their company, and it turned out to be worth-less." The experience was valuable nonetheless. It alerted NCNB to the quicksand of Texas financial dealings.

In October 1987 the FDIC had called to see if NCNB had any interest in Western Bank, another troubled Houston institution. (While state laws prohibited NCNB from buying a Texas bank in an open sale, they did not apply to acquisition of failed banks managed by the FDIC.) No, Gentry said, but he asked if Charter could take a look at it. Make your offer and we'll see, the FDIC replied.

"We said that if they let Charter bid and Charter was a winning bid-der, then NCNB would invest another $7 million in Charter and take an active role in management," Gentry recalled. "That would raise our ownership from under 25 percent to about 40 percent, and we would have board representation.

"They asked, 'Are you willing to commit to that?' I said, 'Yes, subject to Federal Reserve Board approval on our investment.' They said, 'Is there some way you could get that in writing before we open the bid?' I said, 'Do you have a piece of paper?' and he handed me one. [NCNB legal counsel] Paul Polking was sitting next to me. He wrote one para-graph saying that if we're the winning bidder, we'll put in $7 million, and I signed it."

Charter won the bid, and the ease of the transaction convinced Gentry that there were indeed bargains in Texas. NCNB now owned about 40 percent of a $500 million bank with a total investment of $13 mil-lion. Gentry had learned that successful bidders had to be light on their feet. He had committed $7 million of NCNB's money without prior ap-proval. McColl, who had been attending a meeting in Miami, heartily approved when he heard the news. Hartman and Gentry joined the Charter board and became regulars on the commercial flights between Charlotte and Houston.

They watched the competition closely, particularly the First Republic-Bank holding company, the result of a desperation merger of InterFirst Corp. and Republic Bank Corp., where heavy losses had been reported for 1987. First RepublicBank was not so much one bank as it was 120 banks that had consolidated to 40 separate banking companies. The merger was designed to save money by consolidating the support staff and "back room" operations, thus eliminating about three thousand jobs and overlapping markets.

During the first quarter of 1988, First RepublicBank's position deteriorated further. While some individual banks were profitable, most were not. The holding company reported a $1.5 billion loss. Total deposits for the subsidiary banks had decreased by $3.6 billion. In March, the FDIC announced a guarantee of all deposits, including those of more than $100,000, and loaned $1 billion to the two largest subsidiary banks. In exchange, the agency took all the holding company's subsidiaries as collateral and the right to control its banking operations.

"As First Republic's problems became evident," Gentry recalled, "our predatory instincts were aroused. We already had begun to mess around with the numbers. It didn't immediately occur to me that we might buy all of the banks. What I really hoped we might do, at least initially, was that we might buy [the holding company's] Houston bank."

Gentry asked Charter's Jerry Finger to explore that possibility. Meanwhile, Gentry talked with Edwin "Pete" Burr, the FDIC regional director in Atlanta, whom he had dealt with in the Florida purchase, about the willingness of the FDIC to consider someone other than the nation's largest banks, which were thought the most likely to help the FDIC in a recovery of this size. Burr was noncommittal but encouraging.

About the same time in March, corporate treasurer John Mack was visiting NCNB's London office when he read about First RepublicBank's emergency assistance from the FDIC and thought that perhaps NCNB might be able to acquire a "wounded animal." If NCNB could protect itself from the bad loans in the First RepublicBank portfolio, Mack thought it would be a good deal.

Gentry believed he had learned something about "good deals" from the work done investigating Allied. This time he was more cynical and dubbed the First RepublicBank plan Operation Calcutta, as in "black hole of." He wasn't sure just what problems a new owner would find in the First RepublicBank loan portfolio if ever a deal were put together. Later, as NCNB's intentions became more focused, the project code name would be changed to "XYZ Corporation," with its less sinister connotation. McColl stuck with the Calcutta code name in his own notes.

Early on March 29, Hartman returned from the Reserve City Bankers meeting, where FDIC chairman William Seidman had been a speaker and First RepublicBank had been a hot topic. Mack and Gentry briefed

Hartman on their thoughts and proposed that NCNB make a bid. Hartman immediately liked the idea. NCNB was back in the game.

The Texas deal appealed to Hartman because it was a real opportunity to improve NCNB's balance sheet by increasing its deposit base. The bank had always lagged behind competitors on this measure, which meant it always paid a slightly higher margin for its operations because it had to borrow cash rather than use money provided more cheaply by depositors. At the same time, Hartman saw that a deal in Texas would greatly expand the bank's market share. After all, the Texas economy was not going to stay down forever, and if NCNB could get in before others did it would be well positioned for the good times. The question was whether a deal could be arranged so NCNB would not have to assume total responsibility for the bank's bad loans.

That evening, McColl, Hartman, Gentry, and Mack met with Marshall Davidson, Jerry Finger's friend at Drexel Burnham Lambert, the New York investment banking firm. At the time, Drexel was making a proposal to First RepublicBank's management for restructuring its operation. Davidson told McColl that a deal to acquire the entire company might be possible.

Davidson told McColl that if NCNB wanted to pursue the deal, NCNB should hire Washington attorney Baldwin Tuttle, a former deputy general counsel for the Federal Reserve Board. Tuttle was well connected and experienced in bank regulatory matters. He had handled the Franklin National failure for the Federal Reserve in 1974. Now in private practice in the Washington office of the New York–based firm of Milbank, Tweed, Hadley & McCloy, he represented bidders on FDIC-assisted banks and most recently had worked on the restructuring of another Texas bank. With high-powered talent like Tuttle involved, Seidman would realize that NCNB meant business. Hartman called Tuttle the next morning, and he agreed to represent NCNB in a possible First RepublicBank purchase through the FDIC.

Less than three weeks had passed since the announcement of the FDIC loan to First RepublicBank when McColl and Hartman sat down across from Seidman, in an introductory meeting arranged by Tuttle. Seidman had not anticipated that the first institution to express interest in buying First RepublicBank would be a bank as small as NCNB. The meeting was cordial and friendly. McColl and Seidman liked each other immediately. "I felt an immediate rapport with him," McColl recalled. "We told him that we were prepared to make an offer and we wanted to take a run at it."

In their twenty-minute meeting, McColl told Seidman that NCNB knew how to merge banks and how to run banks, but if he expected NCNB to buy the bad loans in First RepublicBank then they might as well head back to Charlotte. NCNB couldn't take that risk. However, if the FDIC was willing to form a partnership with NCNB to work through the loan portfolio, separating the good from the bad, then they would share the profit from the good ones. Bad loans would be written off as losses by the FDIC. If that sort of deal made sense, McColl said, then NCNB was willing to put $200 million into Texas and commit the manpower necessary to turn the bank around.

Seidman was interested—and a little intrigued. NCNB was important to the FDIC. The list of banks that might be interested, or able, to take on the largest bank in Texas was going to be a short one, and any serious suitor was valuable. McColl's deal was different from anything the FDIC had tried before, but that didn't matter. Seidman wanted different. This time, the FDIC was not going to devise a plan and then have banks bid on it. He wanted bidders to arrive at their own solutions. And what McColl outlined was novel enough to be considered.

For McColl and Hartman, who would become the principal strategist and negotiator with the FDIC, the session with Seidman was an encouraging first step. If the chairman was listening to NCNB, then McColl believed he had a chance.

Texas was just the kind of challenge that excited McColl and Hartman. If it worked, the deal would install NCNB in the big league of banking virtually overnight, bringing total assets to more than $60 billion. Using the FDIC's authority to override regional and state interstate banking restrictions, NCNB could leap over two states and enter a major market that would otherwise be barred to it. And the thrill of competing against some of the nation's biggest banks in what looked like the deal of the century made it all the more exciting. Hartman and McColl talked about nothing else on their plane trip back to Charlotte.

When the two returned, McColl began organizing his team and a base of operations. A small, nondescript conference room on the executive floor of the NCNB Tower was chosen as the war room. Hartman would handle finances and negotiations in Washington. Senior Vice President

Bill McGee was assigned logistics as part of a three-man Charlotte-based team that included the bank's communications and public affairs executive, Senior Vice President Joe Martin, and its chief personnel officer, Chuck Cooley, who became the team leader.

Martin and Cooley constructed a calendar arranged with the beginning denoted as D day, similar to the way NCNB had planned for Florida. Key players and their assignments were listed down the left margin. "It was really audiences, people we had to communicate with—directors, news media, FDIC, internal officer group and employees, internal landing team, investors, political leaders, customers," Martin recalled. "We listed all of those and every constituency we could think of."

Cooley concentrated on personnel needs. The entire affair took on a somewhat surreal character. "The objective was to involve nearly a hundred people in a highly secret operation, develop detailed plans to be executed at a moment's notice, and pretend that nothing was going on," Cooley wrote in an after-action report that he wryly titled "What I Did Last Summer."

Secrecy and tight security were essential. Employees involved signed a pledge of confidentiality. They were called in one by one, given their assignments, and instructed not to tell anyone about their work. In some instances, their immediate superiors were not informed of the details; they were simply on an assignment for the chairman. A burn bin in the basement of the Charlotte headquarters was pressed into service. Organizers realized they had gone too far when the custodian asked if it was necessary to burn Hardee's hamburger wrappers and napkins that sometimes were delivered for disposal along with more sensitive documents.

McColl and others worried that if word leaked that the bank was interested in Texas, the news would spook investors and prompt impulsive sales of NCNB's stock. Jim Thompson also worried that if the bank's major funding sources learned prematurely about the plans, the bank's credibility would suffer. He feared that the bank would not be able to explain its position and calm concerns without disclosing information to competitors bidding for First RepublicBank. Thompson believed the market would see NCNB's venture as an unnecessary credit risk because nobody really knew "how deep the hole was in Texas. The market saw credit risk, and up until that time banks had not been able to insulate themselves from credit risks." Thompson carefully adjusted the bank's position and borrowed money for longer term to hedge against the market turning against them and the cost of capital going up.

McColl stepped up his civic activities and public appearances to convince his rivals at First Union and First Wachovia that he was not involved in another major project. "This was the most clandestine, covert operation ever conducted in this company," recalled Senior Vice President Russell J. "Rusty" Page. "I never told my wife what I was working on—nobody did."

First RepublicBank employees never saw anyone from NCNB, even after the FDIC authorized the bank to conduct a close inspection of the books in Dallas. McColl did dispatch a team of credit experts to review the files in the FDIC Washington offices; for five days, four NCNB loan specialists pored over fifteen boxes of loan review reports and documents on the bank's financial condition. They weren't allowed to photocopy the records or take them from the room, so they entered as much of the data as they could into a laptop computer for later analysis in Charlotte.

McColl was not being cavalier in trading secrecy for on-site examination in Texas. He didn't believe it was necessary to review First RepublicBank's books in detail since the deal NCNB was preparing did not depend on current losses.

NCNB's low-profile strategy left reporters to focus on two other principal contenders for the deal—Citicorp of New York and Wells Fargo Corp. of San Francisco, the nation's eleventh-largest bank, with $45 billion in assets—whose interest had become known early.

On April 15, Frank Gentry and his team had scheduled a wrap-up session with FDIC officials following their review of the bank's loan packages and assets. The team included Bob Shaw, Tom Sadler, Cal Hunkele, Denise Sawyer, and Frank Murphy. McColl arrived unexpectedly and went with them to a meeting with FDIC chief negotiator Tony Scalzi. "He surprised the hell out of Scalzi," Gentry said.

After outlining their plan, McColl emphasized that NCNB had other takeover opportunities, including banks closer to home in Tennessee, so he wanted a commitment that if NCNB submitted a proposal the FDIC would respond within ten days. In addition to concerns over public disclosure of NCNB's interest, the NCNB team also worried that, as time passed, more and more of First RepublicBank's deposits would be drained by nervous customers. Scalzi told McColl that his request was impossible. He didn't have the authority to make such a guarantee.

"Well, who does?" McColl shot back.

"Only the chairman," Scalzi replied.

"Is he in?" McColl asked. Scalzi asked him to wait while he found out. A few minutes later, McColl was ushered in to see Seidman. The chairman was not moved by McColl's argument for a ten-day response, which on a government timetable was virtually immediate. "He said he would try for a month," Gentry recalled. McColl hoped to have a firm answer by the Memorial Day weekend.

Four days later, NCNB's first written proposal arrived at the FDIC. In constructing the plan, NCNB took a cue from Seidman's public comments that the FDIC was looking for new ways to deal with the problem. He was open to suggestions. "He told us the things he wanted," McColl said later. NCNB proposed the use of a relatively new type of recovery program involving something called a "bridge bank." It would be formed by the sale of the subsidiary banks of First RepublicBank Corp. to a new bank that would be owned jointly by NCNB and the FDIC. The holding company would be left as little more than a shell, its investors' stock worthless.

The bridge bank concept had been used only once, less than six months earlier in Baton Rouge, Louisiana, to save the $372 million Capital Bank & Trust Co. It had its proponents, however, including former FDIC director Irvine Sprague, who argued in his 1986 book, *Bailout*, that the arrangement was best suited to winding down the business of a large, failing bank in order to preserve the franchise until the assets could be sold.

After the embarrassing First City episode, in which the FDIC had been pressured by arbitrageurs to settle on their terms, Seidman had begun to make it clear in speeches and in congressional appearances that the FDIC would provide no assurance to shareholders and bondholders of bank holding companies or other nonbanking subsidiaries. The bridge bank did just that.

The new bridge bank that NCNB proposed would take over First RepublicBank's forty operating banks with their 178 offices across the state. During a ninety-day transition period, NCNB would determine the fair-market value of all assets and liabilities. Then, with a $210 million initial investment, NCNB would become the owner of 20 percent of the new bank and have an option to buy the remaining 80 percent from the FDIC within five years. NCNB's exclusive option was pegged at a price of 107 percent of book value, which was set at true fair-market value. All other things being equal, NCNB would be buying the bank at about half the prevailing asking price for banks in the Southeast, and doing it on an installment plan.

All assets of the new bridge bank were to be marked to fair-market value and put into two components. The bridge bank would receive the performing loans or those that had acceptable risks of paying out, and a special asset division would hold all the assets for which there was little or no hope of recovery. The costs of the special asset pool, including funding and loan losses, would be absorbed by the FDIC. NCNB could put an unlimited amount of questionable loans in the special asset pool by the end of the first year of the agreement and up to $750 million in bad loans during the second year. NCNB's loan losses were capped at 35 basis points of all the losses in the first year. (One hundred basis points equal one percentage point.) Anything more would be absorbed by the FDIC. All other costs associated with the special asset bank, including funding expense, administrative and legal, also were to be absorbed by the FDIC.

"Just as we discussed," McColl wrote Seidman, "the proposal indirectly leaves substantially all of the financial risk which could arise from a further deterioration of the market with the FDIC. Even so, NCNB will share a portion of the risk since the questionable assets will be on the books of a bridge bank in which NCNB will have an interest. Frankly, we believe that this division of risk is appropriate since neither NCNB nor any other party than the FDIC has a current obligation to undertake that risk and since the full extent of the magnitude of the problems may be impossible to assess."

McColl gave Seidman until noon on April 25—six days away—to reply.

Although the bridge bank proposal would prove crucial, it had not been part of NCNB's first draft. Treasurer John Mack and other members of the core team first arrived at a traditional open-bank type of bid, spinning off some bad assets into a separate bank and recapitalizing what was left under new management. That was before he looked at First RepublicBank's fourth quarter report.

"I took it home one night and read it, and it became obvious to me that performance liabilities [debts] were just awesome," Mack recalled. "There was no way you would want to step into the shoes of this company or to join with this company and be exposed to the shareholder and debtholder liability that was going to take place."

Mack soon came up with the outline of a new plan. "It was a very skinny schedule, one page, that essentially took the First RepublicBank as we saw it on December 31, 1987, wiped out the debtholders, wiped out the shareholders, wiped out the loan-loss reserve, wrote down the loans rather dramatically. By using the billions of dollars of equity and loan-loss reserve and debt that they had, you could recapitalize the company for substantially less than would be required if you were to have to go in there and save the existing company and pay the existing shareholders anything. It was kind of nasty and ruthless [to shareholders and debtholders, who would get nothing], but it was just a plain old fact that it was a whole lot cheaper. It was just obvious that this ought to have an appeal to the regulators."

Mack's outline was shaped and refined with Hartman and others and became the heart of NCNB's first proposal. Also included was a request to the FDIC to invoke new federal legislation, the Competitive Equality in Banking Act, giving regulators emergency power to suspend certain state legislation that restricted bank operations across state lines.

McColl believed that the refined NCNB proposal would appeal to Seidman. "By using the bridge bank, it gave the FDIC face," McColl said later. "I mean they got to stick it to Wall Street one time and remind everybody that they were the federal government and that they had power. So we gave them a weapon. We showed them how to use one of the weapons that they had not used. That really paid off big for the FDIC and for us, because what you do is leave behind all the creditors and the legal liability."

Seidman didn't immediately jump at the idea of a bridge bank, though it solved some of the problems the FDIC had faced in other transactions. His reply on April 25 turned down NCNB's proposal. "Our principal areas of concern were the limited upside potential available to the FDIC and the inability of the FDIC to cap its outlay for two years," Seidman wrote. However, he left the door open and asked McColl to try again.

In the meantime, Hartman had virtually relocated to Washington from Charlotte. His home became the Madison, a plush hotel just a few blocks from the FDIC offices. He and Gentry met daily with FDIC officials, NCNB's attorney Baldwin Tuttle, or specialists at other governmental agencies who would review all or a portion of the NCNB plan.

Hartman, a tall, lean Midwesterner with black, curly, close-cropped hair, had just turned forty-nine on March 1. He had been at NCNB since 1982, when he was hired as corporate executive vice president and chief financial officer. Hartman had not heard about NCNB before he got the call from Chuck Cooley asking if he was interested in the job. McColl had been looking for a new CFO and had bumped into Hartman's former boss in a buffet line at a dinner in Charlotte.

By the time Hartman left Baldwin-United Corp., he had seen it grow from a successful piano company into a diversified financial services conglomerate headquartered in Cincinnati, Ohio. "We bought fifteen banks in Colorado; three savings and loans; about nine insurance companies; Top Value Stamps, the yellow stamps; S&H Green Stamps; Coldwell Banker, a real estate company; Empire Insurance Company in New York; and so on."

Not all of the acquisitions paid off. Once Hartman had worked hard to corner the market on, of all things, solid body guitars, and in 1964 he finally did it, buying the world's leading solid body guitar company in London. Unfortunately, the Beatles popularized a different guitar model and destroyed Hartman's strategy.

An intense, energetic, organized man, Hartman arrived in Charlotte totally committed to NCNB and immediately converted his savings into NCNB stock. Hartman had never made a loan or checked a customer's credit references, but he knew how to put together a deal without dwelling on the social side of the transaction. "I've often made the statement that if you buy Shell Oil gas, you're not buying Shell Oil gas because the oil comes from Texas versus Saudi Arabia, or the company is headquartered in Florida versus wherever it is located. You buy Shell Oil gas because you need it. Our shareholders do not care where our banks are located. They care what our return on equity is. They care what our dividend payout is, and they care what our earnings per share are. They don't care whether we have banks in Florida, North Carolina, South Carolina, Vermont, Canada, or Texas, if they can get better earnings per share."

When he and McColl were returning from Washington after their first meeting with Seidman, one of the deals from his past came to mind. Ten years earlier he had been involved in a savings and loan that went bankrupt. The company that took over the failed business had gotten a tax ruling from the Internal Revenue Service that said the losses belonged to the depositors, not the shareholders, and they had been able to use them to offset future tax liabilities. The company that continued the business could therefore use the losses from the previous year. The circumstances were similar enough that when Hartman returned to Charlotte he immediately contacted a Charlotte tax attorney.

Hartman didn't know if the same application of the tax laws would work for NCNB. It was worth a try, he decided. "Some days you're out fishing for blue gills, and some days the red worm works and some days it doesn't," Hartman said later. "You remember, one day, the sun was up and the red worm worked."

Hartman laid out the tax concept to NCNB's outside tax lawyers and asked them to work on it. If his recollection was correct, this ruling could apply to NCNB. Something approved for an Ohio savings and loan could be sought by a carpenter shop in Arizona or, in this case, a bank holding company in North Carolina.

One of NCNB's tax lawyers met in Washington on April 25 with the IRS. The discussion was encouraging, and NCNB's lawyer was invited back for further talks. On April 27, NCNB's lawyers were back in Washington for another conference with IRS attorneys. They discussed whether NCNB's proposed transaction could be treated as what is known in the tax code as a G Reorganization, an insolvency reorganization under a provision in the tax code that came in 1980. It's designed to allow companies that are in court-supervised bankruptcies to emerge from the bankruptcy proceedings still able to utilize their built-in losses. The idea is that the tax code will allow them to, in effect, recover something from the economic losses they had incurred by being able to apply these favorable tax benefits to their future years' income and income tax returns.

Next came more meetings with the IRS and conferences with the FDIC lawyers, the FDIC outside counsel, the FDIC outside investment bankers, and representatives of the Office of the Comptroller of the Currency.

The lawyers refined the tax concepts as quickly as they could. But progress was slow. McColl became increasingly impatient with what seemed like interminable delays in dealing with the FDIC, though Tuttle had warned him not to expect immediate action. It had taken nine months to settle the Franklin National case.

For NCNB, time threatened to undermine their entire deal. First RepublicBank's net worth was dissolving like a sugar cube in a cup of hot tea. On one particularly bad day when the bank lost $200 million in deposits, Hartman wondered if there would be enough left to salvage. While he wasn't concerned about the bad loans, he knew NCNB needed a significant portion of the sound bank to make its deal work. The delays also diminished the losses that could be carried forward.

McColl had wanted to have the Texas deal settled before mid-May when he was to leave on a three-week trip to the Far East and Europe. The first leg of the trip, which had been arranged months in advance, was extremely important. McColl would be completing plans to list NCNB's stock on the Tokyo Stock Exchange, the first regional bank ever to raise equity capital on the Japanese market. McColl, Hartman, and investor relations specialist Rusty Page also had planned stops in Hong Kong, London, Amsterdam, and Zurich to lay the groundwork for raising more capital. McColl decided that there was no need to reschedule the trip because Gentry and the other members of the takeover team were doing all that needed to be done.

Frustrated at the delays, McColl visited Seidman on May 6 and asked point-blank whether he was going to get an answer by May 15, the second deadline he had set for an answer on NCNB's proposal.

"He was cool, very cool, not an unfriendly cool, but just unruffled," McColl said later. McColl was unable to get the commitment he had sought, and he told Seidman in a huff that NCNB was withdrawing from the competition.

Seidman took McColl's posturing in stride. "They were in a big hurry because they thought they had an advantage because they had started earlier and done a lot of preparation," Seidman recalled later. "I said, 'Hey, that works in the private sector, but you can't do that here.'" Seidman believed McColl would not actually walk away from the deal. "It was a great deal and he knew he wanted it, and so did I, so it never bothered me that he walked out."

Unable to budge the FDIC and anxious about leaving so many people in limbo while he was on his trip, McColl notified nearly all of the NCNB employees who had been drafted into the Texas project that the deal was off. Privately, however, McColl instructed his inner circle of top executives to keep working. The level of tension was more pronounced than anything any of them had experienced before. "I'm telling you," Page recalled, "that you could have driven railroad spikes through their heads and they would have never felt it." Some doubted privately that the deal would fly and believed that NCNB's resources were being drained from more productive ventures.

McColl's morale was low on May 11, when, shortly before 8:00 P.M., he, Hartman, and Page lifted off from Charlotte on a commercial flight bound for Hong Kong, the first leg of their trip. On the way to San Francisco, an intermediate stop, McColl played gin rummy with Page, winning about $15, and he worried about the events of the past two months and whether his organization, and NCNB, could sustain a prolonged contest for control of the Texas bank.

Hartman waited too. A linchpin in the deal, an IRS ruling, was still in limbo.

Chapter 15 **A Waiting Game**

As he traveled west, toward Hong Kong, McColl remained tethered to the United States by his anxiety over the Texas deal.

The first few days of the three-week trip were scheduled to give McColl and his traveling companions time to recover from the Pacific crossing. They arrived just ahead of the weekend, giving their body clocks time to adjust. Hartman visited a tailor, and McColl picked up some linens in the market, along with freshwater pearls. He also accepted an invitation to attend the horse races on Sunday with officials of Hong Kong–Shanghai Bank.

On Friday, May 13, Gentry and Mack called McColl to report on their latest conversation with an FDIC official who indicated that the deal might be closed by Memorial Day and that NCNB's bid looked strong. At 2:00 A.M. Saturday, Hong Kong time, McColl contacted Gentry again. This time the news was not so good. A top FDIC negotiator had reported he would recommend against NCNB and was going to look elsewhere for other bidders. On Sunday, McColl learned that the FDIC was literally looking for new bidders all around the world.

In addition, McColl found out that the FDIC wasn't going to wait weeks for proposals from competitors to come in. The agency had asked six to twelve banks to make a bid within a few days. McColl noted in his diary that the "timetable has obviously been moved up by events. Two weeks versus five weeks. Gentry very discouraged. Article in *WSJ* [*Wall Street Journal*] re: small Texas banks suing FDIC for closing small banks but using open bank assistance for large ones."

What McColl did not know was that the FDIC, in an abundance of caution, had hired outside counsel to advise the agency on its handling of the deal. The first thing the outside lawyers discovered was that the agency had not followed the bidding procedure as it was outlined in the Competitive Equality in Banking Act. The process therefore had to begin anew.

The discouraging news only increased McColl's anxiety. Still mentally wobbly from the Pacific crossing, he held his first meeting with the chairman of the National Australian Bank. The two talked about the Australian bank's buying as much as 25 percent of NCNB's stock for cash that McColl could use in Texas. "We had a very bad meeting," McColl recalled. "I had jet lag, the room was cold. He talked like he wanted to take over the company. I'm sure I offended him. He offended me."

On Monday and Tuesday, the NCNB trio talked with the Hong Kong–Shanghai Bank about a similar deal. The response was immediate. "They got so excited that they went on red alert," McColl said. He offered to bring the bank in if NCNB would be permitted to manage all the Hong Kong–Shanghai's United States business, which included Marine Midland Bank. In exchange, NCNB would receive about $500 million for its stock, which was more than enough to cover the Texas deal. The sessions ended without anything definitive, and the NCNB group flew on to Tokyo, where Hartman received a phone call from the Hong Kong bankers asking if they could return and talk further. The schedule wouldn't permit backtracking for all three of them, but Hartman returned alone to continue discussions.

On Wednesday, McColl rose early, as he did during most of the trip. He worked off some nervous energy with thirty-five minutes of hard exercise in a nearby park and was back in his hotel room at 7:00 A.M. when he received word that Seidman would call the following day at 10:00 P.M. Tokyo time.

Seidman's call lifted some of the clouds. McColl noted in a diary he kept on the trip that he told Seidman "A) Time works against tax benefits, B) Time destroys the management team, C) Time erodes customer confidence." Later McColl wrote: "Seidman gave me the clear impression that he expects our deal to win. He is very much aware of the loss of customers and management. The tax benefits loom large to them. He made it clear that he will deal with us exclusively post May 31 or not at all." Seidman left it that one of his deputies would contact McColl later in his trip.

Hartman rejoined McColl and Page in Japan, and the three went on to Geneva for meetings with investment bankers at Salomon Brothers and later to Paris for talks with representatives from Groupe Bruxelles Lambert, a major European investment banking power. Finally, in London, after meeting with Barclay's Bank, McColl talked with the FDIC. He didn't get the warm reception he had expected. His spirits dropped. The call had come a day late, and McColl felt less of a sense of urgency by the FDIC to NCNB's position than he had believed was evident earlier.

McColl returned to the United States on May 27 and traveled immediately to his Litchfield Beach, South Carolina, condominium for the weekend, where he met with Hootie Johnson, chairman of the NCNB executive committee. Together they reviewed McColl's proposed organization of the Texas operation. On the following Thursday, he went back to Washington for more strategy meetings with Hartman and Tuttle and meetings with FDIC officials.

The time passed slowly, and the lack of movement at the agency frustrated the NCNB team. Hartman, who had remained with the deal daily, except for the Far East trip, had learned how to read the bureaucratic signs. He believed the FDIC was stalling NCNB and the other bidders. With a deal of this magnitude, the bureaucrats did not want to be wrong.

"They were more interested in being sure their legal case was perfect than they were in the financial aspects of the transaction," McColl said. "They don't want to be embarrassed. If they seize something, they want to know that they did it legally and without question. They don't want to be in court the rest of their lives. They want to do it perfectly."

The unstructured bidding process did create delays. Since all the proposals were different, they could not be easily compared.

The deal also included some very high political stakes. McColl believed he could count on the support of FDIC director C. C. Hope, Jr., a former top executive with First Union National Bank in Charlotte. While McColl and Hope had been competitors in North Carolina, Hope was familiar with NCNB, its management, and its capabilities.

Hope, a gregarious, gracious Southerner, had been appointed an FDIC director in 1986 after his term as president of the American Bankers Association. When Hope first learned of NCNB's interest in First Republic, he was one of the few who believed the bank had a good chance. "One of our major considerations was management," Hope said. "That's where perhaps I played a very significant role, because I was well aware of the management structure of NCNB on a person-to-person basis. After all, I had been a competitor for many years. I lived in the same town as the home office. I'd grown up there. I came across the years watching them, always struggling to compete and charging hard against their competition.

"NCNB never understood why it was taking us so long. We had so few bidders that we didn't want to lose them, and we didn't want to lose NCNB, just like we didn't want to lose Wells Fargo, but Wells Fargo was not threatening to pull out. NCNB kept threatening to pull out if we didn't move faster. And we just couldn't move any faster. Ol' Hugh, he didn't care about our problems, he just wanted it done."

In deliberations, Hope usually deferred to Seidman's lead. As he put it, "You don't fly too close to *Air Force One*."

Director Robert Clarke was another matter. A lawyer from Houston, Clarke was Comptroller of the Currency. Clarke's support was essential, not just because he was one of three votes on the FDIC board but because, as Comptroller of the Currency, the banks could not be formally "failed" without his approval.

If NCNB believed it had an edge with Hope, Texas interests had equally strong connections with Clarke. Unknown to NCNB, two Texas groups were organizing, one around former U.S. senator John Tower, a close political friend of Vice President George Bush, who by June was the likely Republican nominee for president. Another group, composed primarily of First RepublicBank's management, had formed around Al Casey, the former president of American Airlines. Clarke's connections with Casey were particularly strong.

Clarke had recruited Casey in March to take over the presidency of First Republic and restructure it at the same time the FDIC extended a $1 billion loan. When Casey moved into the executive offices in April, morale was at rock bottom. Rumors that the bank was folding or being taken over by outsiders from New York or California were rampant, leaving First RepublicBank's 15,000 employees anxious and frustrated. Commercial lending officers had no money with which to do business, and employees wondered if the business would survive. Corporate communications officer Martha Larsh in Dallas got a daily telephone call from her mother, who inquired if she still had a job.

Casey brought a fresh hope for survival and a sense of humor to his new assignment. The grateful First Republic employees saw him as a savior, and he took that in stride too. Once, riding down the escalator from the inner sanctum management level on the third floor of the headquarters building, an employee waved and said, "Hi, Mr. Casey. We're glad you're here." Deadpan, Casey shot back, "You can just call me God."

Hartman believed that Clarke had staked himself out behind Casey and would do everything he could to keep the bank open and in the hands of Texans. "Failing First Republic was an anti-Republican event in Texas of the highest degree," said Hartman. "And that was an enormous impediment we had to get over."

After the Memorial Day holiday had passed without any action, Hartman also worried that the FDIC might delay until after the November presidential election, to avoid the political damage to Bush of turning the bank over to a company from outside Texas, a move that would surely wound the pride and the pocketbooks of some powerful Texas interests, including Jerry Fronterhouse, a leading Republican fund-raiser and principal stockholder in First Republic. "They just didn't want to upset any apple carts. They wanted to wait to make their decision, hoping that it would go away," Hartman said.

As the process ground on, the balance of NCNB's Texas team, the folks who would have to make a deal work from the first minute after the announcement, believed they could not leave things in limbo any longer. They had to move. Cooley, Martin, and logistics chief McGee believed they could not wait to begin gathering facts and making real plans for on-site operations in Dallas. If NCNB's bid was accepted, the organization wanted to move quickly and efficiently in the transition. The winning bidder would have only a matter of hours to reopen the First Republic offices and begin conducting banking business.

Any arrangements Martin and Cooley could make had to be done with the utmost secrecy, and Martin needed someone from outside NCNB whom he could trust to operate on NCNB's behalf in Texas. He called his longtime friend Tom Drew, a Durham-based public relations consultant, but he didn't tell Drew what he had in mind. He just asked Drew to meet him in Charlotte.

Drew, a tall man with a frequent and hearty laugh, glasses, and a shock of blond hair, was Martin's first choice for the assignment. The two had become close friends at Duke University nearly twenty years earlier when Drew was treasurer of the student government and Martin was director of student activities. In 1983, before returning to Durham to open his own business, Phoenix Communications Ltd., Drew had served a stint as finance director of the Democratic National Committee. In that job he had developed extensive contacts with Texas politicians, their staffs, and the Texas media.

When Drew arrived on June 7, Martin greeted him, pushed a paper in front of him and said, "You've got to sign this before I can talk to you about the project. Only about five people in the entire bank even know about this project." The document pledged Drew to secrecy. "You cannot tell any of your employees what you are working on at this stage or anybody you run into," Martin warned.

Drew still had no idea what his role would be until Martin introduced him to McGee, who asked if Drew could accompany him on a trip to Dallas on Tuesday and Wednesday, continuing to Houston on Thursday.

As the three men talked, Drew learned that he and McGee would scout Dallas and Houston for intelligence about First Republic, competitive bidders, and the FDIC. He also was to help arrange for telephones, hotel rooms, and office space for as many as several hundred NCNB officials who might be needed instantly if the FDIC turned First Republic over to NCNB. In addition, Drew was to begin preparations for news coverage and to arrange for NCNB to contact leading political figures in Texas within minutes of the announcement of the winning bid. Martin wanted as much favorable and knowledgeable comment as possible from public figures.

"We can't let anyone know we're working for NCNB," McGee told him. "We'll need a cover."

Drew concocted a story that placed his company in Dallas to bid on a large public relations contract. The job would possibly require as many as sixty hotel rooms for an indefinite period, up to 15,000 square feet of office space and hundreds of thousands of dollars of telephone and communications services. The NCNB folks were just guessing. At the time, no one knew whether NCNB would need to set up twenty or five hundred people to handle the transfer of assets and equipment.

Drew and McGee flew to Dallas, rented a car, checked into the Crescent Hotel, and then walked around downtown Dallas to reserve hotel rooms and office space located as close to First Republic headquarters as possible.

McGee also walked around the main First Republic building and looked at the registry of officers and noted the location of their offices in the First Republic tower. If NCNB won the bid, McColl planned to meet immediately in person with Chairman Casey to consummate the transfer. It would be bad form and an awkward beginning if McColl arrived in the lobby and had to ask directions.

McGee and Drew chose the Dallas Sheraton Hotel as NCNB's downtown base of operations. The hotel was less than a block from the bank's headquarters, and the adjoining Southland Building had available office space. The Sheraton's hotel manager and Southland's leasing officer were eager to please, pledging up to sixty rooms on a moment's notice and offering 18,000 square feet of office space at $6 per foot, a rock-bottom price even for Dallas, which was suffering from a severely depressed economy and had 18 million square feet of vacant office space.

With these facilities arranged, McGee returned to Charlotte and Drew flew on to Houston to check on hotel and office space there. He also sought out Houston public relations consultants Ann Macy and Andi Behlin to help with the other arrangements. He called other contacts in Austin, telling all of them he would reveal the client's identity later.

When Drew returned to Durham a few days later, he began receiving copies of leases and agreements for the hotel rooms, office space, furniture, and telephone equipment in Dallas, Houston, and Austin for him to sign and return. Southwestern Bell had calculated that Drew was considering a $70,000 to $90,000 three-month lease of $700,000 worth of telephone equipment, and the company wanted solid credit references before installing lines.

With his obligations on behalf of NCNB mounting, Drew called McGee to find out how he was supposed to cover these expenses. McGee told him to put them on his VISA card and that he would arrange to increase Drew's modest $5,000 credit limit to $100,000. Before the assignment was over, Drew would sign his name to more than $119,132 in VISA charges, including $1,085.77 in finance charges.

The cover story was beginning to wear thin with some vendors. "With all those telephone lines in three different cities, they thought I was setting up a dial-a-porn operation," Drew recalled with a laugh.

While Drew made arrangements in Dallas, Cooley, McGee, and Martin decided that at the moment of decision NCNB would have to send an NCNB officer to each of the 178 First Republic branches, including an office in Singapore, to reassure both employees and customers and to receive the keys to the property. They figured that two hundred people would be needed for at least a week, with fifty more in reserve.

They organized the team with men and women from offices primarily in the Carolinas and Florida. Senior vice presidents served as team captains. They would all be "warm, friendly, extroverted, sales-oriented" and, just to make sure things ran smoothly at their home offices, some of the best would be left minding the store. The candidates were notified to be ready to leave quickly. McGee planned to assemble this mobile force in Hangar One of the Tampa airport, away from the eyes of the North Carolina reporters, where officers would be briefed and then dispatched to their assignments scattered all over Texas.

These arrangements were expensive and required days to prepare. All the while, NCNB didn't know for sure if its proposal even remained in contention. Most important, top executives had not heard whether a key component of their bid would pass muster at the Internal Revenue Service.

On June 10, good news arrived. NCNB learned that the IRS had ruled in its favor. Without the ruling, the NCNB position was interesting but not compelling. With it, the bid might provide an edge over offers from other candidates. In essence, the IRS ruled that if the FDIC created a bridge bank, the owners would be able to carry forward losses and use them to offset future profits. Hartman had estimated initially that the tax advantage for NCNB would be worth $1 billion to the FDIC.

A few minutes after Hartman heard the news, McColl walked in. McColl decided a celebration was in order and immediately ordered in crystal glasses into which he poured healthy portions from a bottle of Japanese liquor he had bought on his trip. Despite the good news, there was still no word from the FDIC. In fact, the tax ruling served only to heighten McColl's anxiety. Now he began to worry that one of the other bidders would finally catch on and seek a similar ruling.

"Monday, June 18, was my birthday," McColl said later. "I remember what was going on in my head the most was that three years earlier we had lost First Atlanta on the morning of my birthday. I had to read about it in the newspapers that Wachovia had First Atlanta. I remember thinking it had happened again—three years apart."

Those old emotions were welling up in McColl. He and his wife, Jane, took off for the weekend to their Lake Norman retreat, an old fishing cabin converted into a three-bedroom home with a boat house that McColl named Fort Defiance. He sweated through yard work and headed out onto the lake for some sailing on his sixteen-foot Hobie cat. He could lose himself on the boat, and he was away from telephones and interruptions to his concentration.

The day passed without bad news or good news. Negotiations and phone calls resumed as McColl's concern continued to mount.

"I was building courage in them," Hartman later said of the FDIC officials, "convincing them that we did have the best offer, making sure that they understood every aspect of our bid. I was also finding out all we could about other competitive bids and bidders, pointing out the negative aspects in those bids. I was convincing them that we were credible, that we had staying power, and that we would do what we said. Some people had said there was no way NCNB can do this." Part of the problem was that the FDIC staff spends most of its time working with managers of banks that have failed, Hartman said, "so their experience with the banking professionals was with bad ones."

"One week we would be up there discussing the allocation of costs and special-asset planning," Hartman said. "And for one week we would write an accounting manual on how to allocate costs between a good bank and a bad bank. Then somebody would write an analysis saying that NCNB doesn't have a good [valid] tax loss. Next week we would spend that entire time writing explanations of our tax ruling, doing examples of what we thought the carryover basis was, how it could apply, doing models on projecting our income up to 1995, how the tax loss would be offset against those years, compute for the FDIC what their share of the gain would be, what the present value calculation would be."

Another reason for the long delay was the fact that four other bidders were involved, so the FDIC would have to meet with all five sets of bidders at each small turn of events. "Every time they met with us, they had to have a meeting with four other people," Hartman said. "So they were working four times as hard as we were. Each bidder was preparing a massive amount of data and educating the FDIC. We would work three days and meet one, work three days and meet one. The days we weren't meeting with them, they were meeting with somebody else." The sessions even continued into Saturday and often Sunday.

FDIC officials say the process couldn't have been done any faster. "We were always conscious of the fact that the sooner we could get this done the better it would probably be for Texas," Seidman recalled. "Actually, when you look at the size of the institution, the time it took was remarkably short. They [NCNB] had every concern they could think of to try to get the deal done fast, before any other bidders got in there. We are a government agency that was required to have a fair and open process in taking care of institutions that failed in order to give everybody an opportunity and in order to get the best protection for the insurance fund. While we were happy that he [McColl] was here to get a deal done, we couldn't change the basic procedures."

FDIC director Hope said the process was so time-consuming because of the enormity and complexity of the deal, the largest ever done by the FDIC. "We didn't want to do one of these deals where we'd get into it and be in it for eighteen months or two years and then all of a sudden the acquirer is beginning to have financial difficulty," he said. "So you want a strong party to come to the table, and you want a strong management team to come to the table. People who knew what they were doing. We knew we were going to catch flak no matter which way it went. We had to have it all buttoned up, everything taken care of, so that we could stand that flak."

Hope's concern was based on trying to avoid as many legal challenges as possible, while protecting the insurance fund as much as possible.

"We don't make decisions here in the same way that the private sector would make a decision because the private sector doesn't have the same constraints that a government agency has," Hope said. "Hugh McColl can decide anything he wants to decide in that institution on a moment's notice. Now he may get the wrath of the board or some of his fellow officers if he doesn't do it the way it should have been done, but nevertheless he has that authority to do that, whereas we are sitting here having government in the sunshine.

"The chairman would not put to a vote this matter until he felt that everything had been exposed that ought to be exposed, discussed what ought to be discussed. I would not have been able to, and did not, go to Bill Seidman and say, 'What do you think you're going to do?' I mean, that is absolutely illegal, and they put you under the jail for that.

"We didn't all see eye to eye from the first day on how this thing was going to go. I don't think the board could have come together as a board any earlier than it did. It might have if we had met until midnight for the last two or three days. It might have resolved itself one or two days earlier, but it wouldn't have been a month earlier."

The FDIC directors also were aware that the closing of the First Republic banking offices would require a tremendous amount of paperwork and coordination because the process required going before a county judge in each of the counties where the banks were located. The FDIC had never moved on forty banks at one time, and all of the Texas banks had to be failed on one day, a time-consuming and tedious process that involved the coordination of local, state, and federal agencies. Those with Saturday banking hours would have to be reopened the next day under new ownership. To complicate matters further, one of First RepublicBank's offices, the credit card bank in Delaware, couldn't be closed at the same time because a different set of criteria was involved.

During negotiations, the FDIC had made it clear that it wanted the winning bidder's name on the banks immediately. "We told all bidders that, if you are the selected party, we want your name on the door the next day," the FDIC's John Stone remembered. "We think it important that the public know there's a new party in town, a recognized name, to build that confidence back up." When he delivered this news to NCNB, Stone said he realized he might have created an awkward situation. "After I hung up the phone, I realized that I'd just asked a company named North Carolina National Bank to put their name in Texas."

Remarkably, as the negotiations crept into the month of July, four months after McColl and Hartman had first talked to Seidman, NCNB's name had yet to surface as one of the potential bidders. It looked like the deal might go to the wire without disclosure.

The betting at NCNB's headquarters was that the FDIC would make its decision on July 8. NCNB officials were at first certain it would come on the weekend of July 4, since most previous FDIC shutdowns had come on long holiday weekends. Hartman and Tuttle had determined, however, by the FDIC official's demeanor that the FDIC would be unable to act by the Independence Day weekend but undoubtedly would on the following Friday, July 8.

"If there was ever going to be a weekend to bring it down, that was the weekend," McColl said later. "We felt that a decision not to bring it down on that weekend would mean a decision not to give it to NCNB, because our whole deal was based on our tax ruling when you get right down to it and cut through all the rhetoric." McColl believed the ruling should be enough to clinch the deal and any delay gave competitors more time to discover the same tax advantage.

With the FDIC apparently stalled, all Hartman, McColl, and others could do was wait anxiously, hoping a competitor would not discover the same tax advantage and neutralize NCNB's position.

Cooley, Martin, and McGee waited, their plans tucked firmly into bright-red notebooks. Finally, on Wednesday, July 6, anticipating the July 8 decision, McColl put the transition team on alert, believing that the FDIC board was going to announce its decision on Friday. All two hundred persons on the invasion team list were called and told to pack and be prepared for at least a one-week assignment out of town.

The following day, McColl, Hartman, and Kemp, whom McColl had tapped to run the Texas bank, were subjected to a mock news conference, complete with video cameras and telephone links to remote locations. NCNB corporate communications specialists played the role of reporters from Washington, New York, Texas, Florida, and North Carolina. They even wrote mock stories with headlines designed to accentuate tactical errors made by the executives. The executive trio then reviewed the bogus news stories to prepare themselves for the diverse perspectives they would face in an actual news conference.

In the midst of all this, the exposure that NCNB had feared finally occurred. A July 7 article in the *Wall Street Journal* quoted Citicorp chairman John S. Reed as saying that NCNB was a bidder along with Citicorp. NCNB released a terse statement acknowledging its interest but reassuring stockholders that there was no certainty that the bid would be successful and that, if it were, earnings would not be diluted. The company's stock fell 62.5 cents, to $24.25 per share.

It was remarkable that NCNB had been able to stay out of the picture for as long as it did. By summer, some well-placed bankers had heard about the deal, and FDIC director Hope had been asked about NCNB's interest on two occasions during visits to North Carolina, once by Ed Crutchfield, CEO of his former employer, First Union. He deflected the questions, and his inquisitors knew better than to push for an answer.

On Thursday, NCNB executives all across the Southeast left their homes and headed for work with suitcases packed. They waited. Noon passed and there was still no word from Charlotte. At the end of the day, they carried their luggage home at closing time.

The next day, Friday, after a particularly frustrating series of meetings and negotiations, McColl's nerves frayed. McGee was in Dallas with Drew and the Texas associates he had recruited. The NCNB team in Charlotte ordered in supper and waited for news. When the telephone rang, it was FDIC lawyer Ross Delton explaining that a decision would take another thirty days. McColl, waiting in Charlotte, exploded with a fury and declared in vivid language to Delton that NCNB was so frustrated by the prospect of another delay that it was pulling out.

McColl hung up the telephone in disgust. After reviewing his decision with the executive group, he went to the twenty-fourth floor to deliver the news to his corporate communications staffers. NCNB was withdrawing its bid, and he wanted them to know how much he appreciated their efforts. When he arrived, the phone was ringing. It was for McColl. On the line was Hope asking McColl to keep the NCNB bid on the table—"after reviewing the strength of your response," Hope said—an acknowledgment that McColl's response had been reported to the director in full.

McColl hung up and quickly relayed the message to the group gathered around him. Cooley, who had accompanied McColl to the twenty-fourth floor, looked at him excitedly, snapped his fingers with an elaborate flourish, and said, "They blinked."

Indeed, Hope's urging held out some promise. The deal was not off.

NCNB was still a viable candidate, but a decision would take time. McColl was depressed and eager to get away with his family. His lieutenants set in motion calls and notices to cancel the alert. McGee, Drew, and their teams in Texas canceled the hotel rooms and office space that had been reserved for Friday night.

In Washington, FDIC officials continued to wrestle with trying to expedite the process. But even if Seidman had wanted to make an early decision in the case, there were other obstacles to overcome and other regulators to join in on an FDIC decision. In addition, the sheer size of the deal was a complicating factor. Forty individual banks, with branches in sixty-three communities, were involved. The Comptroller of the Currency had never closed more than six banks in one day, and officials didn't know if they could simultaneously close them all. A few were profitable, and profitable banks usually aren't "failed."

Moreover, regulators were cautious and concerned about possible missteps involved in implementing new law. "We had to step our way through some land mines to get to the point where the Comptroller of the Currency finally felt justified in saying all forty of these banks are insolvent," Hope recalled. "The FDIC has no authority to close any bank. We are the insuring agent for the banks, and the only people who can close banks are the same people who charter banks. And the national banks are chartered by the Comptroller of the Currency."

If the air wasn't tense enough around the offices in NCNB's office tower in downtown Charlotte, McColl's hometown newspaper, the *Charlotte Observer*, charged it further on July 18 when it published a front-page story detailing the bank's interest in Texas. "NCNB Takes On Texas-Size Gamble," the headline declared. Business writer Steve Matthews outlined the substantial risks in the reach from North Carolina to Texas, and the article reported what others thought of the gamble. It was not all positive.

"The path is littered with people who have bet on the bottom in Texas," Carlsen Huey, senior vice president of Atlanta-based Citizens & Southern Corp., was quoted as saying. "It's a risky course."

George Salem, banking analyst with Prudential-Bache Securities, said NCNB was "just not large enough to pull off this kind of rescue."

While some observers quoted in the story believed the attempt could bring a gusher of profits for NCNB, other analysts predicted that the acquisition would stretch NCNB's management resources and require two hundred to three hundred people to restructure operations in Texas and add new products.

Other risks were listed in the article. A deal of this size would divert NCNB from the growing, prosperous Southeast. "Top management has only so much time," Citizens & Southern's Huey was quoted as saying. And doing the First Republic deal might mean that NCNB would be so distracted that it would miss out on "a second wave of consolidation" among banks closer to home in Tennessee, Alabama, and Virginia, according to James McDermott, research director of the investment banking firm of Keefe, Bruyette & Woods in New York.

The skeptics were balanced by an optimist. John Mason, a banking analyst with Johnson Lane Space Smith & Co., summed it up by saying, "They have a reasonable shot of hitting a home run."

None of the articles and coverage of the First Republic difficulties did what McColl and others feared most: expose their tax ruling. At one point, however, the Wells Fargo negotiators came close to learning of NCNB's hole card. In late July, Wells Fargo officials asked the FDIC officials if there was any way to structure the deal to capture some of the tax benefits. "But," recalled one FDIC negotiator, "since there was only a week left in the bidding process they knew they couldn't get to the IRS. They asked, 'Will we be disadvantaged if we have a competitor that has been to the IRS with such a structure?' In other words, will you, the FDIC, look at the total cost to government [instead of just to the FDIC]? The board discussed this and [decided] we could not disadvantage NCNB [by divulging the tax deal to other bidders]."

FDIC officials said they were under no obligation to explain NCNB's tax ruling. It was considered proprietary information, just like any other component of a bidder's proposal. Had any of the other bidders learned of the deal late in the game, officials doubt they would have had time to restructure their bids to take it into account.

NCNB's strategy all along had been to stay out of Texas and avoid the attention that was focusing on the major bidders. Now that the news was out, McColl sent a team headed by Kemp to Texas, mainly for appearances. Kemp, an engaging and personable NCNB veteran, and his colleagues on the "due diligence" team surprised the First Republic officers with whom they met. Other bidders had approached their task with the stern, no-nonsense demeanor of loan administrators dealing with a defaulting creditor. Instead of cross-examining First Republic officers whose business had come to a standstill because of the bank's financial condition, however, Kemp asked those he met with to tell him about what NCNB could do to help them accomplish their goals for moving the bank forward. NCNB already knew the numbers on the deal; Kemp was preparing to get First Republic back into the banking business with its management intact.

As the waiting stretched into late July, the NCNB strategists settled on Friday, July 29, as the next most likely date for closure. As before, the two hundred bank officers were alerted and told to stand by. This time the staging site was changed to NCNB headquarters in Charlotte so the entire team could be briefed. They would then leave the building in small groups. In Dallas, landlords of optional office space were alerted.

On Thursday, July 28, McColl had not heard anything. Meanwhile, NCNB had learned that the FDIC was not going to require the successful bidder to staff all 178 branches immediately, only the 41 existing First Republic main bank offices. But Kemp decided to send an NCNB officer to each facility anyway, as a show of support and reassurance to First Republic employees and their customers.

Still with nothing certain from the FDIC, Cooley instructed the NCNB team to gather in the briefing room on the twelfth floor of NCNB's Charlotte headquarters on Thursday afternoon. There, each of the 217 officers received a 146-page loose-leaf notebook bound with a bright NCNB-red cover. Each was asked to sign a confidentiality pledge on the first page. In the front pocket of each book was an airline ticket and a hotel reservation. This was the first indication to any in the group as to their destination and the assignment. Inside the notebook were five sections, outlining details of the deal with the FDIC, what to say to First Republic employees and customers, background on First Republic, a brief description of Texas and the assigned community, and background on other banks in the state. In the back pocket of the notebook were a four-page brochure on NCNB, biographical sketches of top NCNB executives, and name tags with the NCNB logo and the words "NCNB Texas National Bank."

At 3:00 P.M., the team members were briefed for an hour and forty-five minutes by McColl, Kemp, and Cooley and then loaded on buses at

NCNB chairman Hugh McColl, behind a lectern decorated with the horns of a longhorn steer, briefs the 217 members of the bank's transition team in Charlotte as they prepare to board planes for Texas on July 28, 1988, before anyone knew if NCNB would win the bid to take over First RepublicBank of Texas.

Charlotte's busiest intersection, Trade and Tryon, and taken to the airport. The entire operation attracted no media attention, although reporters had been inquiring for days about the First Republic speculation.

After the briefing, McColl, McGee, Martin, Cooley, and Kemp boarded a new Cessna Citation III jet that McGee had lined up as a demonstrator from Cessna and headed to Dallas. On the flight, McColl lost 59 cents to Cooley in a gin game and considered it a bad omen. The five arrived about 7:50 P.M. at the command center that Drew had established in room 2207 in the Sheraton. McGee taped up four sheets of newsprint listing the names of the 217 team members, with space for the status of each one. As team members reached their destinations and called in, each was checked off. These sheets, a vivid demonstration of the efficiency of the operation, would later be encased like trophies behind glass in the foyer of the twelfth-floor conference room at Charlotte headquarters.

McColl decided it was too quiet that Thursday night, so he called his friend Jerry Finger at Charter Bank in Houston, just to chat about a deep-sea fishing trip they had taken earlier in Guatemala.

One by one, the transition team members reported in from Mineral Wells and Midland, Lubbock and Lufkin, Corsicana and Conroe. The phones stopped ringing at 2:30 A.M., but not all team members were in position. Some had to drive long distances across the Texas plains after a night's layover in order to reach their assigned city or town.

Friday brought more time to kill. The FDIC announcement was not expected until near the close of business in Dallas, probably right at 5:00 P.M. Kemp went off to find an Oriental rug shop. Ken Lewis, another NCNB executive who would be assigned as president of the new bank, and Hugh McColl took a drive. They wound up in the expensive Dallas suburb of Highland Park, looking at houses that Lewis might buy when he moved to Dallas.

"Hugh kept telling me what great deals you could get on houses in Dallas," Lewis recalled later. "We came across one for sale, a mansion with beautiful grounds, tennis courts, and a pool. Hugh says, 'Lewis, you are going to love this place. You can get that house for $600,000.' I said I couldn't afford the little house out back, much less the thing in front, but he insisted, so I said, 'I'm calling you on this one.'

"I called the number on the sign, and a woman says, 'Yes, I know the property, and it's been on the market for some time. We have had to dramatically reduce it.' I thought, 'Hugh is right again.' Then she says, 'We have reduced that house from $5 million to $3.6 million.'"

NCNB officers all over Texas scouted their assigned branches, trying to look inconspicuous. By mid-afternoon, they were waiting by telephones at their outposts across the state.

At the Sheraton in Dallas, McGee, Drew, and others were still trying to find out whether the FDIC was going to act that afternoon. McGee walked to the FDIC's Dallas headquarters to try to wangle some information out of Mike Newton, the officer in charge. Although it was only 11:30 A.M., McGee was told Newton was at lunch, as was his chief assistant. *Hmm*, McGee thought, *today might be the day.*

Drew discovered an FDIC official's card left behind in a car that he had rented. He guessed that the man might be staying at the Dallas Sheraton, so he called and asked for him by name. The man had already checked out, Drew was told. Drew asked what company the man had been with, and the clerk told him the International Investment Corp. "We knew right away that something definitely was up by now, because the FDIC wouldn't have been acting that way."

NCNB security chief John Williams, McColl's and Kemp's assistants Pat Hinson and Brenda Meredith, and others were staffing the phones as questions and observations flowed in from transition team members all over the state. At 2:50 P.M., the last slot on the list was filled as Jim Gehling, a Greensboro-based officer, called in from Victoria, 350 miles from Dallas. He called back five minutes later to say he had just gotten a call from an FDIC man who wanted to verify that he was with NCNB and was in place in Victoria. The Dallas team was encouraged at this report.

By 4:00 P.M., McColl's team was back at the hotel. At 6:10, the phone rang in McColl's suite. It was Hope. "Hugh, I've got some good news and some other news," Hope said. "Bill Seidman wants to talk to you."

Seidman came on the line and said, "We've decided to go with you."

Seidman said the FDIC was going to have a press conference in Washington and NCNB needed to have a man there. McColl told him Hartman was standing by and would represent NCNB. Seidman told McColl of rumors that some members of the local boards of directors of First Republic were threatening court action to stop the deal. He suggested that McColl get his people to act immediately to calm the directors down and stop their threatened action.

"Mr. Chairman," McColl replied, "we'll handle it."

Chapter 16 **Who Is He?**

After getting the word from Seidman that NCNB was the successful bidder for First Republic, McColl started making arrangements. He relayed the news to his lieutenants, who set their plans in motion. Then he called the FDIC's director of supervision, Bill Roelle, who said he would be waiting for McColl at First Republic headquarters, two blocks away. Together the two would take control of the bank.

Twenty minutes later, McColl had slipped on a clean shirt, knotted his tie, and was on his way. Roelle had said they would meet at the bank's main entrance and enter together. When McColl reached the street, the heat from pavement baked by a hundred-degree Dallas day hit him in the face. Friday afternoon had drained downtown of pedestrians, and the streets were empty. McColl felt a comic sense of being in a

Grade B movie in which two spies in blue suits meet each other for an exchange.

Roelle had warned McColl that there would be television cameras and reporters at the front doors to the First Republic office towers and had asked that McColl walk on in without speaking to reporters. McColl responded that no one would recognize him anyway. He hadn't set foot in Dallas since NCNB had become a bidder.

McColl and Roelle made their way to the bank's plush wood-paneled and carpeted third-floor executive level, where they found people standing together at the end of a long hall. A tall, white-haired man, wearing large, thick glasses in round frames, was the focus of a group of about twenty bank officers gathered at the doorway of one of the executive offices. It was First Republic's chairman, Al Casey. As they approached, Casey turned to greet Roelle.

"Who is he?" he asked, pointing to McColl, not recognizing the man who had come to pick up the keys to his bank.

Roelle and McColl had arrived just as Casey was telling his management team that he had, for the first time in his life, failed and that he regretted disappointing them in their effort to assume ownership of the bank. They had fought a valiant battle together, he said, and more than a few now had tears in their eyes. McColl was taken aback by the drama of the scene. As he was introduced by Roelle, he greeted each executive gently but earnestly, then disappeared into the office with Casey. When the two emerged, McColl found that the entire executive group had waited to congratulate him and offer a welcome to Texas.

One of the executives standing with Casey was someone who knew McColl well. Joe Bowles was a former corporate communications officer for NCNB who had left Charlotte in 1976 to join Barnett Banks in Florida, later moving on to Dallas with InterFirst in 1981. He had stayed with the business after the merger with Republic Bank less than a year earlier. Immediately, Bowles began to feel as if his prospects were about to improve.

"We had all just given Casey an ovation," Bowles recalled. "There wasn't a dry eye in the group. I looked over my shoulder and saw Hugh coming down the hall with the FDIC guy. Although I've got tears in my eyes for Casey, whom I truly respected, I had to stifle a giggle. I was very, very happy to see Hugh coming because I knew NCNB was one hell of a company."

Casey and the management group had been a leading competitor in the bidding process. The sixty-eight-year-old former chairman and CEO of American Airlines and Colgate-Palmolive Co. had been teaching business at Southern Methodist University since 1986 when he stepped down as U.S. postmaster general. His tenure at First Republic had been brief, but Casey had helped rebuild morale and he believed that management's plan had a chance as the decision went down to the wire, with Comptroller of the Currency Robert Clarke holding out for a Texas-based rescue.

Casey had maintained that his group's position was the best until the end, arguing his case even as FDIC officials told him NCNB had been chosen. Bowles recalled Casey was "so upset he was using anything he could to try to talk them out of it, including telling them that they had just lost Texas for George Bush in the election."

Casey had managed the company through its most trying time and had never lost his sense of humor. It didn't fail him at the end. When the Federal Reserve Bank of Dallas representative asked for repayment of the $1.5 billion in government loans, a formality necessary for the FDIC to take control, Casey quipped, "Well, if you had asked for a billion, I could handle it, but I can't do a billion and a half."

In McColl's brief hallway meeting with the bank's senior executive officers, he assured them that he wanted them to continue with the bank. While he was there, he got a call from the popular Texas businessman H. Ross Perot, who told McColl he was pleased at the outcome. During the FDIC's consideration of bids, Perot had phoned Seidman to lend his support to NCNB's bid. McColl asked Perot to join him at the Sheraton, partly to discuss how to head off the possibility of revolt by local directors that Seidman had reported. Meanwhile, Hootie Johnson, chairman of the NCNB executive committee, had telephoned Reece Overcash, a former Charlottean who headed a large Dallas financial company called Associates Corporation of North America, and invited him to join the NCNB executives at the hotel.

While McColl was meeting with First Republic executives for the first time, FDIC officials at their Washington headquarters were facing reporters at a hastily called news conference. The first question came from Mike Cozza, a Washington-based reporter for WBTV of Charlotte. He asked how the FDIC could choose NCNB when it was much smaller than Citicorp and Wells Fargo. Director Hope took the question, telling

Cozza that a certain size was not a requirement in the bidding process, but strength of management and innovation were. "These people were really ready to move and had their game plan in order," Hope said. "They knew what they were doing."

Seidman and Clarke stressed the point that no depositor at First Republic would lose a dime, and the chairman told reporters, "This is not a bailout." He asked them to reexamine their use of the phrase that had grown so unpopular at the FDIC and that had generated searing criticism of the FDIC. He said Texans should be pleased that NCNB was eager to take over the business and get it running again after months of uncertainty.

The complete details of the deal would not become clear for several days, but Seidman got to the nut of the decision when he told reporters that NCNB had bested the biggest banks in the country because its proposal would cost the FDIC $1 billion less than those of other bidders, primarily because of the tax ruling, and because of the aggressive way NCNB had pursued the deal, convincing the FDIC that it would be a worthy and capable partner.

NCNB had ninety days in which to decide whether to accept the deal or to conclude its arrangement for temporary management of the bank's operations with the FDIC.

Immediately after the decision was announced in Washington, Dallas reporters began pressing NCNB executives for details. Television crews and reporters were jammed into the Sheraton lobby, ready to pounce whenever anyone arrived from the upstairs floors. Deadlines were approaching, and reporters were hungry for new information for the evening broadcasts and the morning editions.

Martin and McColl were both anxious about how to handle the meeting with Perot, who was on his way downtown. McColl and Perot had met only once before, in a brief encounter over dinner earlier in the year at a banquet in Charlotte. The two had talked by telephone in June, when McColl called Perot to tell him about the bank's bid for First Republic. Perot told McColl he was delighted, saying that he believed it would be a successful venture. McColl also asked Perot if he would be willing to buy and run the operations company of First Republic and if he would be interested in serving on the NCNB Texas board. He said he normally didn't serve on boards of directors but might make an exception in this case. Perot was sufficiently interested in the deal to call Seidman and let him know NCNB could count on him as a partner in Texas.

Perot was an important Texas ally. The pugnacious billionaire had burst onto the American scene in September 1968 when stock in the company he had founded in Dallas, Electronic Data Systems Corporation, was offered to the public for sale for the first time. His 81 percent stake was immediately worth $154 million. Six years earlier, he had left his job as a salesman for IBM and started EDS with $1,000 of his own money. In 1970, when he was only forty, his stake was worth $1.4 billion. In 1986, Perot sold his share to General Motors and in 1988 started another company, Perot Systems.

His reputation for success was enhanced further when it was learned he had succeeded in rescuing EDS employees hiding in Iran while the U.S. military had failed to retrieve hostages held at the American embassy in Tehran. Perot's exploits were popularized by Ken Follett's book, *On Wings of Eagles*.

Perot eluded reporters when he arrived at the hotel and slipped upstairs to McColl's suite. He talked with McColl and Overcash before the three headed downstairs to the waiting knot of cameras and questioners. When they stepped off the elevator, they were met with bright lights and microphones. Perot called NCNB the hero of the moment for having enough faith in the Texas economy to buy the bank. Overcash also delivered a solid endorsement. The comments perfectly complemented NCNB's strategy to reassure employees, investors, and depositors, and to immediately establish connections with familiar Texas names.

After seeing his guests off, McColl returned to the upstairs command center to accept the accolades of his coworkers and to congratulate them on their hard work. He also called former NCNB chairman Tom Storrs and Vice Chairman Jim Thompson, but, he confessed later, "I forgot to call my wife."

The evening was just beginning. NCNB really wasn't in business in Texas until the FDIC was assured that all branches in the First Republic system had been officially failed. That wouldn't be accomplished until after midnight.

Finally, at 1:30 A.M., after word from federal banking officials, McColl called the first meeting of the board of Texas's newest bank. Buddy Kemp was named chairman, and the first board members were McColl,

Hartman, Hootie Johnson, and veteran banker W. J. Smith. A short while later, when McColl learned that Hartman and Baldwin Tuttle, the bank's Washington attorney, would be arriving at Dallas's Love Field at 3:00 A.M., he got a driver, a car, and two bottles of champagne and rode to the airport to meet them when they stepped off the plane.

By this time, McColl had changed into a pair of khaki pants, deck shoes with no socks, and a "Don't Mess with Texas" T-shirt given to him by John Hill, an MBA graduate student from Chapel Hill who was working for him that summer. Back at the hotel, the celebration was in full swing.

McColl was still going strong at 5:15 A.M. when his associates convinced him that he should get some sleep. Saturday was going to be a busy day. He headed to bed, but told Hill to rouse him by 6:00. At 5:45 A.M. there was a knock on the door, and a waiter rolled in a cart with steak, eggs, orange juice, and the rest of a mammoth breakfast.

The morning press was excellent. Under a banner headline reporting NCNB's selection was a large color photo of McColl flanked by his Texas friends, Overcash and Perot. "Tomorrow," the story quoted Perot as saying, "we start rebuilding Texas."

After a 7:00 A.M. meeting, McColl, Kemp, and Hartman went to look over NCNB's new property. They found style and opulence beyond anything they or their predecessors had ever built. On the executive level in the fifty-story headquarters tower, they found expensive oil paintings, including a Gainsborough, hung in the spacious offices of the top executives. The chairman's quarters were large enough to accommodate a couple of dozen visitors. In addition to this office tower, decorated with the First Republic symbol, huge, four-pointed stars in shiny aluminum, there was an adjacent thirty-five-story building, which with its 150-foot spire was the tallest building west of the Mississippi when it was built in 1954.

That wasn't all. InterFirst had a fifty-story tower, built in 1965, and had occupied an adjacent fifty-six-story building in 1974. Then, in 1984, InterFirst became the lead tenant in a new seventy-two-story headquarters tower that dominated the Dallas skyline. Outlined in green argon lights, the building was known by some as "the green pickle."

McColl, Kemp, and Hartman spent the morning in meetings with top executives before their formal introduction to the full First Republic officer corps at a special midday conference called by Casey. At noon, the three listened from the back of an auditorium in the First Republic building as Casey delivered his farewell. Standing on a low stage at the front of the gently sloping rows of seats, Casey concluded his remarks by saying, "Texas is going to do well. And who in here can tell me the three reasons why Texas is going to go up?" he asked, his voice breaking slightly. The group of several hundred bankers responded in unison: "Land, water, and people." Casey paused and then said, "You have a good friend and one who enjoys you and who wants to stay in touch."

The bankers, some dressed in suits and others in sports clothes, gave Casey a standing ovation as McColl walked briskly forward, his suit coat flapping behind him. Casey met McColl at the front. "Good luck," Casey said, "and good-bye."

As a parting shot before leaving the hall, Casey warned his former subordinates, "Get your résumés up to date."

Casey's remark angered McColl. The last thing NCNB needed now was a walkout of First Republic officers. "It was a real downer for him to do that to us," McColl said later.

McColl quickly tried to boost the spirits of the First Republic officers seated in the auditorium. He wanted to relieve fears that the new owners were going to clean house or make massive changes, a reputation that lingered from Florida. "We are excited to be in Texas, and we're glad to be here. We understand it is a difficult time. What we need is you and your other teammates. What you see here, plus a couple of others in the back, is what we've got here," McColl said. It was vintage McColl. No script, no notes, spontaneous, upbeat, with sufficient self-deprecating humor to put his audience at ease.

Now was the time for NCNB Texas National to get moving, to charge with all guns blazing, he said. Referring to news articles and magazines that had made much of his Marine Corps background, McColl said his military training had taught him that "when all else fails, attack. You know the Marine Corps has simple solutions because the truth is that most Marines are not real bright. They taught us there are three ways to take a hill—frontal assault, frontal assault, frontal assault."

At one point he referred to accounts that portrayed NCNB as aggressive, even hostile. "That's true. I don't like my competitors," he told the group. "I don't eat with them, don't do anything with them except try to waste them. To me it's a zero-sum game. When I lose business, it's like taking bread off my children's table."

At first, McColl's audience was cautious. Seated together before the NCNB executives, who were entirely new to Texas, were the remaining members of two former competitors—one group from the conservative Republic Bank and one from the high-flying InterFirst. Loyalties to the former institutions remained strong; the merger had only begun. At the Greenwood, Texas, branch the new First Republic sign had just been installed.

One by one, questions from the floor broke the tension. First one person, then another raised a hand to be recognized by McColl or Kemp, who roamed the stage responding to the concerns. Hartman sat close by to provide answers about finances of the new bank. The questions covered the entire operation—personnel policies, loan policies, branching, the new idea of one bank instead of a coalition of many, and, of course, job security. Kemp assured the group that there was no army of NCNB employees waiting at the border for the signal to invade. Most of the 250 NCNB people who had come in for the transition would be gone by Tuesday, he told a square-jawed young bank officer in a polo shirt, who had posed the question in a deep Texas drawl.

Kemp, sensitive to the problems that NCNB had encountered in exporting its operations to other markets and other cultures, said, "What we do in North Carolina doesn't make sense in Florida. We're going to run our own bank here in Texas, and Hugh is going to fuss at us if we don't."

What about the legal lending limit on Monday, someone else inquired? "Whatever you want it to be," McColl shot back. "NCNB's limit is $280 million on top of what you had on Friday."

What role was the FDIC going to play? The FDIC had turned the bank over to the new board, Kemp explained. NCNB Texas National Bank was the cleanest bank in the country, under the new arrangement devised to dispose of nonperforming loans.

Would credit policies change? "We plan to keep things the same way until you want to change them," Kemp answered. "Our plan is to start going out into the marketplace. We turned the bank around at one o'clock last night. You won't find anybody who likes to do business any more than I do."

McColl was nervous at first, but as the session was concluding, he relaxed and rocked back in a chair while Kemp took questions standing in front of a large NCNB Texas National Bank logo projected onto a screen behind them. As the questions lagged, McColl ended the session, reminding the officers that he wanted new vigor and a competitive spirit in the bank come Monday morning. "I want you to come out attacking. That's what I want. Walking tall."

A 2:00 P.M. news conference at the Sheraton followed immediately. For seventy minutes at the Saturday press conference, with reporters from the major networks and newspapers from all over the world, McColl and his colleagues deftly answered questions, despite the drain of the long night and the revelry. Kemp told reporters: "The bank customers and bank employees of Texas deserved better cards than the ones they were dealt by a series of economic events. We want to participate in the recovery we believe is already happening. We start with a very clean slate. We're not looking back."

"We were dead-flat perfect," McColl remembered. "Sometimes you get it right. We had it right that day. We had the adrenaline level right. We had had a mock press conference that turned out to be tougher than the real one, so we were ready. All along the wall were our people, so that everywhere I looked I was looking at NCNB officers. My college fraternity brother, Paxson Glenn, lives in Dallas, and he had come to the press conference. He was giving me all this encouragement. We were really riding high."

McColl, Kemp, and Hartman all reassured the media that NCNB planned no layoffs or drastic changes in banking practices and that the acquisition was a healthy sign for the Texas economy. "The biggest change is there's going to be money available at NCNB Texas National Bank," McColl said. "The first thing [Texans] are going to notice is we're back on offense. People who are quite capable bankers are going to be out there lending money again."

Perot also joined McColl at the press conference, where he pledged his support to the bank's new owners. "First thing Monday morning," he said, "I'll be putting my money in Texas National Bank." NCNB chairman Hugh McColl immediately quipped, "And we'll be expanding the vault."

McColl hadn't been sure what Perot would tell reporters. But the endorsement of NCNB Texas National Bank was just what McColl had hoped for. Perot personified the Texas spirit, and his endorsement of these North Carolinians, who now owned what was left of one of the oldest banks in Texas, played well across the state.

Buddy Kemp, president of NCNB Corp. (left), was named chairman of NCNB Texas, and Tim Hartman was named vice chairman following NCNB's takeover of First Republic.

"We're going to turn a corner Monday morning," Perot said. "Those small and medium-sized businesses that are starved for financial lubrication are going to get it."

Perot explained that First Republic had called him for help earlier in the year and he had said then that his first choice for someone to run the bank was Hugh McColl. He never called McColl because he didn't think he could persuade him to leave NCNB, but he was ready when McColl called him on June 6 and asked him to contact Seidman and endorse NCNB's bid. Perot said he not only endorsed NCNB but offered to underwrite the bank's entire cost if necessary. He wasn't speaking solely out of friendship, Perot insisted, but because he liked NCNB and the way it did business, "grinding it out the hard way by making thousands of loans to medium-sized businesses."

After the press conference, McColl and his team spent the rest of the day in individual media interviews and conferring on personnel deci-

NCNB's Texas team logistics chief, Bill McGee (left), and personnel head, Chuck Cooley, at a party in Dallas on July 29, 1988, to celebrate the announcement that NCNB had been named the successful bidder for First Republic.

Hugh McColl addresses the troops on a bus ride to the party marking the success of NCNB's bid to enter Texas.

sions and dozens of other pressing matters. Then it was time to continue the celebration. About a hundred NCNB employees went to the Cadillac Bar & Grill in Dallas. Before the evening was over, McColl and Kemp were standing on tables with flaming tequila drinks in their hands. Another contingent ended up at the Palm Restaurant, where they enjoyed six bottles of champagne sent by diners at other tables who were welcoming them to Texas.

Only an hour or two before dawn Sunday, as the evening's party wound down, McColl pulled Bob Kirby aside and asked him if he would take Ken Lewis's place as head of the Florida banking operations when Lewis moved to NCNB Texas. Kirby had less than two minutes to make a decision, about the same amount of time he had had when McColl named him to head the NCNB trust operations in 1983. Kirby, the one-time personnel officer who thirty years earlier had told McColl there wasn't room in the American Commercial trainee class, accepted on the spot. Both rejoined the party, where McColl announced the appointment and said, "It ain't bad that I'm giving you a bank larger than the bank Storrs gave me and you were the one who turned me down for a damn job."

McColl awoke Sunday to a favorable editorial in the *Dallas Morning News*, the state's largest daily. Noting that the takeover by an out-of-state corporation was a blow to Texas pride, the lead editorial said, however, "There are plenty of things to be glad about the winning 'rescue team.' The NCNB takeover offers the potential of a new beginning, not just for the beleaguered bank, but for Dallas. The NCNB commitment is a major vote of confidence in this city and this area. From the adversity of the last few years, a more diverse, stronger economy is arising. In order for Texas to pick up its pieces and move on to a better tomorrow, the state's financial institutions had to be righted. So, welcome to town, NCNB Texas National Bank. Let's get to work."

Even rival Houston-based First City Bancorp thought the move was good. "We are delighted that the situation at First RepublicBank has been resolved. It will be good for the state, and will help fuel the recovery that is already well under way," First City's chairman, A. Robert Abboud of Chicago (another out-of-state owner), said through a spokesman.

Beyond Dallas, away from the euphoria and bright lights of television cameras, hundreds of NCNB executives were experiencing the moment from a more personal point of view. The executives who had picked up the keys to First Republic offices across the state had been carefully chosen for this assignment. NCNB depended on their tact and confidence to overcome the fears of First Republic employees who were uncertain about the future. They also were expected to handle the resentment among the fiercely proud Texans whose bank was now owned by outsiders.

"So Then, What Does NCNB Stand For?" was the headline in an Abilene newspaper that greeted NCNB's scout there. Elsewhere, NCNB people found confusion and disappointment over the relative obscurity of NCNB. Susan McDonald of Charlotte found that employees in Beaumont had been betting on one of the big-name bidders, Wells Fargo or Citicorp. "Many branch employees had never heard of NCNB and were pulling for a merger with a bank with some name recognition for [job] security purposes."

In Brownwood, Bob Buckner from Wilson, North Carolina, spent most of Saturday talking with the local branch officers, only to be confronted by the local board of directors, who gathered for dinner at the Brownwood Country Club. Resentment against the FDIC and its action with an out-of-state bank was heaped on Buckner until finally one local board member turned to another who had been complaining the loudest and said, "Damn it, Jack, NCNB didn't ride into town on a mule. These folks wear shoes and obviously know how to run banks."

The strategy of covering every bank in person went far beyond what the other bidders had proposed. Wells Fargo had planned to send a mailgram to executives of each bank. The mailgram was to have said that effective Monday, August 1, Wells Fargo would be managing First Republic. It included a letter from Carl Reichardt, who would have been named chairman and chief executive officer of Wells Fargo Bank Texas, and asked bank executives to make copies of the letter and distribute one to each employee. "If the FDIC's 'closed' sign was posted at your bank, please replace it with the temporary Wells Fargo Bank sign enclosed."

In addition to the personal visits, NCNB already had $500,000 in new signs on order. Brad Iversen, NCNB's new marketing specialist, had arranged with First Republic public relations chief Joe Bowles to replace First Republic's newspaper advertising space with NCNB Texas National ads for the Sunday papers.

Mostly good news flowed back to the Dallas command center as people reported in. Laura Taft Kane and Tom Anderson said they received the keys to the bank from the FDIC representative on-site and then immediately turned them over to the two senior officers from First Republic who had been there when the bank was closed. In Carrollton, Wade Sample of Asheville, North Carolina, was told by employees that they were pleased to be part of a banking organization from the South, because they thought they would fit in better than with one based in New York or California.

All was not rosy, however. Danny Dowell of Hendersonville, North Carolina, found that the Lubbock branch had been drained of approximately $150 million in deposits in the last eighteen months. The loan portfolio had shrunk, in part because of the bank's problems and in part because the bank had lost its chief executive two years previously. He had taken much of the business with him when he joined a group of investors and purchased another bank in town. Fourteen of the bank's management team had followed him.

"From our standpoint, timing could not have been worse," Dowell wrote in his after-action report. "From [the ex-executive's] side, timing could not have been better. He has been in a position for eighteen months to hire whom he wanted, pick the customers he wanted and certainly grow his new bank. An aggressive calling effort is needed immediately to stop the 'bleeding.' "

David Darnell, a commercial lending officer from Greensboro, North Carolina, encountered a similar situation in Austin. During the previous week, the Austin bank's senior lender had resigned to become the new president of Texas American Bank–Austin.

As NCNB employees in Texas began sorting out the pieces Sunday, McColl and Hartman left Dallas on an afternoon flight for New York, where the following morning they were to meet with 113 banking analysts, investment portfolio managers, and large shareholders. As McColl had awaited word from the FDIC on Friday, Rusty Page, NCNB's senior vice president in charge of investor relations, had been on the telephone to securities analysts in New York alerting them of a possible press conference Monday morning. "I had to make these calls Friday afternoon because I could not reach these people over the weekend," Page said. "I'm telling them we may have an analysts' meeting on Monday morning. 'What's it about?' I can't tell you, but it'll be at 7:30 A.M. at the

Intercontinental Hotel if we have it. 'How will I know?' You'll read about it over the weekend."

When they arrived in New York, McColl and Hartman remained as invigorated as ever. McColl met his son and daughter for dinner and then walked forty blocks back to his hotel. "I didn't sleep a wink," he said.

Monday morning, with microphones carrying their words from Japan to Europe, McColl and Hartman met their toughest audience to outline details of the deal. "The structure of this investment provides NCNB with the opportunity to manage approximately $20 billion in acceptable assets for an initial investment of $210 million," McColl said in his presentation. "This unusually high level of leverage is supported by the strength and the viability of our 80 percent co-owner, the FDIC. The transaction provides NCNB with the opportunity to test the viability of the Texas market for a five-year period before any additional investment is required."

McColl told the group that the deal would allow NCNB to immediately exceed its corporate objective of five-year compounded growth in earnings per share of at least 10 percent, with long-term results well in excess of the objective. The contribution to earnings generated by the Texas bank was expected to add 3 cents to the $2.83 a share in 1988 and 9 cents a share, to $3.17, in 1989, Hartman said, adding that the deal could contribute 38.5 percent to the company's earnings by 1994.

"Viewed another way," McColl told the analysts, "imagine for a moment if NCNB had been able to buy our Florida and South Carolina banks at a nominal premium, which would minimize goodwill amortization, and had a two-year put [option to refuse] of questionable loans. Our returns today would be even more impressive than they have been. This is the opportunity presented to us with this investment: the price is right, we have walled off the credit risk, and the rewards are substantial."

The new bank was insulated from all existing legal and contractual liabilities related to the old banking company. Hartman told the analysts that he expected the pool of questionable assets to total at most $5 billion out of the new bank's total fair market value of $25 billion.

As further incentive, the FDIC agreed to share with the new bank a portion of the gains resulting from the liquidation of assets associated with bad loans. NCNB's share of these gains was targeted at 5 percent, but performance criteria could vary this base to a range of 3 percent to 8 percent—after adjustment for its ownership percentage. "What this does, of course, is ensure that NCNB has the opportunity to acquire controlling ownership of a 'healthy' Texas bank," Hartman said, noting that the analysts probably thought "healthy" and "Texas bank" were contradictory terms.

McColl told the analysts that for the past two and a half years NCNB had been concentrating on fine-tuning its acquisitions in Florida and was now ready to move into another new geographic region. "Given today's highly competitive and deregulated financial services environment, banks cannot afford the luxury of shifting into a no-growth or harvest mode," he said. "Future earnings growth will be achieved only by superior management, careful planning, and bold execution. Gone are the days of simply riding the coattails of a favorable economic climate."

NCNB chose Texas for expansion because of its population of nearly 17 million and bank deposits totaling $150 billion, but the success of the First Republic acquisition was not contingent upon an upturn in the Texas economy, McColl said. "With the burden of today's bad loans removed, we are highly confident that we can manage a healthy Texas bank even through a period of slow economic growth, if indeed this occurs," he told the analysts.

The reaction from analysts and the market was immediately positive. Before the market closed Monday NCNB stock had climbed $1.625 per share, closing at $25, with 923,400 shares changing hands.

"NCNB got a great deal," banking analyst Thomas Brown with Smith Barney in New York told the *Charlotte Observer*. "Unlike most acquisitions, this will add to earnings per share right away. And it will significantly add to earnings in later years. Some people will say, 'What's a North Carolina bank doing buying a bank in Texas?' We wouldn't ask that question of a retailer. It doesn't necessarily follow that their expansion should be in contiguous states. They should go for profit opportunities."

Goldman, Sachs & Co. gushed, "This marks a new era, in our judgment, for regional expansion. Among the largest regionals, NCNB is arguably at the forefront of true, broad national expansion with its Texas move." The deal removed NCNB from its Southeastern peer group into one of its own making, the investment banking company said, terming the move "a well-structured, long-term Texas play—with a strong Southeastern franchise."

First Boston, Fox-Pitt Kelton, Oppenheimer & Co., and Salomon Brothers were nearly as admiring. Salomon Brothers called it "the right bank, the right people, the right deal" and said it "will go down in the annals of bank history as one of the finest transactions ever consummated."

PaineWebber was less enthusiastic, saying, "NCNB has struck a good deal, but we think that the euphoria is too much, too soon." And the brokerage house said: "Concern remains regarding NCNB's ability to turn First RepublicBank around without impairing NCNB's momentum. We also expect the Texas market to be extremely competitive over the foreseeable future, creating margin pressure as recapitalized banks vie for market share in a still-sluggish Texas operating environment."

Dean Witter had similar reservations, saying that moving Kemp, Hartman, Lewis, and other key executives to Texas "stretches credulity to think that Charlotte operations will not be disrupted as a result. This occurrence should enable NCNB's major competitor—First Union—to make some good inroads into its market share."

During the following week, the details of the NCNB bid and the competing forces began to become clear. Hartman later credited Seidman for building the case among the FDIC staff for trying a new approach. "I contend that had you had a long-tenured government employee at the helm, this would have never gotten done. He was a unique man who arrived at the right point at the right place in Washington and demonstrated the right amount of courage and withstood the criticism."

In Washington, critics arose quickly. The House Banking Committee, chaired by U.S. Representative Henry Gonzalez, a Texas Democrat, convened hearings immediately and called Seidman to explain what had happened in Gonzalez's home state. Seidman told the committee on August 3 that he was satisfied that the FDIC had achieved success in its mission to preserve confidence in the nation's banking system: "In the late afternoon of July 29, the FDIC Board of Directors concluded that NCNB Corporation's plan represented the most effective, most viable and least costly approach for preserving existing banking services in the affected communities and promoting stability in the Texas banking system."

U.S. Representative Toby Roth, a Republican from Wisconsin, was not impressed. He criticized the venture as a "sweetheart deal born in a crisis." NCNB "doubles its size for a mere $200 million investment," he said.

Committee member Fernand St. Germain said, "That's a pretty good deal. You put up $200 million and get $3 billion in tax breaks."

At the hearing, a Dillon, Read & Co. tax specialist hired by the FDIC said the net tax benefit to NCNB would be $2.1 billion and the actual savings over a period of years would be about $700 million.

Seidman told the committee that the NCNB bid was $800 million less costly than any other bid and met other criteria of good management and good business for Texas.

After the hearings, Seidman elaborated on the FDIC's reasons for choosing NCNB. He said the bid was unique among all bids ever received in the history of the FDIC. "They had done a lot of homework and had gotten the tax ruling, which was very favorable," Seidman said. "We had nothing to do with [the tax ruling], and it made their bid very unusual."

Seidman was delighted with the fact that NCNB had received the tax ruling from the IRS in advance of the purchase, since—in every other case—the tax advantages weren't made clear until long after the purchase of a failed bank.

The FDIC did not reveal the details of the individual proposals. Neither did the losing bidders. But the *Wall Street Journal* reported that Citicorp was understood to have asked the FDIC to inject about $1 billion to erase First Republic's negative equity and then Citicorp would raise additional funds to recapitalize the bank with about $20 billion in assets.

While there were many other factors favoring NCNB's bid, the offers from the Wells Fargo and First Republic management also came closer than it appeared publicly. Citicorp had dropped out of the bidding in the final week, never giving a reason, although FDIC officials said they believe the New York giant decided to withdraw because it had determined it was not going to be the winner. (Citicorp was the winner in the bidding for First Republic's Delaware-based credit card bank, however.)

Casey's group had studied the effects of the First City deal on the FDIC board and had structured its bid to take advantage of lessons learned in that episode. They wanted to use the "open bank" approach, in which the bank is not officially failed but would be given assistance to recover.

The First Republic plan, presented to the FDIC on June 30, consisted of a "collecting bank," a new entity funded by the FDIC and investors, that would have bought the problem loans from First Republic. Relieved of its problem loans, First Republic then would convert $1.1 billion of debt and preferred stock into common equity and raise $1 billion of new equity in public markets. The plan envisioned $4.8 billion in problem assets going into the collecting bank, through which the FDIC would stand to collect in excess of 30 cents on the dollar. The FDIC would be exposed by $5 billion and would end up owning 5.8 percent of the new First Republic common stock.

Since the First Republic plan followed the open bank concept, it included a drastic write-down of debt and a recapitalization of the new holding company using FDIC funds.

"They said, 'We want a margin—a cost of funds plus,'" according to one FDIC negotiator. "We said, 'That's costing us,' and we tried to scale that back, but that would have affected their future earnings and made it harder for their stock to sell. But I thought Al Casey and his people did an admirable job to put together as good a transaction as they could under the circumstances. They put their heart and soul into it. They did everything imaginable on behalf of their shareholders and their creditors."

The major difference between the Wells Fargo and NCNB offers was in the nature of the way nonperforming loans could be put into special collection in the second year, according to a report from Dean Witter on August 4, 1988. "The language of NCNB's agreement states that the 'put' of such loans must be 'mutually agreeable' with the FDIC, while Wells Fargo sought the right to put back any loans during this period," the *Dean Witter Money Managers' Weekly Research Review* said. "WFC also told us that the FDIC approached them with this deal, while NCNB sought out the FDIC to make the bid."

NCNB's proposal concentrated on the new, "clean" bank, rather than on what would happen to the bad loans. The bank wasn't trying to make money on the collection of the bad loans but simply to recover its costs in collecting them for the FDIC.

And the NCNB bid was attractive to the FDIC because it presented a clear-cut deal that could be put into play immediately without a vote of creditors, as the First City deal required.

The deal set several precedents, especially with its provision for FDIC ownership of a bank. The decision to award the First Republic deal to NCNB marked the first time ever that the agency had entered into a partnership with an outside party. It also was the first time the FDIC had guaranteed the risk on the loan portfolio and other real estate retained on the balance sheet of the restructured company. The agency liked the way NCNB proposed handling the bad loans because, by having NCNB care for the pool of assets, the costs involved were below the FDIC's internal costs.

The NCNB bid also was unusual because it set out the purchase of First Republic over a period of five years. Normally, transactions like this one are handled all at once. "It was a little different than anything we had done before because of the step transaction where they bought 20 percent and then moved with an option to buy the rest," Seidman said. "The basic approach was the same—a good bank part and a bad bank part. My reaction was I would have preferred not to have done it that way. I would have preferred to have done it all at once. But unfortunately we didn't have a bid on hand that allowed us to do that at comparable cost."

The FDIC liked the fact that NCNB had the capital readily available to help recapitalize First Republic, which meant no complications or delays. NCNB had prepared its finances carefully for the Texas move, lining up potential investors months in advance in case they were needed.

NCNB had several potential big investors, including Hong Kong–Shanghai Bank, Groupe Bruxelles Lambert in Belgium, North Carolina businessman C. D. Spangler, Jr., the National Australian Bank, and Jefferson-Pilot Corporation of Greensboro, North Carolina. Any one of the five could have put up the entire $210 million to $220 million needed to meet NCNB's commitment in Texas. Perot also had said he would put up the entire amount.

In the end, approximately 15 percent of NCNB's initial $210 million investment, or $30 million, was raised through the sale of holding company assets or borrowings against these assets. The remaining $180 million came from a private placement of convertible preferred stock, an offering made in September that actually raised a total of $400 million.

The placement was the market's confirmation of the NCNB gamble. Even so, Hartman knew that no one would know exactly whether the deal was a success until NCNB credit officers had finished combing the loan files. And that job was just beginning.

Chapter 17 **The Richest Poor**

People I Ever Saw

A few days after the First Republic deal was announced, Ellison Clary in NCNB's Charlotte communications office received a call from a reporter at the *Deseret News* in Salt Lake City, who asked about the bank's plans for the Tracy Collins Bank & Trust Co. of Salt Lake City. Clary was stumped. No one in NCNB knew that a bank in Utah, 2,147 miles from NCNB's headquarters in Charlotte, was part of the First Republic package. Clary's boss, communications vice president Dick Stilley, said later, "We had no idea what the answer was."

The Utah bank was just one of many surprises that NCNB officials began to encounter as they became better acquainted with First Republic. What NCNB thought it had purchased was a fully operational banking business with 178 banking offices in forty cities throughout Texas. NCNB knew that the banks' loan portfolios were stuffed with bad deals.

That's what all the negotiating was about with the FDIC. But the new owners had never seen anything like what they discovered about the flamboyance of Texas business.

Buddy Kemp, the man McColl left in charge as chairman of NCNB Texas National Bank, had little time. The bank's deal with the FDIC provided NCNB with a ninety-day examination period, during which it would decide whether to complete the purchase of the bank.

The initial glow of victory faded quickly in the reality of business in the wobbly Texas economy. Kemp and his team of top executives met daily to survey the landscape and check their progress. They had calculated a tolerance for errors, and Kemp was determined to keep moving, rebuilding confidence in the people and in the bank. What he feared most was what he called some "off-the-wall, uncontrollable event."

In Kemp, McColl had on-site his most trustworthy lieutenant. Kemp had more than twenty years of experience at NCNB and had handled every line of business in the bank. During the 1970s, he had worked at McColl's side through NCNB's own difficult period in working out bad loans. The two had developed an immediate affinity for one another. Both were competitive bankers. Both were reared in small towns. Both were challenged by the difficulty of complicated banking deals. And both could motivate coworkers to higher levels of performance than they thought possible.

A native of North Carolina, Kemp was raised in the town of Reidsville, just a few miles south of the Virginia border, where his mother managed a small savings and loan. The town's economy had depended largely on textiles and tobacco until Miller Brewing Company opened a plant nearby in the 1970s. Most of the old American Tobacco Co. cigarette manufacturing plants were quiet now, but some of the finest domestically produced Oriental design rugs come from the Karastan factories in nearby Eden. Such rugs, domestic and foreign, woven in intricate detail and rich in color, were Kemp's hobby, along with filling scrapbooks with memorabilia.

Kemp joined NCNB as a credit analyst in 1967, after earning a bachelor's degree in history from Davidson College and an MBA from Harvard University. During the problem years in the mid-1970s, he had gathered experience on the bank's credit side. In 1977, he had taken over the retail bank when he was named to head the North Carolina Banking

Group. In 1983, the same year McColl became chairman, Kemp became president of NCNB's entire North Carolina operation.

Kemp had volunteered for the North Carolina Banking Group assignment. His colleagues couldn't understand his interest in the move that would take him out of the commercial lending side, NCNB's traditional fast track to the top. Kemp, however, believed the assignment gave him a chance to demonstrate a broader range of ability. Later, he said, "It would prove I could do something else, if I didn't screw it up."

When Kemp took over, the retail business was sleepy and sluggish. Growth was slow. Kemp invigorated the place with a few associates he brought with him, and together they wrote a new plan. "We just started over again," Kemp recalled later. "We built up training programs and measurement systems. Ironically, none of that was there." He carried the reporting on operations and profitability down to the branch level; previously, detailed reports had covered only operations in a single city.

In addition, the new strategy was put in terms that every officer could understand. Kemp wanted NCNB people to know not only what was expected of them but also what was in it for them personally. "Until the early 1980s," Kemp recalled, "we did not have incentive programs that allowed us to differentiate those who were doing the expected job and those doing their job in a significant way." The program added another degree of precision in personal accountability that later was expanded to the rest of the business.

Kemp was as driven in his desire to build NCNB as McColl was. Even when he underwent open heart surgery in 1985, he slowed his pace only temporarily. He spent only a few weeks in recovery and then started walking three miles a day.

In Texas, one of Kemp's first tasks was to motivate employees, few of whom had ever heard of NCNB before July 29. Many were nervous about their future, and the last thing Kemp needed was to have to replace large numbers of the 15,000-strong First Republic work force. To be successful, Kemp needed to assure Texas employees of NCNB's interest in keeping them on the job.

He jumped at the suggestion by NCNB assistant vice president Jan Boylston, who said a nice introduction would be a red rose on the desk of each person. Aside from its traditional meaning, red also was NCNB's color. The gesture certainly wouldn't go unnoticed, but Ann Macy, the

Houston public relations consultant hired by the bank for the transition, suggested they change to a yellow rose, since they were in Texas.

On Thursday, just four days after most employees reported for work under the bank's new owners, Project Yellow Rose was launched. Macy ordered 17,000 flowers from a Houston florist, who had to wire Holland to find enough at the weekly Friday auction to fill the order. When the roses arrived in Houston on Saturday, they were cleaned and arranged so they could be easily slipped into vases for delivery Sunday night and Monday morning. It was a hectic all-night job, but the vases were all in place by 7:00 A.M. Monday.

The roses were a hit. More than 7,000 employees sent thanks to Kemp. "Just as the Yellow Rose of Texas reaches its full bloom, may our relationship reach full bloom so that we as individuals and as members of a team may encourage the growth of NCNB Texas National Bank. Thank you for the roses," wrote the ten members of the new bank's trust department in Lufkin.

In Charlotte, NCNB headquarters staff got a different kind of message: "Don't Mess with Texas." This slogan, borrowed from an anti-litter campaign in Texas, suddenly appeared in several places at the bank, even as a bumper sticker that McColl stuck to the rear of his black BMW. McColl became the only executive who could deal directly with Texas. "And they tell me to stay out of their business," he told a reporter in Florida. "We have some very powerful managers in Texas who will let you know in a heartbeat when to stay out." The idea was to give the Texas bank time to organize itself—from forty banks into one—before attempting consolidation with the rest of NCNB.

What some of the Texas employees who received flowers from Kemp did not know was that they actually didn't work for the bank. To his surprise, Kemp learned that about 4,000 of the 15,000 employees actually were on the payroll of the holding company, not the subsidiary banks now owned by NCNB. Some employees had been shuffled onto the holding company's books at the end of 1987, while the newly merged banks were trying to reorganize their departments. The 4,000 people included some tellers, trust investment officers, computer operators, and even attendants in the parking garage. Complicating matters further, Kemp learned, some employees who worked side by side were being carried differently on the books. One might be a holding company employee while the other worked for the bank.

Many of the 4,000 employees involved didn't know what company they worked for. In some cases, their pensions were in jeopardy because they had worked for the bank for twenty years and then in January 1988, at the time the Republic and InterFirst merger took effect, their jobs had been transferred to the holding company. They had never been told of the change.

NCNB knew that some services remained part of the holding company, an arrangement that had scared some bidders off from even looking at First Republic, but the number of essential employees involved was the "off-the-wall" surprise that Kemp feared.

"It wasn't until August 21 that we realized that we didn't have a whole bank," Kemp recalled. "There were twenty-two nonbank subsidiaries. I spent the majority of my time trying to negotiate either the purchase of subsidiaries or the transfer of those employees or the replacement of those functions. The first three or four months here, my job was trying to get control, get those things in place."

That was no simple matter that would be settled easily. First Republic-Bank Corp., the holding company that controlled the support functions vital to the bank's operation, filed for bankruptcy on Monday, July 31. The bankruptcy lawsuit threw everything into a state of uncertainty. "When that happened, you then had to take everything through a court process," Kemp said. Ultimately the holding company would go through three sets of lawyers, finally having to hire a Los Angeles law firm, and two different bankruptcy judges (the first judge removed himself from the case for potential conflict of interest reasons).

NCNB appealed to the FDIC and the Comptroller of the Currency to step in and use their powers to transfer the services company, which processed checks and handled electronic data systems for First Republic's offices and another 136 banks outside the First Republic system, to NCNB Texas. The regulators declined, saying they could not take over until a crisis occurred, such as the services company's failure to perform.

The holding company responded with an offer to sell the services company, but at a hefty price of $200 million to $250 million. Kemp dug in for a fight. He was working from estimates that the business was worth between $6 and $10 million. Recalled Kemp, "I think they really thought that they had us in a difficult position and they were going to exploit that." He and others within the bank began referring to the inflated price as "ransom."

Emotions were raw, and negotiations became acrimonious. "We didn't know who would flick the switch off," Kemp said. If the services company withdrew completely, the banking business at NCNB Texas would come to an abrupt and very messy halt, with documents and electronic transactions piling up on one another.

Some NCNB officers believed that part of the holding company's strategy was designed to leave NCNB frustrated and disgusted enough with the impasse to walk away from the whole deal and return to North Carolina before the ninety-day period was up. Kemp knew that if NCNB walked out, that would give Casey's management team a shot at regaining control of the bank. "I think somebody gave them advice that if you play hardball with these guys, you could kind of jerk them around," Kemp recalled. "They underestimated our resolve, our follow-through, that we were going to take control of our destiny."

As the negotiations over ownership of the services company dragged on, NCNB fought back. During a two-and-a-half-day blitz in early November, personnel specialists signed up 3,300 of the 4,000 disputed employees as NCNB Texas employees. In effect, the 3,300 employees, whose jobs had been identified as directly related to the banking operation—such as tellers and computer operators—quit their jobs with First RepublicBank Corp. and were immediately rehired by NCNB Texas.

When the holding company learned what had happened, its lawyers went straight to the bankruptcy court, because major changes in a business involved in a bankruptcy workout must have the approval of the judge. The judge ruled in favor of NCNB and set the holding company's complaint aside.

"We had documentation that most of those jobs had been moved out of the bank into the holding company at the end of 1987," said Walter Elcock, NCNB Texas personnel executive. "We felt there was some basis for saying that was an inappropriate or illegal transfer of assets and violated the law, and that certainly the FDIC would look into it."

Finally, on November 14, the holding company agreed to accept $55 million for the services business. The $46 million difference between what was paid and what Kemp believed the business was worth wasn't justified, Kemp and others maintained. NCNB and the FDIC paid the price because their internal studies showed that it was going to cost $50 million to $60 million to replace the computer hardware and programming software being provided by the services company.

In the joint news release that reflected none of the acrimony that preceded the settlement, First RepublicBank's Al Casey said, "We have believed all along that NCNB Texas is the logical purchaser and we are delighted that a mutually satisfactory arrangement has been worked out."

Seidman later said the FDIC had anticipated that control of the services companies would end up in court and that future transactions would be less complicated. "That's another thing we have learned. When we take these institutions out, we have to have the services covered," Seidman said. "The whole transaction was the first real break in the feeling that the holding company and the banks are the same entity with the same interests. It becomes clear when you fail banks in a holding company that they generally have adverse interests and that the holding company has to treat the banks at arm's length in terms of the way that transactions between them take place, or else they may be liable for not doing so."

All during the negotiations over the services company, the NCNB team's attention was focused on the much larger task of determining which of the $21 billion in First Republic loans would be classified as good loans in the NCNB Texas portfolio and which would be assigned to the special assets division. It was a major undertaking; the real estate portfolio alone included more than 100,000 pages of documents. And the decisions made on which loans to assign to the special assets division would determine whether NCNB would make a profit in Texas or prove its critics right and lose money.

From the very beginning, CFO Tim Hartman had pegged the success of the Texas deal on finding enough good business to produce sufficient cash flow for the new bank to be profitable. "We knew we had to have $8.5 billion to $9 billion in performing loans," Hartman said, "but we had no way of getting an answer to that question short of going through the process."

The loan review assignment fell to a tight-knit group of credit officers headed by Fred Figge II, chairman of NCNB's credit policy; David Rhodes; Bill Kelley; Chan Martin; and Robert J. Shaw, a meticulous credit officer who had led the first foray into the FDIC's records pertaining to First Republic when NCNB began looking closely at the bank in early April. Now the team was sent to Dallas to examine all loans of $100,000 or more. Altogether, about 16,500 loans would have to be reviewed.

NCNB had ninety days to determine which loans went to whom, but McColl said he wanted the credit analysts to complete the work in half that time. Shaw was doubtful at the outset that he could make McColl's deadline, but he was pretty sure his team could wrap things up within sixty days. Even that would mean the other senior credit officers would need to work virtually nonstop for two months.

Chan Martin led a team of 44 analysts who scoured the records on real estate loans. Bob Shaw and Richard Douglas headed a team of 74 analysts who were responsible for the commercial and international portfolios. The teams began the day at 7:30 A.M., with team leaders gathering earlier for breakfast. The analysts daily worked as late as 9:00 P.M., and sometimes office doors weren't closed until after midnight. Work continued into Saturdays. On Sundays, everyone usually rested.

The job was all-consuming, requiring patience as well as stamina. Some of the credit officers and analysts from the NCNB offices in the Carolinas and Florida had left home for a two-month assignment on a day's notice. One analyst finished training on Monday and was shipped out four days later to Texas. Another had just finished credit school when he flew to Austin, only to be summoned to Dallas on the same day. One woman took her lengthy assignment a week after returning from her honeymoon.

NCNB commercial lenders with special expertise were brought in for three-week rotations, but the analysts were there for the duration. They did have every other weekend free for a trip home, but Sundays were the only real days off. Even holidays were ignored. The Austin team packed and moved to Waco over Labor Day.

In addition to bank employees, NCNB Texas had hired the accounting firm of Price Waterhouse and other outside accountants to help with the process, paying them a total of $10 million per quarter.

Working in rooms they called the Pit and the War Room, the credit analysts sorted through the paperwork, evaluating collateral placed on loans and examining the documentation. "We called ourselves moles working in the mole hole," Robert Shaw recalled, "and we got one of those posters that said, 'The Job That Ate My Brain.'"

As they sifted through the documents, they found that as a result of defaulted loans the bank owned lots of things—houses, furs, expensive sports cars, boats, airplanes, jewelry, horses, even part of the Dallas Cowboys professional football team. One of the NCNB team quipped,

"These are the richest poor people I have ever seen," and it immediately became the auditors' motto.

The demands of the job, and the urgency of the assignment, created a camaraderie among those detailed to Texas. In Austin, the group ate together, worked out together at a nearby health club, and prowled Austin's Sixth Street watering holes together. One weekend they met their counterparts from San Antonio for a day of tubing on the Guadalupe River. Being part of the largest bank acquisition in history kept them going and even sparked enthusiasm.

Teams were assigned first to Austin, San Antonio, Houston, Fort Worth, and, of course, Dallas. When work was finished in those major cities, the teams packed up and moved on to smaller cities, like Corsicana, Baytown, Waco, El Paso, and Odessa. The job was the same in each location. Loans that were sound were classified as "A." The next category, loans that NCNB might want to assign to the special asset pool, were classed "B." Losers to be assigned to the special asset division were classed "C." The final decision on placement of a loan was made by a committee in Dallas chaired by Figge.

Analysts working on real estate loans found that lenders' biggest nightmares had come true. Bankers and developers had flooded the market with new office buildings, residential subdivisions, and shopping centers. Many were unfinished, or finished and unoccupied. More than 40 million square feet of vacant office space was on the market in Dallas–Fort Worth alone. In fact, Texas had more vacant office and retail space than all existing square footage in the Carolinas.

For their part, Texas banks had viewed real estate development as a way to attract business to the state. With the economy growing at such a rapid pace in the early 1980s, no one had bothered to assess the real needs of the marketplace. One developer after another borrowed money to pay for building projects that changed ownership frequently, the price increasing with each signing of a new deed.

"The loans that we had were based upon appraisals, faulty appraisals, that were founded upon properties in the area whose viability was less than well founded," Hartman recalled. Hartman had moved to Texas with Kemp, as vice chairman and chief financial officer. "As oil went up and as you hired more and more people to chase the energy boom, that created a real estate boom. When energy topped out, you had layoffs and you didn't have people filling up these buildings."

About one-third of the Texas bank's assets were in real estate loans before the FDIC deal, compared to less than 10 percent at NCNB, which was doing business in such booming economies as Florida and the Carolinas.

Some of the problem grew out of the chummy relationship bankers shared with developers and builders. One analyst said he found that certain large borrowers "had our damned loan documents—legal documents on the word processing systems of our borrowers—and when they needed an $8 million loan they just wrote it up and it was signed off by officers of First Republic. Now if that isn't a lack of control to the nth degree, I don't know what is."

Such departures from normal procedures arose out of the fiercely competitive Texas lending industry. One of the things that bankers could do to be more responsive to potential clients was to increase the speed with which they gave them a yes.

The situation was bad, recalled Calvin C. Hunkele, NCNB Texas executive vice president for control, who worked through the loan portfolios with the team. "Every piece of property that was either bought or sold or used as collateral was overpriced by 300 to 400 percent when we first came down here."

When the team had finished its work, it had reduced the original $5.5 billion First Republic real estate portfolio to around $200 million for good loans. The rest were placed in the special asset bank for collection.

In addition to the bad real estate loans, NCNB Texas officials had yet another unwelcome surprise—loans to other bank holding companies. Hartman said that in addition to the $425 million that First Republic had out to other bank holding companies, it had pledged another $480 million in further loan commitments. The bank's exposure amounted to about $800 million to $900 million of potential liabilities, much of it to other banks that were already in trouble.

"I became ill that day," Hartman said. "I knew we had problems in real estate. I knew we had problems with energy and other areas. But this was ten pages of banks in Texas that we had loaned money to and you had less than 5 percent good loans. That was the day I got concerned, because if those ratios applied everywhere else, we didn't have $8 billion [in good loans needed to keep the bank running], and no matter how hard we worked, you couldn't make any money."

After looking through the portfolio, he and other bank officials determined that NCNB would classify about $45 million of the $800 million to $900 million as good loans, with the rest going into the special asset division.

His concern dissipated, however, as the new bank began to sell certificates of deposit through Merrill Lynch. "By about September 15, money started to pour in, and people across America, not just people in Texas, said, 'This is a neat story,' and they started to buy our CDs. We sold $1.1 billion in CDs through Merrill Lynch in about six weeks, and then we introduced a high-yield CD program. Between then and the end of the year, we sold another $3 billion."

When interest rates went up, the new bank had $4 billion, on which it paid 8.8 percent and bought government securities paying 9.5 percent. With the added advantage of the tax credits, the NCNB Texas balance sheet began to look pretty good, Hartman said.

The logic of the deal was not lost on investors. NCNB was hot. In fact, the offering was so successful that NCNB did not have to use any of the financial backing that McColl had carefully cultivated during his trip to the Far East and at home with Jefferson-Pilot and North Carolina investor C. D. Spangler.

The response of the market was a boost, but Kemp was still worried. He had approached the situation in Texas believing that NCNB would be able to work out many of the difficult loan situations. A decade earlier, he and the wholesale banking division had done that for many NCNB customers. At times, NCNB had taken risks to avoid bankruptcies in the face of judgments from other banks that the only way out was to shut down a customer's business. That experience was helpful, but it couldn't overcome what NCNB officers found on the books in Texas.

"There were big issues we didn't understand," Kemp recalled. "The number of problem [loans] just overwhelmed me. There was no way we could handle the care and feeding in Texas as we did in North Carolina. The problems were just so awful that we had no conception of how bad it could be. These deals didn't make sense when they put them on the books in the first place. If you had waited on these loans for five or ten years, they still wouldn't get better."

The challenges weren't sufficient to cause NCNB to back out, however. On November 22, 1988, NCNB bought its 20 percent share of the bridge bank, with the FDIC as its partner for the balance. Included in the deal was an exclusive five-year option to purchase the rest of the FDIC's 80 percent share. NCNB paid $210 million for its share of the business. The FDIC put in $840 million, which raised the new bank's equity to a level that allowed it to begin normal operation.

Based on the credit analysts' work, about $6 billion in loans and real estate acquired—assets that previously had been carried on First Republic's books as being worth $9.3 billion—were transferred to the special asset division. NCNB credit analysts said these deteriorating loans could have resulted from the overvaluation or a soft Texas economy.

"It really just signaled a turning of the page, because the real work was just starting," said Frank Gentry, who signed the purchase documents for NCNB. "Since this was now our bank, we really had a mammoth job ahead of us."

One of NCNB's jobs, a job it was paid to do by the FDIC, was to collect on the bad loans. With all its other problems at the outset, loan collection had not been a priority. At least, not until Seidman called McColl shortly after the first of the year and told him the bank was not fulfilling its collection duties under the agreement. "They just weren't cutting the mustard," Seidman said. "I told him, 'You can't run our bank for your benefit.'" After that call, Seidman said, NCNB began to move. "He was a man of his word," Seidman said.

NCNB's collection efforts drew protests and hard feelings. In Florida, when customers became angry with NCNB, they complained that NCNB stood for "No Cash for No Body." But the bank had not seen bad publicity until it began collection efforts in Texas.

Some of the risky loans were owed by businesses that had met their repayment schedules but whose collateral was less than the value of the loan. Those notes were called, and, when necessary, foreclosures ensued. Former customers began picketing the bank's offices and angrily complaining to reporters. North Carolina may have sacrificed more lives to the Confederate cause during the Civil War, but in Texas NCNB's bankers were accused of being Yankee carpetbaggers. Local politicians took up the cry, and legislators at the statehouse accused NCNB of denying credit to small and medium-sized business.

Kemp was prepared for the bad press. What frustrated him was a lack of good news to balance the complaints. At one point, the constant harping became depressing not only to the pride of those at NCNB Texas but also to the business of the bank.

Gradually, some success stories began to creep into the media's coverage of the Texas economy. One was the Susan Clark Co., a middle-market, upscale gift wrap manufacturer with $30 million to $40 million in sales. Ken Lewis, president of NCNB Texas, personally called on the company and then had McColl approach the management about moving the company's accounts. In Grand Prairie, a Dallas–Fort Worth suburb, the bank loaned the two new owners of the Blue Ribbon Cafe $55,000 to renovate the former K-Bob's Steak House, a First Republic loan that had been foreclosed, and even threw in the first three months rent free. That story made the newspapers and cast the newcomers in a different light.

In March 1989, Hartman said he knew the deal was a success. "We began to get a profit and loss statement that said we would make money." In fact, Hartman said, the deal began to look good enough that NCNB could accelerate its buyout schedule. His only concern was whether the FDIC would agree. The money NCNB was making for the agency in Texas was reducing the FDIC's overall cost of rescuing the bank.

Hartman's concerns were for naught. Based on the early strong performance, the company added to its 20 percent stake on April 28, 1989, by paying $310 million to the FDIC for an additional 29 percent. Just more than three months later, on July 31, Kemp sent 17,000 yellow roses to NCNB Texas employees marking the end of the first year's operations. But, if the sun was beginning to shine on a corner of banking in Texas, storm clouds were building elsewhere.

Chapter 18 **Eye of the Tiger**

By the end of 1988, the FDIC had closed 206 banks—more than three-fourths of them in Texas—and had given financial assistance to 21 more so they could remain in business. It was the agency's busiest year since its creation in 1933. And 1989 was shaping up to produce a record almost as dismal.

Virtually ignored during the fall presidential election, the implications of the collapse of the country's savings and loan industry now were inescapable. More than 200 thrifts had failed in 1988, and it appeared that about 600 more were insolvent or potentially insolvent and would likely be shut down in the next three years. The Federal Savings and Loan Insurance Corp. was broke, with losses exceeding $750 million. Congress was talking about closing down the FSLIC and turning the regulation of the nation's entire financial system over to the FDIC.

The system was under its greatest strain since the Depression. Even powerful New York banks, the biggest in the financial community, were facing mounting loss reserves to overcome defaults on massive foreign debts and real estate deals that had gone sour. Bankers in the largest institutions were, for the first time in decades, announcing major cuts in personnel and selling off pieces of their operations just to raise money.

The storm clouds that had first appeared in the Southwest now were gathering in the Northeast, where the overbuilt real estate markets were collapsing as they had in Texas. Trouble seemed to be everywhere— everywhere, that is, except in the Southeast, where the region's largest bank, NCNB, was expanding its position in Texas with the acquisition of failed savings and loans and capturing major attention on Wall Street with its capital offerings. After raising $250 million from the sale of preferred stock immediately following the First Republic acquisition in 1988, NCNB raised another $300 million with a private sale of debt called subordinated notes in March 1989.

Other banks in the region also were performing well. With the U.S. Supreme Court's approval in 1985 of a regional banking compact, major Southeastern banks had expanded across state lines. North Carolina's First Union National Bank was a major contender in Florida. Wachovia, after its merger with First Atlanta, maintained its position in North Carolina and had a major foothold in Georgia. Citizens & Southern, whose headquarters was Atlanta, dominated the Georgia market and was a ranking competitor in Florida and South Carolina, two of the fastest-growing states in the region.

C&S, a proud institution, had celebrated its centennial in 1987. Founded in Savannah, the bank was the leader in the South's premier city, Atlanta. Its chief executive, Bennett A. Brown, a courtly South Carolina native and son of a tobacco farmer, had joined the bank in 1955. He followed in the tradition of the venerable Mills B. Lane and his son, Mills. B. Lane, Jr., who over the course of seventy years had developed the bank into a statewide bank similar in reach and stature to Wachovia in North Carolina.

In 1989, Brown presided over a bank with $21 billion in assets, after acquiring the $4 billion Landmark Banks of Florida in 1985 and the similarly named Citizens & Southern Banks of South Carolina in 1986. During a precarious period in the mid-1970s, the bank's stock had dropped to $4 a share in 1978, the same year Brown was named chairman (after a year as acting CEO). When the overheated Atlanta real estate market had collapsed, C&S had found itself overextended in its operations and its lending. Brown led the bank through a remarkable recovery; he and his colleagues had weathered the worst and won. Now, C&S was more than seven times larger than in those dark days, with a work force of 13,900 employees. Brown was not impressed when he learned that Hugh McColl wanted to buy his bank.

The union of the two banks made good sense to McColl. The new, merged bank would dominate the market in four states and insulate itself from becoming a possible acquisition target. The rich deposit base of C&S, now at $16.1 billion, would give NCNB the capital needed to finish the purchase of NCNB Texas National from the FDIC.

The deal also would fulfill a dream. "Truthfully, I always dreamed about acquiring C&S and Sovran [in Virginia], not because I am some sort of seer or genius, but because I wanted to build a bank that dominated the South, and they were the biggest banks in their states," McColl would say later. "I dreamed about acquiring them. They literally never left my subconscious or my conscious mind."

In early March 1989, McColl began talking with an old friend who sat on the C&S board in Atlanta. Craig Wall, a tall, slow-talking South Carolinian, had known McColl since 1963, when the young banker called on Wall's Canal Industries in Conway, South Carolina. McColl was one of several bank peddlers who made the rounds in South Carolina. Another had been Bennett Brown. Brown was six years older than McColl, but the two often wound up at the same hotels and watering holes, particularly when country bankers were gathering for a meeting.

Wall, the chief executive officer of a large forest-products company, had been on the C&S of South Carolina board when it was acquired by the Georgia bank in 1986, and then he moved onto the bigger board. His position made him a natural conduit for McColl, who by now had convinced himself that C&S was the next natural acquisition for NCNB and the last link in McColl's trans-South network.

McColl believed the time was right. NCNB's stock had climbed steadily, to $35.50 a share from $23.38 since July 29, 1988, the day of the First Republic deal. He was flush with victory in Texas and his instincts, which had rarely failed him in a decade of mergers, told him to move. So did the team of investment bankers and attorneys McColl had consulted. They recommended a frontal assault, and the old Marine knew how to count that cadence.

Through Wall, McColl approached Brown with a proposal that they meet at Litchfield Beach, South Carolina, where Brown and McColl each owned a house. McColl asked Wall to tell Brown he wanted to bring him up to date on the Texas deal. Brown declined, because McColl had talked before about how a combined NCNB and C&S would make a hell of a franchise. Brown wanted to hear no more discussion on the subject.

Stonewalled on his initial approach, McColl wrote Brown a long letter telling him details of the Texas success and again inviting him into a discussion about a possible merger. Again Brown declined.

Finally, at 1:00 P.M. on Thursday, March 30, McColl telephoned Brown to tell him the NCNB board was to convene later that day to discuss a possible takeover of C&S. He called again three hours later and said, "I hate to do this."

"Well, don't," Brown retorted.

Undeterred, McColl told Brown, "My board is meeting, and we've gone too far. I've got to launch my missiles."

"You do what you have to do. We'll just hunker down," Brown replied.

Shortly after eleven o'clock that night at Brown's home in the Brookhaven neighborhood of Atlanta, a young NCNB associate from Charlotte handed Brown a note from McColl notifying him that NCNB wanted to buy C&S for $2.4 billion, at the time the biggest buyout in banking history.

Other NCNB couriers took the same message to other powerful C&S board members and shareholders. NCNB's strategists believed that even if Brown didn't want to sell the bank that he had resurrected, perhaps the stockholders would.

Brown and his troops, who had been preparing for the annual shareholders meeting just two weeks away, did more than hunker down. They prepared for war. Using codes names like Peachtree for themselves and Tarheel for their aggressor, C&S immediately launched an intensive internal and external blitz of anti-takeover publicity. They hired Rodgin Cohen of New York, one of the top anti-takeover attorneys in the nation, to orchestrate a campaign that portrayed NCNB as a risk-taking company with an uncertain future, while C&S was a solid, responsible company with a policy of managed growth.

Brown and his staff prepared a strong case, raising the specter of antitrust issues because of the two companies' overlapping South Carolina business, and lined up the political power among state regulators against NCNB. The company attempted to rally other banks in the region to seek new legislation barring NCNB from acquiring it or other Southeastern banks, asserting that NCNB's Texas acquisition now made it ineligible to operate within the Southeast compact.

"C&S will also urge further scrutiny of the projected tax benefits being attributed to NCNB's Texas acquisition," Brown said in an April 11 news release. "Although NCNB obtained certain rulings from the IRS at the time of its Texas acquisition, certain key points were not ruled upon; tests still must be met for the benefits to be realized; and non-Texas income cannot be transferred to Texas to take advantage of Texas losses."

In addition to those arguments, C&S said the proposed deal would be bad for banking. "The banking industry does not need an acquiror who uses a government assistance program to inordinately boost earnings so that it can acquire stronger, better-performing banks, first in the Southeast and then elsewhere," the press release said.

The company's cry of foul in Texas was heard all the way to Washington, where the NCNB challenge reopened the suggestion that something was amiss in the Texas deal. Ironically, some of the critics who complained that NCNB could not successfully manage the bank now said that NCNB had been given unfair advantage in Texas.

Brown, whose public relations portrayed him as a much more sympathetic figure than McColl, criticized NCNB for wanting to put C&S assets at risk in a merger that would be taking place while the Texas deal was still unproven. "It's not easy to run a good bank in today's environment," he told the *Wall Street Journal*. "Yet NCNB says it will take on [First Republic] in a bad economy, run competitive operations in North Carolina and Florida, and then turn and take on a hostile attack against this organization."

C&S publicly raised questions about NCNB's commitments to lend to companies with operations in South Africa. Eventually, the charges became more focused on McColl. "I like Mr. McColl," Brown told the *Wall Street Journal*. "I just don't want to be in business with him."

Brown told shareholders that McColl had offered him 100,000 shares of stock, valued at about $3.6 million, and salary and benefits worth more than $1 million to facilitate the merger. McColl said later that the figure was closer to $10 million, but he acknowledged that the offer "turned out to be a very bad tactic, because it insulted him."

Brown told *Business Atlanta* magazine that he was unswayed by McColl's offer to make him chairman of the new, merged bank. "There is only one guy in charge, and he has run that bank in a very aggressive and effective way, and he's been successful at it, and that's Hugh McColl," Brown was quoted as saying. "And if anybody thinks he's going to change, then they don't know Hugh McColl."

Shareholders and employees started wearing green-and-white "I'm for C&S" buttons. Letters and telegrams of support for Brown's position poured into his seventh-floor office in the C&S headquarters building on Broad Street in downtown Atlanta. The Atlanta newspapers wrote editorials and columns generally backing Brown and lamenting the fact that Charlotte probably would win out over Atlanta as headquarters if the deal went through.

McColl repeatedly defended the Texas deal in an effort to convince C&S shareholders that they would be losing out on a good deal if the two banks weren't merged. NCNB proposed to swap 1.075 of its shares for each of C&S's 61.7 million common shares outstanding, a deal worth about $2.4 billion. "We kept thinking that what we had to do was basically make sure that all the board members knew we were out there and helpful," Frank Gentry recalled. McColl and NCNB's chief lobbyist, Mark Leggett, called on Georgia's legislative leaders to try to smooth the way for any possible challenges.

Almost as suddenly as the attack had begun, it ended. Just three weeks after he had launched the bid, McColl announced that he was withdrawing it. He told the media that he had expected Brown ultimately to accept NCNB's bid. "We thought he would catch the excitement of the opportunity," he said.

McColl said later that some of the charges had offended him and his family. Reflecting on the campaign, he said he felt betrayed by advisers who had designed the frontal attack and then had second thoughts after it began. "Our lawyers showed the white feather," he said. At that point, he realized it was pointless to continue.

McColl believed that if NCNB had been willing to go through a long battle, it could have forced the merger, but to do so would have jeopardized completion of the Texas acquisition and could have stopped the bank in its tracks.

"If we had stayed the distance we might have won. Our stock was very high," McColl said. "But, we had a huge bonanza to be harvested in Texas and we just decided it was not in our interest to continue.

"Our investment bankers advised us to take the course of action we did. They sort of thought better of their advice after it didn't work. It was the charge of the Light Brigade and nobody was following. You know, the Egyptians periodically attacked the Israelis, but no generals were out there. I found myself out there by myself."

McColl kept these thoughts to himself. At a press conference he said, "Atlanta is a very important city in America, not just the Southeast. One of my successors will sooner or later try to get into Atlanta."

In Atlanta, on the day of NCNB's retreat, Brown was clearly elated as he mounted a podium in the main C&S lobby to talk to employees. One who had heard McColl say he fed his associates tiger meat handed Brown a stuffed toy tiger and a paper bag marked "Tiger Food." Brown choked the tiger and then grabbed it by the tail. "Let's go for a sail," he said, referring to McColl's favorite pastime, and then swung it around in a circle over his head and flung it to the crowd.

However, a writer in a *Business Atlanta* article observed in the last paragraph of a July 1989 story on the interbank combat: "The tiger, looking none the worse for wear, now patiently sits in Brown's office. Day in and day out. Watching."

The challenge from NCNB was enough to wake Brown and his board to the potential for other takeover attempts. Even before McColl had withdrawn his bid, speculation began on whom C&S might turn to for merger protection in the future. The *Wall Street Journal* reported on April 3: "One top candidate appears to be Sovran Financial Corp., a Norfolk, Virginia, banking company with $20 billion in assets and operations in Virginia, Maryland and Tennessee. The banks have virtually no geographic overlap and share the same conservative philosophy."

Sovran itself was a relatively new bank. It was formed in 1983 when two of Virginia's leading banks, Virginia National Bankshares of Norfolk and First and Merchants Bank of Richmond, merged. In 1987, Sovran had purchased Commerce Union, based in Nashville, Tennessee.

C&S and Sovran officials had discussed a possible merger in 1987 and again in 1988, but nothing had come of the talks.

Discussions were renewed in August 1989, and on September 26, 1989, the speculation became fact when C&S and Sovran announced plans to merge into a new $48 billion asset company to be known as Avantor Financial Corp. Brown was to be chairman, and Dennis Bottorff, a forty-six-year-old Nashville banker with an engineering degree from Vanderbilt University, was to be president. The bank would have dual headquarters in Norfolk and Atlanta.

At the board meeting approving the merger, Craig Wall announced: "Gentlemen, you have just done what Hugh McColl would have wanted you to." The merger made the company all the more appealing, as NCNB had virtually none of the Virginia banking market. There was no rebuttal.

Meanwhile, NCNB Texas demonstrated its new market strength in June with a $300 million sale of subordinated capital notes. In July, NCNB Corp. went to the American market and raised $410 million in new common equity. In September it sold 5 million shares on the Tokyo exchange and raised $245 million. That same month, the company raised another $400 million through subordinated notes. It was a stunning record achievement for the NCNB team of CFO Jim Hance, treasurer John Mack, legal counsel Charlie Berger and Rusty Page and Susan Carr from the investor relations office. When combined with the earlier spring placements, the summer offerings accounted for a third of the total of all equity capital raised in the U.S. banking industry in that year.

The new money allowed NCNB to complete the purchase of NCNB Texas. On August 9, 1989, more than four years ahead of schedule, NCNB paid the FDIC $800 million for the remaining 51 percent interest in the bank. The final payment included a $270 million profit to the FDIC on its investment in the bridge bank deal.

The situation deteriorated to the point that NCNB hired outside lawyers and got ready to defend itself. Then Hartman called FDIC chairman Seidman and proposed a one-on-one meeting of negotiators to settle the dispute. Gentry, representing NCNB, and an FDIC representative were named to find a solution and eventually hammered out a new agreement.

With completion of the Texas acquisition, NCNB became the nation's ninth-largest bank, with assets of about $60 billion, more than double its 1988 assets of $29.8 billion. The accelerated buyout was made possible by better-than-expected profits from the NCNB Texas operation. It earned $63.1 million in the second quarter of 1989, with $28.8 million going to the parent company.

By the end of the year, the FDIC's workload had increased. During the same month that NCNB completed its purchase of First Republic, Congress adopted legislation creating a new insurance fund for the savings and loan industry and put it under Seidman's management. As chairman of the newly created Resolution Trust Corp., he also presided over an expanded agency faced with selling assets worth three times the size of all bank failures and assistance transactions in the last fifty years. His new powers clearly established the chairman of the FDIC as the top banking regulator in the United States.

Seidman became a regular on Capitol Hill. His frank, blunt analysis of the banking industry was in sharp contrast to that of some others called to testify about the problems of the financial industry. Once, when asked why he opposed merging the FSLIC with his agency, he said simply, "Because they're broke and we're not."

By midwinter, however, the FDIC would be looking at another section of the country where major banks were in trouble. In December, officials of the FDIC, the Office of the Comptroller of the Currency, and the Federal Reserve Bank—all the banking police—had informed the Bank of New England that problems in its loan portfolio were far greater than had been imagined.

At the beginning of the year, the Bank of New England appeared to have reached its goal of primacy in the New England market. In just three years, with a series of mergers, it had expanded its branch network from 100 to 450 offices, doubled its employee work force to 20,000, and increased its assets to $32 billion under the aggressive direction of Walter Connolly. But by the end of the first quarter of 1989, the bank would report losses of more than $1.5 billion, one of the largest quarterly losses in banking history.

Throughout 1990, bank troubles increased. By midyear, problems also were beginning to surface in the Southeast, where bankers, under increasing pressure from regulators to do so, were shoving more and more real estate loans into the nonperforming category and increasing loss reserves.

NCNB continued to feed on the failures. NCNB Texas bought nine banks from National Bankshares Corp. in San Antonio, adding \$1.5 billion in deposits. Also in Texas, it bought an \$8 billion home mortgage servicing company and a \$3.5 billion savings and loan in Houston. It picked up a \$460 million credit card portfolio from a Maryland savings bank. At the same time, it formed its NationsBank subsidiary in Delaware—the first time the new name was used—to handle credit card operations. NCNB's Florida subsidiary purchased a \$1.1 billion thrift.

"We bought the thrift of the week," said Gentry, who was the bank's principal contact with the FDIC. "In Texas, we went from being number one in deposits to being overwhelmingly number one in the number of branches of any of the banks."

But after a euphoric 1989 and a bold start in 1990, NCNB's problems would begin increasing as federal regulators introduced rigorous new requirements that would affect the loan portfolios of NCNB and every other bank in the country.

Chapter 19 **A Softer, Gentler Cat**

The late summer and early fall of 1990 were the most depressing time in McColl's career. Examiners were looking at NCNB's loan portfolio with an ever-critical eye, and the reserves against losses were growing daily. For the bank's critics, the situation was merely confirmation that NCNB had overstepped its size. To make matters worse, McColl had to face the problems without the aid of his chief credit officer, Fred Figge, who was out of action because of heart surgery.

Compounding all that, McColl suffered personal setbacks. In early August, while on a hiking trip up a glacier on the Eiger mountain in Switzerland, his leg broke through the ice, and he injured his left knee badly enough to require an operation. Immediately after he returned home, his sister, Frances, died. And he and the rest of the NCNB family watched helplessly as cancer drained the life of Buddy Kemp, the odds-on favorite as McColl's successor.

Kemp, a twenty-two-year veteran of NCNB, had been sidelined with an illness shortly after moving to Texas as chairman of NCNB Texas. Doctors discovered a brain tumor. Texas vice chairman Tim Hartman had succeeded Kemp as chairman in January 1990, but throughout the year McColl had stayed in close touch with his old friend. He was a regular visitor to Kemp's home and hospital room.

In the late summer, when Kemp's condition became grave, McColl would fly to Dallas from Charlotte and spend the afternoon with Kemp, talking business, people, the markets, whatever. On McColl's last visit, Kemp had been impatient for someone to bring him barbecue for supper. McColl finally left the family in the room, drove to a nearby restaurant and ordered several servings of everything on the menu. He gave the waitress a $100 bill without waiting for change and carried the feast back to Kemp's room.

"I remember that [it was my last visit] because as I left I said, 'I'll see you next time,' and I got to my car when I realized I had left my briefcase in his room and I had to go back in and get it," McColl said. "He always kidded me because we never talked about his dying. I would always say, 'I'll see you next time.' " Kemp died in November.

McColl was still disabled from the August accident, and he underwent surgery on his knee in November. The next day, however, he climbed into a wheelchair and with the help of Pervis Lee, an NCNB employee for more than twenty-five years, he made it to the White House for an economic summit arranged by President George Bush.

McColl's troubles continued to mount. The bank's third quarter in 1990 was dismal, with earnings of $56.9 million, or 51 cents per share, compared with $143.6 million, or $1.45 per share, for the same quarter in 1989.

Taking a lesson from the Texas experience, McColl created a special asset bank within NCNB and shoveled NCNB's bad loans into that vault. William P. Middlemas, NCNB's president for Southeast banking, was told to get rid of the problem, which now amounted to more than $1 billion, with much of the business in Florida and North Carolina, two states that the NCNB bankers were supposed to know well.

As the recession worsened, so did NCNB's balance sheet. The company's stock continued to decline in value. Before the year was over, it reached a low of just under $17 a share, a fall from $55 per share the year before. The amount of nonperforming loans had nearly doubled during the year, compared with the 1989 figures. Earnings fell to $365.7 million, or $3.40 per share, in 1990 compared with $447.1 million, or $4.62 per share, the previous year. McColl and other top NCNB executives forfeited bonuses.

The rising crisis in the banking industry was eclipsed only by the increasing tension in the Middle East. Behind the headlines on the looming Gulf war, the FDIC reported that the additional $11 billion that banks had set aside for possible loan losses in the fourth quarter of 1990 was the highest in history. The annual total for loan losses was $31.7 billion, an increase of $670 million over 1989. Real estate loan losses had increased 84 percent in the past year, and lenders had their worst record of nonpayment since 1982.

The FDIC had an ever-declining balance with which to deal with failing banks. In December, Seidman said the fund would fall to a meager $4 billion if new money was not added. The agency would end 1990 with a $4 billion loss.

The problems now extended across the entire range of banking. Before year's end, Citicorp chairman John S. Reed announced that his huge bank would cut its dividend 44 percent. Losses for the year might reach $400 million, largely because of money the bank was setting aside for commercial loan loss reserves. In an effort to cut expenses, he also said the company would be reducing its work force by 8,000 by the end of 1992. At Chase Manhattan Corp., chief executive Thomas Labrecque had already announced similar economy measures and a cut in dividends.

As the new year began, NCNB slowly began to climb out of its hole. The bank had set aside $505 million in provisions against credit losses and nonperforming loans in 1990, more than twice the amount for 1989. This strategy depressed earnings, but it helped clear the decks for the future.

In January, NCNB received a significant vote of confidence. C. D. Spangler, Jr., whose wife, Meredith, was an NCNB director, filed a report with the Securities and Exchange Commission revealing that he had purchased $100 million worth of NCNB stock in recent weeks. The purchases left him the largest single shareholder in the corporation, with 8 million shares, or 7.78 percent of the total number of outstanding shares.

Spangler, a Charlotte construction company owner who became president of the University of North Carolina in 1986, had been a major NCNB stockholder since early in 1982, when he sold his controlling interest in Bank of North Carolina to NCNB. Negotiated one morning at the Greenbrier resort in West Virginia, the deal had been one of McColl's early triumphs and one of the cleanest purchases.

Spangler said he made the January 1991 purchases simply because he saw a good deal. The stock was tremendously depressed—he bought some shares at $19—but he believed in the bank's primary market and had confidence that McColl and NCNB's management would work out of the depressed situation.

In February, McColl and his salesmen were back trying to raise money, this time in Edinburgh, where the bank sold 1.2 million shares. "The Europeans saw the turnaround before the Americans. It was April before New York had decided we were okay," McColl said.

The recession was cutting particularly deep in Florida, where NCNB had taken serious losses. Despite problems at home, McColl had been eyeing the situation in Florida for several months. He saw opportunity to improve NCNB's position, which was fifth in market share in the state.

Nearly ten years earlier, in 1982, when NCNB was building its Florida base, McColl had made a pass at Southeast Banking Corp., headed by Charles J. Zwick, and had gotten a slap in the face for his interest. Zwick wrote McColl a tightly worded letter letting him know that any overtures would be considered hostile.

Recent contact indicated a change in attitude. While attending a meeting of financial leaders in San Francisco in the fall of 1990, McColl noticed a definite warmth in Zwick's manner. Southeast, a $12 billion bank that once was Florida's leading corporate lender, was facing its fourth consecutive quarter of losses. Federal regulators had urged the bank's board to fire Zwick, but in October the board voted to keep the twenty-two-year veteran. Through Zwick's friend, former Federal Reserve Board chairman Paul Volcker, who was now with the New York investment banking firm of James D. Wolfensohn, Inc., McColl arranged a meeting to talk about buying Southeast. Zwick was interested, but he said he wasn't ready to sell.

In January, Zwick's board fired him as chairman. Later, he claimed that federal regulators had threatened to seize the bank unless he was removed. McColl, Hance, and Gentry continued to meet with South-east's new leadership, including a session in New Orleans, where they could gather without being recognized.

One or two NCNB directors asked McColl about the Bank of New England, which the FDIC had taken over in January. McColl told them it was "a bridge too far," recalling a World War II phrase used to de-scribe a disastrous overextension of Allied forces in Holland. Some of the subsequent bidders for the bank did talk to NCNB about managing the bad-asset portion of the recovered bank.

Before making a final decision on Southeast, McColl reviewed the situation with the executive committee of his board, chaired by Hootie Johnson. The directors were fully supportive, but suggested that McColl check all possible options before committing to Southeast. So began a round of calls to competitors and adversaries throughout the South, with dramatic surprises in several cautiously receptive responses.

McColl kept his executive committee apprised of developments with Southeast, which offered potential as a deal if the FDIC would assist in taking over the bad loans, now amounting to about $1 billion. But McColl decided to take another look at C&S, which had never left his list of potential merger candidates. His executive committee supported McColl's desire to try again.

After turning back NCNB in 1989, C&S/Sovran (it had discarded the Avantor designation) was suffering from the recession in the Southeast, and it had been particularly hard hit by mounting losses on loans in the District of Columbia metropolitan area. These problems surfaced in the fourth quarter of 1990, when the bank had added $237.5 million to its loan loss reserve as a result of nonperforming real estate loans there. Earnings for 1990 plummeted to $229 million, or $1.60 per share, com-pared with $507.2 million, or $3.67 per share, in 1989. Real estate loans made up 32 percent of the company's $34 billion portfolio at the end of 1990, with Washington, D.C., accounting for 21 percent of the real es-tate total. The stock price had dropped from $35.88 at the close of the first quarter of 1989, when NCNB first announced its intentions, to $15.63 at the close of the fourth quarter in 1990.

C&S/Sovran officials insisted that the massive real estate problems in the Washington area had not started to surface when they announced their decision to merge in September 1989. "The loan demand was good in that area," Brown said later. "Past dues were not out of line. Foreclosures were not a problem. It almost turned in the fourth quarter of 1990. If you look at the FDIC trends of all the banks in that area, it was the fourth quarter of 1990 that it started."

Brown said his bank's problem was the result of the fact that there were too many banks competing for too few possible large real estate customers. "There was no demand in the Southwest. It had dried up. In New England, you couldn't find a good loan market. The Florida market had already been through some difficulty. The D.C. area looked like a hot spot. The government always expanded. The government never had any problems. That held true for I don't know how many years, a hundred years. Finally it created a glut, everybody chasing what appeared to be a very lucrative market."

The C&S/Sovran problems were deeper than that, however. The merger was not going smoothly. One headquarters, with President Bottorff in charge, was located in Norfolk. The other headquarters, with Chairman Brown in charge, was in Atlanta. This arrangement had worked no better than the one attempted thirty years earlier when NCNB was created from banks in Charlotte and Greensboro, North Carolina. Loyalties to old institutions remained in place. In addition, with command of the new bank divided between cities, the task of eliminating duplication in systems moved slowly. Further complicating matters, regulatory approval had taken eighteen months to complete.

McColl also learned that the board of C&S/Sovran was divided between directors supporting Bennett Brown and those supporting Dennis Bottorff, who was to succeed Brown at the end of the year. The time appeared to be right for an overture to Brown.

McColl assembled his team. Hance, who would emerge as team leader, would handle finances. Personnel chief Cooley had been down the road before. So had corporate counsel Paul Polking, Joe Martin, whose corporate communications staff was one of the best in the business, and Bill McGee, who handled logistics.

Investment bankers were recruited. "We hired Morgan Stanley because they were big and tough and had a reputation that when they went after somebody it happened," McColl said. "We also hired Merrill Lynch and Salomon Brothers. We wanted to have on our side the cannons that said, 'We're going to win this.' We were carrying on peace negotiations while we had the tanks massed at the border."

That part of the strategy was vintage NCNB. This time, McColl added a new twist. He had previously handled mergers by instinct. Even when he was an understudy to Tom Storrs and the two were buying banks in Florida, he never followed a script. He took pride in his ability to read body language and to adjust to changing circumstances in negotiations. He believed he had a feel for those things. His instincts had failed him in 1989, however, when his style had clearly been used to defeat him. This time, he decided, he would approach Brown differently.

McColl called Cooley in for help and advice and told him, "I am going to buy C&S/Sovran. I don't know when. I don't know how." He told Cooley to hire the best talent available and deliver a complete psychological profile of Bennett Brown, Dennis Bottorff, and all the key players at the bank.

Cooley considered the directive and returned to McColl with an alternative. Cooley would do it himself. Within a few weeks, after reading everything he could find about Brown, he handed McColl a profile of Brown and, to McColl's chagrin, a profile of McColl as seen by Brown.

Cooley told his boss that the keys to Brown's relationships with people were honesty, sincerity, warmth, and friendliness. He also observed that each trait was just the opposite of the characteristics that McColl had portrayed to Brown. From Brown's vantage, McColl was arrogant, crude, and ungentlemanly. Moreover, Brown was turned off by McColl's use of words suggesting power.

"What we focused on was Bennett's need to retire with honor," Cooley said. "That meant he did the right thing for all the employees, all the shareholders, for everything that he represented. While it sounds personal, it is a manifestation of real success."

After McColl had digested Cooley's report, he, Cooley, and Martin began an intense series of role-playing sessions. With Cooley or Martin performing as Brown, McColl was schooled to avoid the use of militaristic terms and other verbal and nonverbal examples of his usual aggressive style. They coached him to become softer, more receptive, and friendlier in his approach.

"I really, really wanted this deal," McColl recalled. It would have fulfilled a career ambition of extending NCNB's range across the entire region and setting it up to become a truly national bank. "I wanted it so much I was willing to submerge my entire personality. I was willing to do whatever was needed to be done. I would even change the name of my bank, give up the chairmanship."

While McColl's attention had turned to C&S/Sovran, the bank continued negotiations with Southeast, with Gentry filling in as chief negotiator. Finally, in early May, when McColl felt he was ready, he placed the call to Brown. "He wasn't in, and I thought he wouldn't return my call," McColl said. Later in the day, Brown phoned. "He told me he would take it to the executive committee. From that time on, Bennett set the pace at which we operated."

Now McColl's anxiety intensified. What if the C&S/Sovran executive committee just said no again? What if another suitor emerged? What if the real estate problems improved enough for the company to remain solidly independent?

As he waited, McColl devised a way to answer questions about progress of the deal. He found a book of Latin phrases and on the morning of May 29, the day the C&S executive committee was to meet, he printed "*Permittre divis cetera*" on a sheet of paper and taped it to the glass wall of his outer office where it was visible to all inquiring associates who were allowed on the floor. Translated, the message said, "It's in the hands of the gods."

On May 30, McColl was late for work. He had stayed home an extra hour to play a little longer with his year-old grandson, John Spratt McColl, Jr. When he arrived at the office about nine-thirty, he received a message that Brown had called. When McColl returned the call, he began by explaining his grandson's role in the delay. Such grandfatherly priorities set precisely the tone that Cooley had suggested he use with Brown. Brown gave him some good news and some bad news. Yes, Brown said, the executive committee had authorized Brown to continue the talks. But, he added, he couldn't continue until after the full board considered the request on June 18.

McColl taped up another message: "*Aureo homo piscari,*" which translates to "Money talks." He now believed that price would drive the deal.

Brown's response was enough for McColl and his team to intensify their efforts. McColl turned the running of the bank over to his staff and spent much of his time on the telephone trying to gather more intelligence about C&S/Sovran. He closed the executive wing of the twenty-third floor to all but a few trusted lieutenants. "We virtually shut the company down during that time," he said. "We wanted this deal badly."

Additional information confirmed early intelligence that portrayed

C&S/Sovran as a leaky ship that was sinking while two captains fought over command.

As credit problems in the metropolitan D.C. area increased, Brown and his board became aware that their exposure there was potentially fatal. Even as the June meeting approached, the bank was in negotiations with the Office of Comptroller of the Currency over how to handle problem loans that were concentrated primarily in one of the banks that Sovran had purchased before the merger.

The Virginia loan problems were an embarrassment to Brown. He and his team at C&S had fought their way out of difficulties in Georgia to regain a position of strength. Now, under terms of the merger, he was scheduled to retire January 1, 1992, leaving the company he had rescued in the 1970s to the man who he believed represented the entity that was dragging it back into a similar hole.

Moreover, board members were choosing up sides, and Brown was not sure if he had a majority of votes. An Atlanta faction coalesced behind Brown, while the Virginia and Tennessee directors formed behind Bottorff. But within factions there were factions. The Virginia directors, for example, divided their loyalties between Richmond and Norfolk.

As McColl gathered what news he could about C&S/Sovran, his confidence increased. From what he had learned, the C&S/Sovran board was badly split, and while both sides preferred to remain independent, a merger with NCNB was the second choice among those on both sides. Another bidder certainly wasn't an option.

"Who could they run to?" McColl reasoned. "First Union and Wachovia were already in Atlanta. They couldn't afford it anyway. The money-center banks were sick and not about to do any more deals like this. We were the only game in town. Size brings with it certain things. You can walk into an auction and be the only player to bid."

For McColl, time dragged slowly on. On June 6, McColl had his executive assistant, Pat Hinson, track down Joe Martin, who was in a car driving from Dallas to Fort Worth, and alert him to an incoming telephone call from the chairman. Martin pulled his car onto the shoulder of the road and waited.

With Gentry and Polking standing with him at a speakerphone in his office, McColl rang Martin. "I just wanted to wish you a happy anniversary," McColl said, remembering that it had been ten years to the day that NCNB had landed in Florida. "I just want to thank you three for a great decade, and the next one's going to be even better."

On June 10, McColl's wife, Jane, left for their beach house with a tongue-in-cheek request to her husband: "Call me when you get your little banks bought." The quip, reported in a news account of the negotiations, suggested that Jane McColl had little to do with her husband's work. Nothing is further from the truth. "I talk to my wife about business all the time," McColl said. "She is very good at reading people. I trust her totally."

A week before the June 18 C&S/Sovran board meeting, McColl put up another message on his outer-office wall: "*Vincit qui patitur*," which translates as "Patience will prevail."

June 18 arrived, McColl's fifty-sixth birthday. While Brown's board met in Atlanta, McColl sat through a four-and-a-half-hour deposition with an attorney preparing a case for former customers of First RepublicBank Corp., the Texas bank's former holding company, who were suing NCNB. McColl enjoyed fencing with the lawyer, who tried his best to shake McColl's testimony with needling questions. The more the lawyer pressed, however, the more McColl's mind focused on something other than C&S/Sovran. The attorney unwittingly helped the anxious chairman through a very tense day.

After the board meeting, Brown telephoned to invite McColl to Atlanta two days later. Brown said he wasn't prepared to talk price, but his board wanted to see what NCNB had in mind. He said he would pick up McColl at noon at a private airport terminal outside Atlanta.

The board meeting had been a trying one for Brown. The directors were briefed on the latest round of negotiations with regulators who were concerned about the loan problems in northern Virginia. Next, discussion moved to what the company could do about the situation, including a possible merger with NCNB. Then, without Brown's consent, a director called for a vote reaffirming earlier plans for Brown to retire in Bottorff's favor at the end of the year. All fifteen former Sovran board members voted for the motion, and all fourteen former C&S directors voted against it. The internal battle was joined. Authority for Brown to begin talks with McColl subsequently passed handily.

Brown was overheard to say after the meeting, "Well, maybe I'll just let Hugh McColl settle this thing."

Suddenly NCNB had assumed the unfamiliar role of aiding Brown because it had become obvious that the C&S/Sovran merger was in serious jeopardy. Brown "was caught between Bottorff trying to take the company from him internally and I was trying to acquire the company externally," McColl said. "He still hoped to escape from that trap by taking Bottorff out and then getting the board to decide to remain independent. As it slipped from his hands, he felt it slipping, it became more important to him that we get a merger. That was the only way to salvage honor."

McColl began preparing for what he believed to be the most important performance of his career—his meeting with Brown. Investment bankers gave him the financial questions to be answered. He was well schooled in the social issues, but Cooley and Martin went through more sessions with him to soften his personality. At the end of the day on June 19, McColl went home to an empty house in Charlotte. His wife was still at the beach. He had planned to go over the merger proposal specifics one more time and then get some sleep so he would be relaxed for his important meeting. But sleep didn't come. A voracious reader whose tastes run from William Buckley to Nadine Gordimer, he picked up a new 450-page spy novel, *Condition Black*, by Gerald Seymour. He read through the night.

At dawn, McColl had finished the book, and he got ready for his trip. For his meeting with Brown, he chose a shadow gray-blue plaid suit, not the power statement of corporate dark blue with chalk stripes. He selected a tie with the University of Georgia colors in it. If the meeting went well, this would be his uniform throughout the negotiations.

The morning was rainy and foggy. "When I got to the airport, I told the pilots I wanted them on the ground in Atlanta precisely at 11:59:50 because I [had] told Bennett I would be there at twelve sharp. But we couldn't take off, because it was foggy and raining and there were geese on the runway, if you can believe that." The delay irritated him, but Martin, who traveled with him to Atlanta, reassured him that he really was ready for the meeting. They talked quietly and comfortably about the objectives, anticipating all the potential variations in Brown's demeanor and questions, matching Cooley's "script" to each imagined circumstance.

The NCNB plane arrived two minutes late in a driving rainstorm. A programmed McColl was fully prepared when Brown picked him up in his car and drove him to his condominium. "When I got there, his wife hugged me at the door, which was good," McColl recalled. "In the South, women have a way of letting you know whether you're offending their husband, and her hugging me like an old friend was definitely good. We sat in the kitchen and ate ham and cheese and turkey sandwiches and pickles and iced tea. I was so nervous, I could barely eat. Then we went in the dining room. He cleared off the table, and we both sat on the same side, which is a good sign because adversaries sit across from each other."

"Well, tell me what you want to talk about," Brown began, in the most straightforward of all the options that McColl had anticipated.

Taking his cue, McColl outlined a vision for a banking merger that he characterized as the model for banking in the years to come. Mindful of the semantics that had derailed earlier talks, McColl chose his words carefully and laid out the plan and the advantages of merging the two institutions.

Brown responded with the same key questions that the NCNB trio had predicted he would. He wanted to know about leadership, cuts in personnel and staff, the name of the new bank, and, most important, the price. McColl ticked off the right answers.

The bank would have a new name, NationsBank, which would ease concerns about the North Carolina flag flying over Georgia. Shortly after the Texas acquisitions, Brad Iversen, who had just joined NCNB as its marketing executive, raised the old question of a new name that would better reflect the company's size and geographic diversity—and perhaps be more acceptable in new markets. Determined not to be stuck with one of the odd computer-generated names being adopted by other financial institutions, he and Joe Martin began working with Lee Ballard of the Naming Center in Dallas. Ballard was an academic linguist who worked with Latin teachers and poets rather than computers to develop potential names with the imagery sought by companies.

Martin vividly recalled the time pressure that had derailed the earlier attempt to change the NCNB name when the company had entered Florida. Now, with the familiar red-and-white NCNB logo applied in Texas by requirement of the FDIC and without the pressure of any other impending merger, he and Iversen began the lengthy process of testing prospective new names for legal registration requirements, market reactions, and linguistic problems in translation to other languages.

On the list Ballard had come up with was the word "Nation." Ironi-

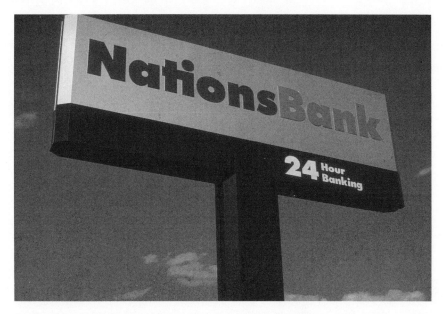

By the time discussions with C&S/Sovran began, NCNB had created the name NationsBank and was using it for its credit card bank in Delaware. The name had already cleared linguistic, legal, and marketing tests.

cally, it had also been considered in 1982 when the company had nearly chosen "NovaBank." Working with poster-size flashcards, Iversen and Martin combined two of them to make the single word "NationsBank," and they were surprised when the lawyers determined that it was not in use anywhere in the world. Even more surprising, "NationsBank" cleared the marketing surveys conducted throughout the country, consistently scoring as one of the most recognized and highly regarded names in banking, although it had never been used. The word carried all the image characteristics that NCNB had sought, and it carried them without even being advertised. The corporate identity firm of Seigel and Gale, with main offices in New York, then developed a graphic look for the word that would reinforce those characteristics.

When NCNB opened a credit card bank in Delaware in 1990, it was given the name of NationsBank. Without fanfare, the new entity began to distribute credit cards throughout the United States, confirming the marketability of the name and, perhaps more important, establishing legal rights to the exclusive use of the name. Unnoticed by the news media, "NationsBank" had cleared all the linguistic, legal, and marketing hurdles and awaited a merger opportunity that would call it into being.

As for the issue of leadership, McColl wanted Brown to take the chairmanship, while he remained as CEO and president.

Then, McColl pulled a sheet of paper from his coat and showed it to Brown. Labeled "For Illustration Only," it showed that an exchange of 0.75 shares of NCNB stock for each share of C&S/Sovran would mean a total payout of $3.99 billion for Brown's shareholders.

Brown was noncommittal. He asked more questions, and three hours after he had picked McColl up, Brown drove him back to the airport, where the eight-seat NCNB corporate jet, a Cessna Citation, sat waiting. Brown gave no hint of whether he had liked the deal or not. He simply told McColl that he would call him with whatever decision the full C&S/Sovran board made.

McColl was pleased with the tone and course of the meeting. Evenly, without piles of notes and memoranda, he had gotten answers to everyone's questions. He was not threatening, and he maintained the composure that Cooley and Martin had trained him for. "I was so low key I didn't recognize myself," McColl said. "My body language was soft and my body was soft. My posture was soft. Not sleeping was helpful."

McColl took his customary seat behind the cockpit, the one from which he could keep an eye on the altimeter at all times, and picked up the telephone to call his office but handed the phone to Martin and fell asleep before Pat Hinson could answer at the other end. It had been a successful day.

McColl and his associates faced another agonizing waiting period, and McColl reactivated his intelligence network, hoping to put more pressure on reluctant board members to accept the deal. His sources told him that the situation within C&S/Sovran was continuing to deteriorate. After the board vote, it was obvious that Brown only had one good alternative—make the best deal possible with McColl.

"Brown's power was draining away from him daily," McColl said. "Meanwhile, Bottorff had brought in his own investment bankers, which was unheard of. First Boston and Robinson Humphrey were the C&S/Sovran bankers, and Bottorff ends up hiring Dillon Read."

On June 25, the news that NCNB and C&S/Sovran were considering a merger and considering changing the name to NationsBank finally became public. The *Business Journal of Charlotte* first reported it in a segment on WBTV in Charlotte on the six o'clock news. The *Wall Street Journal* reported it in the June 26 editions. The nation's financial media focused on the possibility of a megabank deal in the South.

When the news broke, executives at Southeast in Florida expressed surprise. Frank Gentry had continued to talk with them about a possible merger until the C&S/Sovran deal looked more certain. McColl told Gentry the Florida bankers should have known NCNB's interest was waning. "Didn't they notice I wasn't there?" McColl told Gentry.

At the regular meeting of NCNB's board on June 26, Hance outlined the proposed merger. That same day, C&S/Sovran and NCNB both issued press releases confirming that talks were under way, and NCNB launched a major advertising campaign promoting the bank's involvement in community affairs. One slogan was, "Our best bankers still spend time in second grade." The ads emphasized work as volunteer tutors by bank employees. NCNB sent copies of it to five thousand political and community leaders throughout the Southeast, including C&S/Sovran's twenty-nine directors. The bank also emphasized in media contacts that the new NationsBank would mean that, for the first time in history, the South would have a bank large enough to handle multibillion-dollar deals on its own, without ever having to approach other lenders. The image campaign was designed to insulate NCNB from the kind of public relations assault C&S had inflicted in 1989.

Finally, on June 27, the C&S/Sovran board met and agreed to continue the merger talks by authorizing Brown and his team to exchange financial records with NCNB, a process known as due diligence. Credit experts, financial analysts, and lawyers from Atlanta traveled to Charlotte, and more than one hundred of NCNB's examiners went to major C&S/Sovran offices during the weekend of June 29 and 30. Tim Hartman in Dallas dispatched analysts seasoned by the Texas experience of identifying "dead horses," his name for bad loans that had filled the bank's books there.

"Texas taught a lot of our people to be realistic," Hartman said. "If a horse is dead, say it is dead. List the five reasons it is dead. They did it 150 times in Texas, and all 150 times the dead horse stayed dead. We developed skill and confidence."

Just before the July 4 holiday, McColl, feeling a bit frisky, walked through the main NCNB lobby in downtown Charlotte wearing a brand-new white baseball-style cap with "Nations" in blue and "Bank" in red. A few employees noticed and asked if they could get one, but there was no fanfare and no media attention. Dick Stilley in corporate communications fired off a message to his boss, Joe Martin: "The person in charge of blurt control has failed miserably."

McColl and Brown and their families retreated to Litchfield Beach for the holiday weekend. On the eve of the holiday, Brown called McColl and invited him to join him for a walk on the beach at seven o'clock the next morning. Brown arrived wearing a blue-and-white-striped, button-down collar shirt over white walking shorts and brown deck shoes. McColl greeted him in a plain white T-shirt, blue walking shorts, and no shoes. Jane McColl snapped a photograph of them shaking hands with her husband wearing an Atlanta Braves cap and Brown in a new NationsBank cap McColl had just handed him.

The two walked south on the beach shoulder to shoulder with the early morning sun warming them. After about a half a mile, McColl picked up a seashell and sketched in the sand a conceptual plan of organization. Hours later the rough-drawn outline, which could have been the result of child's play in the sand, disappeared with the tide. Before the walk was over, McColl believed the deal was settled except for the price.

The next day, the two men, accompanied by Bottorff, met at Craig Wall's nearby beach house. And on July 6, Brown and his wife invited the McColls and analyst Jon Burke and his wife to dinner at the Brown house on the Waccamaw River. Burke worked for the Robinson-Humphrey Co. Inc. in Atlanta, which was representing C&S/Sovran. All the meetings were cordial, and the deal proceeded.

The C&S/Sovran board met in Norfolk on July 16. McColl was invited to speak. He waited five hours before Brown asked him in. He stayed less than ten minutes, answering questions about how he would deal with the problem loans in the Washington area and how he saw reductions in the work force taking place in the event of a merger. McColl left the room to wait for the board's decision. It came in ten minutes. The discussions were to continue on price. C&S/Sovran also said in its press release that it still fully intended to stay independent.

McColl flew on to New York that night to prepare for final negotiations. After a day to organize strategy and assign negotiating roles at the offices of Wachtell, Lipton, Rosen & Katz at 299 Park Avenue, the NCNB team met Thursday for the first time with the C&S/Sovran team

Wearing an Atlanta Braves baseball cap, Hugh McColl presented a NationsBank hat to Bennett Brown. Photographer Jane McColl snapped their picture at Litchfield Beach, South Carolina, on July 4, 1991.

at the offices of First Boston Corporation. The NCNB team, led by Steve Waters of Morgan Stanley, trotted out its arguments for sticking with the offer of 0.75 of an NCNB share for each share of C&S/Sovran stock. The C&S/Sovran team balked, and after separate meetings between Hance and C&S/Sovran's financial chief, Jim Dixon, Hance came back with the C&S/Sovran counteroffer—0.90 or 0.95. The two sides remained about $500 million apart, a wide gulf on a $4 billion deal.

McColl and his team decided to stick to the original offer as negotiations resumed the next day, Thursday, July 18. McColl stayed at the Wachtell Lipton offices. Waters, who had been involved in the $25 billion RJR Nabisco leveraged buyout in 1988, walked the C&S/Sovran team through the offer. A key point was that NCNB believed the real estate problems in the Washington area would get worse before they would get better.

The C&S/Sovran team was unmoved. They accused Waters of holding McColl and NCNB back from raising the offering price enough to make a deal possible. The talks broke off again, with no apparent hope of movement. The next morning started out the same way, with Waters reiterating NCNB's position. There was no progress, but Brown agreed to meet McColl again at 3:00 P.M. to fly to Washington to see Bill Taylor at the Federal Reserve.

At 3:00 P.M. Brown was nowhere in sight. McColl was trying hard to contain his temper as he called Taylor to apologize. At 4:30 P.M. he decided he had waited for Brown long enough. "I had decided that the deal wasn't going to happen. We're not going to get together. I said, 'The hell with this. We're not going to sit around here any longer.' Somebody said, 'Let's go over to Brooks Brothers and buy a tie.'" On the way out with Hance, Figge, and Cooley, McColl stopped off in the men's room. Only because of that delay, they were still in the elevator lobby when Brown called.

McColl took the receiver. Brown said, "Let's go to the beach. Let's forget it and start over on Monday."

"I'm not going to the beach," McColl shot back. "I'm staying here. I'm going to make you an offer whether you are here or not."

Brown replied, "Well, I've got a number in my head, and I'm willing to do the deal, but I'm not sure you're willing to do that. And I'm not willing to tell you that number over the phone."

About 5:30 P.M. Brown and Bottorff arrived and went into a conference room with McColl. The room was stiflingly hot, since the air conditioning apparently was malfunctioning. Moreover, New York was in the grip of one of its summer heat waves, with temperatures in the nineties.

"He put a price forward, which I thought was ridiculous," McColl said. The haggling began. Finally, at 6:33 P.M. on Friday, July 19, they agreed on an exchange rate of .84, pegged to the day's price of NCNB stock, $31.08 per share, which made the deal worth $4.26 billion. Brown would be chairman, and McColl would be president and CEO. Both agreed to set meetings of their respective boards for that Sunday to approve the deal officially.

After the meeting, McColl wasn't elated, just drained. He felt like it had taken forever to put the merger together, though it had required less than sixty days. He departed for his hotel, leaving a corps of lawyers working through the night to put the final deal in the proper form. The paperwork had to be ready for approval by both boards of directors, which would gather for special meetings on Sunday.

Brown and Bottorff exited quietly, but when they reached the street level, "Denny and I shook hands and did a high five," Brown said.

On Sunday, McColl opened the NCNB board meeting in Charlotte at 1:00 P.M., telling the directors, "The risks are manageable and the rewards are great." Then he turned the session over to Vice Chairman Jim Thompson, who asked Hance to outline details of the proposal.

As McColl prepared to leave for a flight to Atlanta to sign merger papers with Brown, Roger Soles, the tough-minded chief executive of Jefferson-Pilot Corporation, whose company thirty years earlier had initiated the merger creating NCNB, called McColl's work a great achievement. He led the directors in standing and congratulating McColl with a hearty round of applause.

The C&S/Sovran board was still meeting in the company's terminal at the DeKalb/Peachtree airport when McColl arrived. He waited until Brown emerged with the merger agreement, which his directors had approved 28 to 1. The one "no" vote was a symbolic protest against the disappearance of the historic Citizens & Southern name.

When McColl received word by telephone that the NCNB board had approved the merger unanimously, the two turned to a table cluttered with aviation magazines and signed the agreement creating Nations-

Hugh McColl (left) and Bennett Brown sign the papers officially declaring the merger of their respective banks on Sunday, July 31, 1991. The scene is the C&S/Sovran terminal at DeKalb/Peachtree airport in Atlanta.

Bank, at the time the nation's third-largest bank, with assets of $119 billion, 59,000 employees, and 2,000 branches.

McColl and Brown held a press conference on July 22 in Atlanta to announce the merger. When Brown was asked about the "culture conflict" he had described during the first merger attempt, he reached under the table on the dais, pulled out a steel military helmet, and put it on. The crowd of reporters and bank employees erupted in laughter.

McColl introduced himself to C&S/Sovran employees in a speech at the historic Fox Theater in downtown Atlanta on July 24. He reminded them that the NationsBank legacy was firmly established in the South. C&S had begun business in 1887, and the beginnings of Sovran could be traced to 1865, with the charter of First National Bank of Richmond, and to the formation of People's Bank of Norfolk in 1867. NCNB's heritage also was more than a hundred years old.

"Southern banks were last powerful during the pre–Civil War days when they supported the cotton trade," McColl said, quoting an editorial in the *Raleigh* (N.C.) *News & Observer*. "But NationsBank sends the signal that the region is back in high cotton."

The deal was a bonanza for the seven New York investment banking and brokerage houses, which collected a total of $40.23 million in fees. Morgan Stanley received $11 million. First Boston made $12.38 million. And James D. Wolfensohn, Inc., $7 million. Salomon Brothers, and Dillon, Read & Co. got $2 million each. Robinson-Humphrey received $3.85 million, and Merrill Lynch's fee was $2 million.

Now that the merger had board approvals, the gargantuan task of melding the two huge banks into one was begun. It was the first time in history that two multistate, multibank holding companies were to be consolidated.

McColl again called on NCNB executive vice president H. A. "Rusty" Rainey, who by now had accumulated ten years of on-the-job training in mergers. His first "large" one had been in 1982, when the Bank of North Carolina, with all of 750 employees and seventy offices, had been brought into the system. "It was a first for us because it was in multiple locations," said Rainey, a wiry, sandy-haired man of medium height. "They had 750 employees, and we knew we could reduce that to 500. It was the biggest job we had ever done."

When he began planning the NationsBank transition, he also had experience from Texas, South Carolina, and Florida behind him. Throughout the 1980s, he had been kept so busy that at one time he owned houses in three cities. He made a $10,000 profit on one of them, even though he and his wife never got to live in it; he was transferred to work in Texas before he could move from his previous assignment. Even after the merger with First Republic, Rainey supervised mergers with eighteen other banks or thrifts.

"Our experience in mergers gives us a big advantage over our competitors," Rainey said. "We have just simply evolved into larger and larger acquisitions." He said a key part of NCNB's transition strategy is to have a recognized manager. "It has to be someone who knows how one piece of the company fits with another, someone with enough delegated authority to make it work. That was my role."

"We've gone through a number of acquisitions over the years, in Florida, in South Carolina and in North Carolina, in Texas," Rainey said. "We have learned a lot about how to handle the people issues. And frankly, some of that knowledge came from our own mistakes."

In Florida, for example, NCNB's aggressive work ethic did not suit the more relaxed and casual style of banking, and NCNB's image suf-

Chief Financial Officer Jim Hance (left) presents NationsBank to financial analysts in New York. With him are General Bank President Ken Lewis (center) and Hugh Chapman, chairman—NationsBank South.

fered after expelled bank executives complained publicly about the out-of-state bankers. The expansion into South Carolina went more smoothly because the corporate culture at Bankers Trust was more like that of NCNB.

With each step, employees from the previous acquisition were deliberately involved in the next one. When NCNB acquired the Texas bank, for example, employees from the North Carolina, South Carolina, and Florida operations were part of the team sent to help orient new Texas employees. All but a handful of these people were recalled home within a few days. "We couldn't afford to move a lot of people to Texas, so we had to use as many Texans as possible," Rainey said.

As Rainey organized the NationsBank transition, Texas employees were involved in orienting Georgia, Tennessee, and Virginia employees. "Texans are all over the transition team, putting together the new NationsBank," said chief planner Frank Gentry. "That's doing wonders to eliminate any remaining 'us and them' that may have existed between Texas and the East."

The transition team was responsible for implementing changes by 1994 that planners originally projected would amount to $350 million in annual savings, much of it from eliminating overlapping branches and operations. About 9,000 jobs would be cut, through either attrition or downsizing.

As Rainey began to pull his new transition team together under the co-chairmanship of Jim Thompson and C&S/Sovran executive Hugh Chapman, McColl continued to try to smooth the way for regulatory approval. He and Brown announced in August that NationsBank was committing $10 billion to community investment lending over a ten-year period beginning in January 1992, when the merger would become official. It was the largest commitment ever made by a bank to promote community improvement in underserved areas. Later, in the fall, NationsBank announced a $40 million sponsorship of the 1996 Olympic Games, to be held in Atlanta, and arranged a $300 million line of credit for Olympic organizers preparing the city for the international event. High cotton indeed for the South.

Chapter 20 **NationsBank**

Hugh McColl began his last day of work under the NCNB banner planning a noontime party for December 31, 1991. Throughout the morning, as he moved about NCNB's Charlotte head-quarters building, he stopped executives and employees and asked them to gather for a farewell to NCNB in the fortieth-floor, gold-carpeted penthouse.

The celebration was to start at noon, when chief legal counsel Paul Polking was expecting to receive official notice of final approval of the NCNB and C&S/Sovran merger. Polking had carefully steered the merger documents through multiple government agencies and through public hearings prompted by complaints that the new bank would not be responsive to the community. It had been a demanding six-month schedule, timed to the last hour, with no room for delay if NCNB was to begin the new year as NationsBank.

Polking was sure nothing was going to derail the deal, but then noon arrived and the call did not come. As the minutes passed, the crowd grew until nearly 150 people stood waiting. Some drifted to the northside windows to watch construction under way on the sixty-story office tower across the street that would be headquarters for the new bank. Some would be moving their offices there by the end of the spring.

Finally, at 12:20 P.M., Polking stepped to the podium and announced the news: NationsBank would begin business on January 1. McColl cheered along with everyone else and then presented Polking with a crystal hand grenade, a memento he had had commissioned for his chief lieutenants in the C&S/Sovran merger. In the NCNB ranks, it was a reward as cherished as any year-end cash bonus.

The crowd watched a videotape of the first NationsBank television commercial, scheduled for broadcast the following day during the Orange Bowl. McColl made a few remarks about the accomplishments of the past and the glorious future, and then Executive Vice President

Hugh McColl (left) signs a $40 million contract making NationsBank a corporate sponsor of the 1996 Olympics in Atlanta as Olympic official Billy Payne provides the pen.

A truck loaded with brand new NationsBank signs heads down the highway following the successful merger of NCNB and C&S/Sovran.

Chuck Cooley handed his boss the symbolic last NCNB flag, folded in the familiar three-corner military style.

The air of triumph within the room was mixed with sadness at the passing of a proud name, itself the only remaining symbol of hundreds of banks that had become part of NCNB during the past thirty-two years. As the hour-long ceremony drew to a close, McColl and the others lifted their champagne glasses in a toast to NCNB.

In addition to the occasion as a call of retreat for NCNB, the ceremony marked a beginning. On January 2, 1992, at nearly 2,000 offices across the country, more than 59,000 workers would report to work for NationsBank, a new bank that would be competing in a world of banking very different from the one that had created NCNB.

"What we are seeing is enterprises that took a hundred years to build up being taken out in one fell swoop," McColl said later. "There is going to be a radical change in banking. Manufacturers Hanover is disappearing. My point is that unthinkable things are happening. We're worried about whether we've cornered the market on the buggy-whip business."

Indeed, the nation had traditionally relied on the large banking houses in New York for financial leadership. Now these banks offered the least attractive investment in history. Banks that had been counted among the top ten in the world in the early 1980s were out of the running altogether in the early 1990s. Citicorp, America's largest bank, ranked only eighteenth in 1990, behind banks from Japan, France, Germany, the Netherlands, and Britain. And Citicorp was not dealing from strength. CEO John Reed announced in 1991 that the bank was downsizing and seeking to cut $1.5 billion in costs, primarily through personnel reductions. Dividends had even felt the knife.

"The industry is in the middle of a total restructuring," said William Seidman after his departure from the FDIC in October 1991. "McColl, Dick Rosenberg at Bank of America, Charles Sanford at Bankers Trust—they are a group that sees banking in transition." Only partly in jest, Seidman added that by the time Congress had finished rewriting banking laws in 1991, banks would face an even tougher future. Banks had received none of the things they had asked for and many new regulations they didn't want.

McColl and his Texas chairman, Tim Hartman, had lobbied for greater flexibility for institutions like NationsBank that had the capital and talent to create a separate, unregulated subsidiary to compete with other large corporate lenders like Morgan Stanley, insurers, and corporate-owned financial powers such as GE Capital Corp. At the same time, however, NationsBank argued that it would continue to serve individual customers as well as small and medium-sized businesses with a traditional bank.

The prototype for this plan was already in place in Texas. Beginning in January 1991, Hartman had reorganized the Texas operation so that his bank officers were concentrating on marketing the business to the customers on the street. The approach was novel for Texas, where banks had left that relatively small-dollar business to the savings and loans while concentrating their efforts on large, multimillion-dollar deals. The failure of that strategy was as clear as the wreckage of financial institutions brought down with the collapse of energy loans and expensive and highly leveraged real estate deals.

By purchasing nineteen failed savings and loans, NCNB Texas had doubled its number of branches across the state and now had a clear advantage in reaching customers. Hartman also scrapped a system by which branch managers had run their offices as independent units. Building maintenance and keeping up with daily reports became someone else's responsibility. "When our branch executive walked in at 8:30 in the morning, he or she was on the phone to a customer, and that was true for everybody in the bank."

"That was like a lightning bolt for Texas banking," Hartman said. "Our people began to go out and say, 'Hey, we're the bank down the street. What can we do for you?'"

It paid off. The Texas banking team made 110,000 calls in 1991 and negotiated 46,000 new loans in nine months. "It's having a good hamburger and putting it in the blue wrapper, putting cheeseburgers in the yellow wrapper, and making sure the french fries are fresh. And having a pleasant person at the register. That's all we're doing. It is nothing fancy," Hartman said.

To compete in this kind of environment, McColl already had told the new NationsBank management to expect something different, whether their heritage was NCNB, C&S, or Sovran. "The question is, what do we want? It occurs to me that the goals of the growth strategies of NCNB, which have driven us so hard over the last thirty years, have been achieved. We have achieved a strong presence in the large and fast-growing markets in the South. We have, in fact, created a company where we can leverage the infrastructure and achieve better profits through driving down unit costs. In short, we have arrived at the place that we said we were going. What we haven't done is prove that we can run it and make it a rewarding venture for our shareholders. That is what we must do.

"To be ranked as the best big bank in America, we need to have profitability results that rank near the top, the most important of these being return on equity." McColl believes the bank will accomplish that by getting back to the basics of banking and by consolidating "back office" operations, where millions of transactions are recorded annually.

Before McColl delivered his marching orders to NationsBank management in October 1991, a leading authority on banking, Lowell L. Bryan, had recognized banks like NCNB as the banks of the future in his 1991 book, *Bankrupt*. He said the Charlotte powerhouse would be among some ten to twenty large, multiregional banks with assets of $50 billion to $200 billion, operating from headquarters outside of New York. "In 1980 the list of most highly capitalized bank holding company stocks was dominated by money center banks; today the list is dominated by super regionals," Bryan said. "Their strength came from serving the core banking needs of individuals, small businesses, and mid-size companies."

A new business focus is not entirely sufficient, Bryan warned. Without legislative changes, the future is uncertain even for the successful super regionals. "Unless we reform the regulatory structure, they too will suffer," Bryan said.

McColl left the 1991 rounds of congressional hearings empty-handed. He also left doubting the efficacy of a united banking front. Even continuing the NationsBank membership in the once-powerful American Bankers Association was negotiable. No one questioned the resolve of the NationsBank effort, or its potential political clout. McColl said it is more than coincidence that he has weekly sessions with his Spanish tutor; U.S. Representative Henry Gonzalez, the chairman of the House Banking Committee, hails from San Antonio, a big NationsBank market with a large Hispanic population, like other NationsBank markets.

As NationsBank began business, McColl renewed his appeal for removal of restrictions on interstate branching and for other changes that he believes are necessary for American banks to remain competitive.

"As our nation focuses so intensely on competition from the Japanese and other nations, we should recognize the simple fact that ours is the only industrialized nation in the world without nationwide branching," he said in a speech on emerging issues that was broadcast on C-SPAN in February 1992. "Let me repeat that. The United States is the *only* industrialized nation whose banks do not have the right to operate anywhere within its borders. Very simply, American business cannot compete globally until American providers of credit are granted what—outside the U.S.—is the global standard in banking laws and regulation.

"My company must spend at least $40 million a year to maintain separate operations in each state. That $40 million represents capital that otherwise could produce $600 million in new loans per year—and that is a conservative multiple.

"The industrywide cost, according to the Treasury Department, is $5 to $10 billion a year," said McColl. "That translates into at least $75 billion in loanable funds . . . $75 billion Congress effectively chooses to keep stuffed in a mattress while our economy struggles to survive."

McColl believes congressional approval of interstate banking that would eliminate the multiplicity of accounting and reporting requirements will come, someday, and NationsBank will be among those banks that will have the muscle to take advantage of it.

In fact, by summer NationsBank had signed an agreement with MNC Financial, Inc., to buy 16 percent of its shares for $200 million. MNC, which owned the largest bank in Maryland, had total assets of $16 billion and 241 branches throughout the District of Columbia, Maryland, and Virginia. Its banking subsidiaries were Maryland National Bank, American Security Bank in the District of Columbia, and Virginia Federal Savings Bank.

NationsBank also had emerged as a major player in the nation's financial markets. The *Wall Street Journal* reported in July 1992 that NationsBank had become the biggest new buyer in the Treasury bond market. "They have become one of the dominant factors in the market," one analyst was quoted as saying.

McColl has said that he was interested in "filling in the gaps." He was speaking of other Southern states, like Alabama and Louisiana, where NationsBank doesn't do business. But when his friend C. D. Spangler, Jr., president of the University of North Carolina, introduced him at a UNC-sponsored issues forum in early 1992, he jokingly accused McColl of including California and Arizona in that category as well.

"This is going to be a decade of consolidation. We have the financial power to make it interesting," McColl said. "I believe that before it is all over there will be nationwide franchises. Bank of America will be one of them. NationsBank will be one of them. We will have a half a dozen major players."

McColl summed up his career in a speech at the lighting of the crown on the new NationsBank Corporate Center in May 1992. Retired bank employees were guests of honor. "The fundamental strengths of our corporate culture have survived nearly thirty-five years of constant mergers," he said, "with Addison Reese's vision, his meritocracy of fairness and equity, his intensely competitive nature, and with Tom Storrs's cool-headed leadership, his demand for perfection with the numbers, his intellect and foresight.

"We are a company that acts on our beliefs that the company will be only as healthy as our customers and communities. We embrace the responsibility to them that has come with our success. And we are a company that truly cares. We care for each other like family—in policy and every-day small gestures. And we like to win.

"Most of all, I believe our company will succeed because of the course charted by my two predecessors at the helm. When Tom Storrs retired as chairman in 1983, I borrowed a quote from Winston Churchill after the Battle of Egypt to sum up the irreplaceable roles that Tom Storrs and Addison Reese played. Churchill said, 'This is not the end. It is not even the beginning of the end. But it is, perhaps, the end of the beginning.'

"As our company goes forward," McColl closed, "we will be wise never to lose sight of our beginning."

Index